Hills of the North, Rejoice!

Always look up!

Ralph.

Hills of the North, Rejoice!

Ralph MacGregor

illustrations by Moira Webster

Curlew Cottage Books

Published by
Curlew Cottage Books
Curlew Cottage,
Hilliclay Mains,
Weydale, Thurso,
Caithness, KW14 8YN

© text and photographs 2004 Ralph MacGregor

ISBN 0-9538703-2-4

Typeset by Samantha Barden
Printed by Bell & Bain Ltd

Contents

Hills of the North, Rejoice!

Introduction

'Live adventurously!' I repeat the advice with which I began my previous book, 'Ralph's Far North'.

For over 20 years I've been writing a fortnightly column for the 'Caithness Courier' entitled: 'Out and About with Ralph'. This book is again largely based upon a selection of the pieces which have appeared over the past few years. It is written from the perspective of one who loves being out of doors, alone, in the wilder and remoter parts of the Scottish Highlands. It is my belief that there are many others who would share this delight if they could but shake off the pressures from society to conform to a false norm created largely by companies wishing to sell items such as cars, fashionable clothing or expensive holidays! The best things in life really are free, or nearly so.

If, like me, you rarely begin a book at the beginning, you can dip into the essays at random. However if you do start from page one, the book will take you from early spring through all the seasons in northern Scotland, with a few ventures further afield. The northern Highlands are still one of the least known parts of Britain and on most of my solitary wanderings I never meet anybody. Nor will you, apart from perhaps on the few munro peaks and Ben Loyal.

A word of warning – the outings described in this book may require a fair degree of fitness and experience, especially in bad weather. Do not attempt my routes unless you are sure they are within your capabilities, unless you can read a map and use a compass, and are prepared for possible severe weather. Walkers and cyclists now have a legal right in Scotland to (responsibly) cross open country and much farmland; please do not abuse this right.

I hope you will not take a mobile phone. Why walk out miles from the road to have one's peace destroyed by the beeps of incoming text messages? Mobile phones are completely out of place in remote country. If you feel you must, keep the thing for emergency use only, switched off and buried in the depths of your rucsac!

Hills of the North, Rejoice!

    My reasons for writing the book? Mainly a human wish to share my experiences with other like-minded people, and with those who would like to do the things I do but for good reasons are unable to. Also it is my hope that more folk may be inspired to make use of their God-given eyes, ears and legs to appreciate the beautiful world in which we live. The book would indeed have been worth producing for the sake of Moira Webster's artwork alone, I hope you enjoy her delightful drawings as much as I do! My other reason for writing is the last chapter, partly inspired by Roger Deakin's wonderful book: 'Waterlog'. There are still some world firsts available to the ordinary person. Live adventurously!

Ralph

Old trainers

Every spring I need a new set of running shoes, my old trainers having virtually disintegrated after a year's cross-country jogging over rough Highland terrain of heather, rock and bog. Last year's shoes were already falling to bits when I took off for a long training run across Ben Alisky. To be honest, 'training' is largely an excuse for enjoying some of these longer runs! From home I could see one tiny patch of white left on Ben Alisky, it seemed a nice objective to visit the last snow of the season (I should have known better – there was plenty more to come). The moors were saturated with rain and thaw, but the water would run out of the holes in my shoes.

So from Loch More, I jogged down the soggy track for two miles out to Backlass (the start of an old drove route to Dunbeath and a public right of way) then on across the moors towards the gentle twin hump of Ben Alisky. Old trainers are ideal for crossing the flow country, there's no need to worry about the bogs as your feet are always soaking wet anyway. It was a lovely mild day in early spring, golden plovers calling, sun on the slopes of Morven, the last snow vanishing fast. A simple moorland crossing (though the Allt Backlass can be a bit tricky to cross dry-shod when full) led to the Dalnawhillan Lodge path. Follow this path down to the lodge and you'll find the River Thurso a major obstacle with no bridge! I rounded the northern slopes of Alisky to reach a miniature grassy corrie where that last patch of snow lay in a little gully, perhaps 30 square yards in size and three feet deep. I made sure to climb over it, then up to the big cairn on the summit with a view which, like many of these flow country hills, is out of all proportion to its very modest height.

I always like to visit the old settlement of Ben Alisky, amid grassy upland pastures to the south. Are there any records of this place? All I know is that the Ben Alisky heather whisky was famous! A fine ruin of a shepherd's house remains, as well as a wooden fishing hut dating from around 1940, this now very much in the last stages of decay and waiting to be blown away by the next storm. The long horizons of the flow country beckoned in all directions, now I headed for another empty house, Balvreed, four miles distant as the greenshank flies. Heather, bog, heather, bog, dubh-lochs, streamlets, sun and vast skies all round – and the shores of Loch Sand, a delectable moorland loch, rippling in the morning sun – then a watery maze of more dubh-lochs, and up over former improved pasture to Balvreed. This old shepherd's house is also now falling down and would make a superb bothy for renovation by the Mountain Bothies Association. There are few houses even in Caithness where you can see dubh-lochs from the window, few houses so much imbued with the atmosphere of the deep flow country. It must have been some place in which to live. The track back to Loch More follows, for two miles, a dismantled forest fence. The fence was erected and then permission for tree-planting was refused. The RSPB subsequently bought the area and decided to take the fence down again. Shades of the Grand Old Duke of York. The same kind of thing on a bigger scale is happening near Forsinard where tens of square miles of forest where planted on the flow country in the 1980's at the taxpayers' expense and are now being removed, at a cost of millions, in an attempt to restore the peatlands to their former pristine state!

My shoes, now in an even worse state, would perhaps do for one more run... I really should have worn my new ones but they were still in their box and hadn't yet even seen a road; I didn't want to ruin them immediately in the heather and slush! Spring had faded to a memory and in the last of the snow-showers I'd driven gingerly over the snow-covered road to Braemore in the early morning. From the end of the road I'd jogged the six miles westward along the track to Gobernuisgeach, crunching the last three miles through a couple of inches of frozen snow. The mountains were completely white but the weather was improving and it still looked possible to do my usual morning crossing of Morven.

If you don't mind fording the river you can cut out a couple of miles by turning down to the Berriedale Water a mile before the end of the track. The river was high and very cold so I preferred a detour to the footbridge at Gobernuisgeach! Once off the track, however, my feet were soon soaked as the snow was deep and very wet. It proved hard going, back down the river for a mile then up through the heather, heading for the col between Morven and Small Mount. Much more snow had fallen than expected, higher up it was at least a foot deep, trapped in the heather, giving a wallow rather than a jog up to the col. The temperature dropped sharply on gaining height and the wind picked up, it was though a little easier going, with boulders and rocks protruding from the now frozen snow. By 2000 feet the snow was forcing itself in through an ever-growing split along my right shoe. Woollen sock or no, there was a great incentive to get over the top as quickly as possible before frostbite struck! I pulled on my pullover and wind-proof top – and even then, wearing thermal underwear and climbing fast, was only just warm enough. Ice pellets blew across, frost-feathers thickly adorned the rocks, miniature cornices were growing out from the ridge, conditions were as cold as any I'd seen that 'winter'. My foot was going numb. The hills to the west looked bleak and white... I can't have lingered on the summit for more than a second or two – I remember a general impression of blues and browns and whites – then jogged down as fast as was safe through deep snow-drifts and across the frozen, stony slope to the subsidiary top. The steep descent from there in such conditions would be tricky with deep soft snow, hidden holes and loose boulders.

Ten minutes later the worst was over, the slopes levelled out and the temperature had risen above freezing. Indeed the wet slushy snow seemed positively warm! The sun was coming out and, as I jogged down beside the streamlets towards Corriechoich, winter gradually turned back to spring. Another three miles along the slush-covered track took me back to Braemore, a flask of hot tea and a very welcome change to dry socks. My right trainer had now split all the way from heel to toe and it was another hour before my foot fully regained its feeling... the shoes went straight in the bin when I got home!

Knoydart heatwave

In a short five hours the winter had turned into summer without my realising it. Stomping up through the snow to the 3000-foot summit came a man wearing shorts and rolled up sleeves – and I hadn't yet realised it was actually warm enough not to be wearing my jacket! The previous day I'd driven 200 miles from Thurso, climbed a couple of munros then walked a long way up Glen Kingie to camp. Not surprisingly I wasn't feeling too energetic the next morning and planned a relatively easy day – over the summit of Sgurr Nan Coireachan, down into Glen Dessary and back over a pass to my tent. But I hadn't counted on the weather or on a hill called Garbh Cioch Mhor.

It was Good Friday, and early frost had given way to thin cloud lapping the 2500-foot contour line. Sleepily I'd sloshed up the boggy path for a few miles, gradually waking up near the 2800-foot summit of An Eag as the cloud broke and cleared to a day as near perfect as one can get in the west. The higher peaks were still streaked and dappled with snow and gleamed, sharp and clear from Ben Nevis to Skye, as the last puffs of cloud evaporated into clear blue. You just don't notice tiredness on the tops on such a day. Scrambling down to the col and up 800 feet of slabby rocks took me to the main top of Sgurr Nan Coireachan, the summit ridge a long white ribbon of wet snow. And it was here that I met the first shorts of the season.

The top was pleasantly cool but already the glens far below looked too warm for comfort. A steep descent of 800 feet took me to the next col and the route down into Glen Dessary. Ahead rose a mile and a half of steep, broken, twisting ridge leading to the summit of Garbh Cioch Mhor. It seemed a shame to leave the high places so soon on such a perfect day; perhaps I'd just climb up along the ridge a little way, eat lunch, and then go down. Now I'd first visited this area a long time before in typical late June weather; steady rain one day, squally showery rain the next. The hills rose, bright green and streaming with water, into a cloud ceiling which went up and down but rarely cleared the tops. I'd set off from Glen Dessary, crossed Sgurr Nan Coireachan in cloud and increasingly heavy showers and made a determined effort to reach the summit of Garbh Cioch Mhor. The ridge was interminable, the weather worsened with gales of hail and sleet which in my innocence I hadn't quite expected in late June. So I retreated and the peak remained an 'almost' for the next 15 years... it would take two hours to reach the top and get back to the col. I'd be pretty tired by the time I was down into the baking heat of Glen Dessary and would still then have many miles to go. I should go down now... but temptation won. The ridge was grand, rocky scrambles, snow patches, tremendous views on all sides. The isles of Rhum and Eigg rose from the shimmering sea while all around was an Alpine scene of range upon range of snowy, craggy peaks.

Hours later and I thankfully reached the shelter of a bothy in Glen Dessary. It was great to escape the heat and sun for 15 minutes! Quite a contrast to that first June occasion, before the roof was reslated, when water plopped and splashed into a dozen or so cups and pans spread out under the worst leaks. Now came the penance for my diversion on the tops. A mile down the glen a couple of youths were sunbathing, cans in hand – and I still had four sweaty miles to go with a pass to cross. I wasn't quite on hands and knees when I finally made it back to the tent but it was not the most enjoyable part of the day. But it was great to laze, brewing tea, watching the evening sun go down behind the hills while the occasional late and exhausted backpacker wended his way down the glen. Winter had gone, summer had come.

Fickle April

Early spring is a fickle time of year. It wasn't yet eight in the morning on Good Friday when I turned off the main road at Hope Lodge onto the twisty single-track route along Loch Hope. Ben Hope rose into utterly black cloud as violent squalls of hail and sleet swept across the bleak landscape. And I was planning a lightly-equipped 'fell-running' attempt on McDougal's Peak – take the mountain by storm, I'd thought. Storm indeed.

Meallan Liath Coire Mhic Dhughaill. Perhaps the longest mountain name in Scotland? It'll just trip off the tongue of Gaelic speakers, but I just call it McDougal's Peak – a remote hill, 2600 feet high, south of Foinaven. On five occasions I'd set out from home to climb the peak but only once, 17 years earlier, had I been successful. It's a long drive on single track roads to get near, then a walk of 15-20 miles over very rough country to reach the summit from the eastern side and return.

Have faith – always set out! In that weather it would be folly to take nothing in the way of spare clothes – so I had to run with a small rucsac holding a pullover and a complete waterproof outer covering as well as food. Otherwise I wore a tracksuit with vest and long-johns, an ancient, battered pair of running shoes as well as gloves and a woolly hat. That should see me through a few blizzards!

The Hope Lodge-Altnaharra Road is not as remote as it seems, with several farms along it. There is also Gobernuisgeach lodge on the Westminster Estate, in the foothills of the extremely rugged country around McDougal's Peak. Down the two mile track to the lodge I jogged, the last mile along the exclusive Strathmore River. It's a very well-kept and tidy estate, with all the paths, tracks and buildings in good order – money is no object here! Nobody was about except for a few tame stags and a crazy jogger. My route led straight into the gale but, almost miraculously, there were no more squalls for several hours. Cloud was clearing to reveal the higher tops white with fresh snow and hail. There would be bitterly cold winds up there! Little more than an hour after leaving the car I reached the crest of the pass and turned south up grassy slopes leading to the first peak of Meall Garbh. That was enough running – besides, it was a bit steep now and the ground was covered in slush. My old running shoes, which were full of holes, gave excellent water-cooling to the feet – so I sheltered behind a boulder to pull on an extra pair of wool socks for the next few miles through the snow.

The circuit from Meall Garbh via McDougal's Peak to Carn Dearg is one of the finest hill-walks in the north, a horseshoe of high ridges above the deep Coire Loch. Views across Sutherland are spectacular, as often is the wild weather. This time it was just a freezing gale, funnelling over the ridge in funny ways so that one minute I'd almost be crawling and a bit further on it would be calm. I was glad of that pullover, under my waterproof top! Black clouds and hail enveloped first the hills to the west, then the hills to the east – but somehow missed me. Things were deteriorating though – the wind on the last summit was stronger than ever and the descent of slippery slopes in trainers a little tricky. Hail blasted across as I tacked sideways across the col while eddies whipped water of Loch na Mang and sent it hurtling up Carn an Tionail. This last top proved a stormy one indeed, not a place to linger – I headed back down the east ridge towards Gobernuisgeach. The map shows little of the contorted nature of the country hereabouts, it's mostly bare rock slabs and perched boulders, rocky basins and low cliffs. Good route-finding is essential for fast progress – hence one of my earlier failures went attempting McDougal's peak by this approach. I could see the spray, eight miles to the north, where a big waterfall off Ben Hope was blowing back on itself in the wind. I hurried. An old stalker's path winds down at the eastern end of the ridge; miss it and you're in for a very slow, rough descent. I noticed a boulder on a rock which looked as if placed by man – a leading light for the end of the path. Heading for it I saw another, a couple of hundred yards off, then a little cairn. From each marker, by looking carefully, another perched stone could be seen – which led, after half a mile, to the end of the path, zigzagging down through the rough terrain. I washed the heather out of my shoes in the river, rejoined the main track and jogged slowly back to the car. For once, I just made it back ahead of the weather, the hail and sleet hammered down for the next 20 minutes as I changed into dry clothes and enjoyed a flask of hot tea.

A week later, another Friday, now into April, and a very ordinary day at Dounreay. Cloud had been thickening all morning and I noticed the haze of snow coming in over the hills around lunchtime. A bit of sleety rain started soon after but I thought nothing of it, and sat happily typing away at my computer as it turned to steady heavy white stuff. I was sure it would soon turn to rain; often after an hour or two it dries up and turns warmer. The trouble was that by going-home time my forecast was obviously completely wrong, snow was lying thickly and coming down harder than ever. I still wasn't particularly bothered, I was well equipped for cycling home in bad weather with cagoule, overtrousers, waterproof gloves and overshoes. (Waterproof polythene socks inside overshoes are the key to warm dry feet whatever the conditions!)

It was worse than I'd expected, cycling down the runway, not only was it very slushy and snowing hard but the wind, force 6 to 8, was straight into my face. It would be a slow plod home. The wind, indeed was the main problem, but I'd seen much worse, and with head down under cagoule hood and helmet pushed slowly on through Forss and up the long straight. Standing on the pedals as the wind increased, the bike shot from under me, leaving me sprawling on the road. Not a safe place to be – in seconds I was on the verge! Under the slush on this higher stretch of road, it had frozen. Another couple of hundreds yards and the strong side-wind, sent me sprawling again, there was not enough friction to balance the bike against it. A car had skidded into the ditch and been abandoned, there wasn't a sprinkle of salt or pellet of grit in sight. I walked. Once over the top I could ride again, gingerly, downhill into a very raw and slushy Thurso. It was still another five miles home though, straight into the driving snow on deteriorating roads. A lorry had jack-knifed, blocking the road and was being rescued by a JCB; I threw the bike over the wall, wheeled through the field and carried on.... April, and my worst ride home of the 'winter'. I was back after six – the poor bike plastered in snow – and it was my good summer bike which I'd just taken out of the garage! Yet the following Monday I was cycling home in warm sun wearing shorts. Fickle weather indeed.

An old man's outing

It was one of those rare, utterly clear early spring mornings of birdsong, blue sky and long distance views, indeed just right for a run over the mountain tops. Unfortunately I was just getting over one of those colds which hadn't been quite bad enough to keep me off work but had left me feeling about 40 years older. It was a choice of either sitting in the sun or doing the sort of morning's outing that would suit an octogenarian. I chose the latter.

Dorrery Hill would be my objective, though I quite expected to run out of energy and turn back halfway. I set off on the bike and pottered, gently, towards Halkirk. It does indeed make a nice change to take, really slowly, routes along which you usually rush. I kept stopping for rests, the excuse being to take photos or just to look – at the wild primroses, the yellow gorse, the new lambs. Many people do not know of the riverside path in Halkirk, which leaves the road immediately north of the bridge and follows the Thurso for about half a mile to Gerston. This is probably the best short footpath along the river anywhere along its length. There are benches and picnic tables, fine views across the rapids to the old mill with Morven beyond, great banks of wild flowers in summer.

The Calder road is usually ridden flat out, head down, hurrying to or from work. This morning it was more at the pace of an old lady on a sit-up-and-beg, but I enjoyed the sunshine and clear views all the more for it. Wild geese were feeding in fields by the road – there have been a lot about this month. Loch Calder was a lovely dark blue, now rippled with waves as the wind picked up from the south-west. Good – I'd have a following wind home! Taking it very easy I carried on towards Brawlbin then slowly up the hill towards Dorrery. A few days earlier, seen from the Broubster road, the hill had looked more like a volcano with smoke billowing off its western flanks and lines of orange flame. The fire engine had then passed, blue lights flashing. Yet another bit of heather burning had got out of control. Just two dry days in early spring and the horizons vanish in a haze of smoke. Grouse management requires controlled burning to keep heather in good condition, but problems seem to arise when estates, desperate

for grouse numbers, take risks or crofters want a bit of fresh green for the sheep and don't mind if a few hundred acres get burnt. The infertile soil is then degraded even further.

Most people walk up to the main top of Dorrery from the lodge at the end of the road, following the track up to the mast. The lower top, at the north end of the ridge, is however much nicer and has not been spoilt by roads and masts. It also gives a much more interesting walk. Leaving the bike near the old Brawlbin school, I set off across fields towards the hill. There are many deserted crofts and cottages here, always interesting places to (carefully) explore. Even abandoned cars can add to the scenery, one wreck here allowed a young rowan tree to grow through its engine some 25 years ago, protected from grazing sheep. The car has now all but rusted away but the tree is a good 15 feet high with a thick trunk – and still surrounded by the chassis of the car!

The fields give way to heather and peat, sheep-paths lead to the remains of the village of Badnabeen, just below the steeper slopes of the hill. In the low broken ruins of a crofthouse, is a monument to John MacDonald, apostle of the North' who was born here in 1779, subsequently became a noted Gaelic poet and was minister of Ferintosh in Ross-shire for 30 years. Sit back against the cairn and close your eyes and you can almost hear the children playing and the women singing the Gaelic songs as they work. It's a climb of only a couple of hundred feet to the crest of the ridge but is steep and (feeling at least 80) I nearly turned back. With the odd rest I eventually made it, well worth the effort for the view Dorrery gives westward across the flow country to Sutherland and back east over fertile Caithness. Dorrery Hill marks a real boundary, hundreds of miles of Highland country stretching from Loch Lomond and Perthshire come to an end here. The short tier of broken crags is, you feel, the very last remnant of the mountains, like the furthest reach of a great wave running up the beach.

With the wind from behind, and the sun still shining, it was a gentle, easy journey home. It had taken me twice as long as usual – but good to take time to stand and stare!

Emptiest Ross

A very great deal can be done in a day. There are, after all, at least 16 whole hours available!

The winter's wild oscillations of weather had swung back to cold north winds and snow showers by Easter, and the train ran through a white landscape all the way from Forsinard to Lairg. April snow doesn't however have the menace of January, and by nine it had already melted from the roads in the sunshine as I pedalled out of the station and on across the lower Shin dam towards Rosehall and the west. I hadn't decided exactly where to go, except that one of my objectives was to visit a remote corrie in the heart of that empty range of mountain country bounded by Ullapool, Dingwall and Bonar Bridge. Of all the Highlands this is one of my favourite parts, although I hadn't been there for years.

The bitter north wind hurried me along the Rosehall road, the sun dazzling off white fields and moors interspersed with dark plantations. Snow had now mostly melted from the grassy south-facing banks of the road, revealing some brave primroses. The main road west to Oykel Bridge was empty and gave a lovely cycle up the valley above the river, the water level was high and salmon-fishermen were out braving the elements. I turned left, swung down past the forestry houses and onto the track leading up into wilder country.

Although roadless, there are several routes right through to Ullapool which I've taken more than once. Today I was going at least halfway there. A forestry road led for four miles to Duag Bridge, recent timber-felling operations had churned this into a sea of mud through which my mountain-bike ploughed, very much in its element. A heavy snow-shower blew in, turning April into a reminder of January for half an hour before clearing again to bright sunshine. The higher hills remained white, but lower levels were thawing slowly and all the tracks were very wet. Two miles on, up a steep stony track, is Corriemulzie Lodge, high on a hillside with views to the mountains further south. The remoteness of such a place is an illusion these days, a 4x4 vehicle would take only 15 minutes to reach the main road and another hour or so to Inverness. I carried on along the Landrover track heading west, another six miles up into the remote Coire Mor, the track becoming increasingly rough and wet with streams running across it. Straight ahead rose the sharp peak of Seana Bhraigh, snow-covered and looking Alpine or even Himalayan. I had considered dragging the bike across the tops and descending into Glen Beag to the south, but this clearly wasn't going to be possible – I had a train to catch! So, towards the end of wide, bleak Corriemulzie valley I abandoned the bike to jog the last couple of miles up into the corrie. Indeed the track was so rough that jogging was both faster and easier than cycling. Two rivers proved minor obstacles, one ankle-deep but the other up to the knees and both containing water which had only recently been snow. Nothing for it but to run straight through, letting the water drain gradually from my shoes over the following miles! It was, however, well worth the effort to reach the high corrie with its spectacular peak rising for another 2000 feet of crags and narrow ridges above the dark loch. It's a place only known to estate guests and those hillwalkers who seek out the remoter parts, surely one of the finest spots in the north.

Back now, back through the rivers to the bike, back across all the bumps and streams and potholes to Corriemulzie Lodge and Duag Bridge, the wind still bitter, even colder if anything. In such weather you cover a lot of ground because you have to keep moving to keep warm! Rather than return to Lairg I took another cross-country route, following a track which meanders across to Strath Cuileannach and comes out at Croick, west of Bonar Bridge. This started well as a beautifully graded forest road but soon deteriorated into the wettest and muddiest route yet. It was bikeable though, and with the wind from behind gave an enjoyable crossing. The main obstacles were three padlocked forestry gates; side gates were provided for walkers but these were too small for the bike which had to be unloaded and lifted across. The ground was still partly snow-covered, with peaks to the south very white. Mud and water splashed up to freeze on the bike, coating the frame and cables in ice half an inch thick, while little icicles dangled off the mudguards. There's been a lot of new forestry planting since I was last in this strath but the shepherd's house at Luibachoinich is still inhabited and the main part of the glen is clear of trees. The post-bus (a Landrover) from Ardgay used to run this far, giving a good start to a walking tour of the area I made nearly 20 years ago. There was still another four miles of rough track to cycle before reaching the tarmac at Croick, but with the wind behind and the sun coming out it was no hardship. I met the shepherd calling his sheep to be fed, further down the track others came running towards me with that plaintive 'baa-aa – I'm hu-ungry – have you got foo-ood for me-ee...'

Suddenly, at Croick, I was back into civilisation with the farm and Croick Church, built in the 1820's. In this churchyard the GlenCalvie people sheltered

when evicted during the clearances of 1840. On the east window you can still see their scratched messages. 'The GlenCalvie tenants were in the Kirkyard. May 2 1840', and suchlike. A nearby plaque states that these are 'poignant reminders of the hardship and uncertainty of the times'. Not quite how I'd have put it. They are reminders that 'ethnic cleansing' happened here, and that some people would do the same again if they had the chance. Another sad message scratched by the people on the window is: 'The GlenCalvie tenants. The wicked generation.' The church of the day led these poor people to believe that their eviction was predestined punishment for their sins. I hope we have moved on. Sombre thoughts left aside, the ride down Strathcarron was one of the best parts of the day in glorious sunshine with a strong following wind. This strath with its rocky river, woods, farms and narrow roads is a cyclists' gem – you don't have to be fit to enjoy pottering round the 18 mile circuit from Ardgay, up one side of the river and down the other!

The train-ride home through the sunlit evening would have made a good tourist advertisement; everything anyone thinks of as the Highlands was there.

Sea, rocky rivers, snow-covered mountains, lochs, birchwoods, castles, crofts, moors, sheep with lambs, buzzards, wild ducks, geese, swans. Seals basked on rocks near Brora, I've met people who have never seen seals in the wild and would love to. Stags were right by the line in Kildonan, gaining the attention of even the small children who were tired after travelling for hundreds of miles. Soon they were all excitedly stag-spotting. 'They're huge!' 'A wabbit!' another kept shouting as Easter bunnies scuttled in all directions. Several stags leapt into the river and began to swim across. Otters, wild goats, ospreys and even eagles can be seen from the train if you're lucky. Dusk came over the flow-country with Morven snow-covered and looking twice its height. One of these days people will recognise the enormous tourist potential of the north line. Who needs funiculars up Cairngorm? I cycled home from the station in hard frost and moonlight. A very great deal can be done in a day. Indeed.

Early spring

The rime on the summit rocks of Morven was inches thick after a fortnight of bitter east winds and cloud. The wind had dropped at last though, and a few hundred feet lower down the snow was melting. Perhaps spring was now on the way! Slushy patches of snow still lay on the plateau between Carn Mor and Smean but the ground was wet, not frozen. The moors stretched northwards, barren and brown, and a column of smoke drifted from where some keen gamekeeper had already taken advantage of the lull in the weather to begin the season's muirburn. Given the shortage of grouse in the previous few years, estates would being doing their utmost to encourage the birds and in a day or two the air would be full of smoke haze and the scent of burning heather. The clear water of the Toberon Fhionn (white well) below Smean was relatively warm, coming from the depths of the mountain, and refreshed me to continue on my way over the moor to Maiden Pap where the long heather growing in the shelter of the steep summit rocks was thickly covered in lichen. Down at Braemore, below the white-streaked slopes of Scaraben, the air was still cold, but the bitter edge of the previous weeks had gone.

I love those rare clear days of early spring; such days are however terrible for working indoors with the blinds drawn against sun-dazzle! The recompense is that with daylight now at both ends of the day, the cycle ride to work can be magic on a glorious clear morning. The sea shimmers blue out to the sharp outlines of the Hoy cliffs and the distant Brough of Birsay, while far to the west, beyond the white Sutherland mountains and the long ridge of Ben Hutig, is the Cape Wrath peninsula. One such morning I set out on the mountain bike, a slow ride past Halkirk then turning south instead of taking the usual route to Dounreay. Caithness abounds in good mountain bike routes which are very rarely cycled and if you are prepared to wheel the bike for a few rough miles there are many excellent through treks to be made. One of my favourites is along a chain of remote moorland lochs, hard going to be sure but well worth the effort. There are sandy beaches where you can ride the bike for a few dozen yards with the knowledge that possibly nobody else has ever ridden a bike there before. Eventually you return to civilisation in the shape of the private road from Forsinard to Altnabreac, with a wide choice of routes across Caithness and Sutherland in front of you. This time I was taking it easy, enjoying the spring sunshine and a rising south wind which, once past the short headwind stretch through Altnabreac, would blow me homewards. The Loch Dhu Lodge had been sold again and new gates erected, somebody's wee holiday cottage! I pottered on past the lochs to Dalnawhillan, past the ever-barking dogs in the kennels then on towards Loch More with a good following wind. A group of hinds easily outpaced me above the track; running over the rough heather they crossed just ahead and cantered down over the river flats. Loch More was high, promising good fishing on the Thurso and several anglers were out plying the early-season waters.

Hills of the North, Rejoice!

For once the Easter weekend coincided with glorious sunshine, so nobody had any excuse for staying indoors! When were you last on top of Ben a Chielt, above the Causewaymire? It must have been 15 years since I'd last visited the prominent cluster of masts and had forgotten just how fine the view was, out over the moors to the mountains with the sea glittering to the south. There is a good mountain bike route from Rumster Forest, up via the hill-climb route to the tall TV mast then a hard push on foot through rough heather to gain a peat-cutting track along the ridge. This allows a ride to the summit, followed by a fine long descent to the Causewaymire road and on down into Latheron. The return route is by Nottingham Mains, up past the Rumster outdoor centre then back through the forest to the starting point. Just the thing for a fine spring morning. The short (and short-lived) Rumster Forest walk has now disappeared under tree-felling, hopefully to be reinstated when the timber operations have ceased. How about replacing the felled sitka spruce with birch, alder, rowan, hazel, whitebeam, sycamore, ash, holly and perhaps a few noble fir and Scots pine?

Two days later and the sun was hot, it was blinds-drawn weather again at work and T-shirt weather on the bike home. Daffodils were coming out in droves. You can be sure though that winter isn't over yet, indeed the rime is building up again in easterly gales on the summit of Morven as I write!

Don't be a sheep!

Our modern society may be deemed 'individualistic' – but the pressures to conform are stronger than ever. In Caithness there are more independently minded people than in many places but even here the insidious influences remain. I've never been one to take much notice of what people say, either directly or behind my back, and will do things my way, even if everybody else does them differently. Some folk just can't understand this and don't realise how much they've been influenced by the pervading fashions and culture. Take weather. Ever since a child I've enjoyed all weathers – rain, wind, fog, sunshine, gales, snow – the more variety the better. I've long since given up arguing with people who say, 'What a miserable day!' just because it's grey or raining. If you want to lie on a beach you obviously want sunshine – but most people actually spend most of the time indoors or in cars, I would contend that rain hammering on a window or windscreen is a lot more interesting than sunshine shining through it – and you can also enjoy the warmth and shelter without feeling you should be outside. Weather doing things – force 12 gales, squalls, thunderstorms, hail, blizzards – is invigorating, exciting, adds adventure to otherwise routine days. Perhaps that's why people don't like it – it reminds them too much that there are factors in life over which they have no control.

Present day culture regards any form of physical exercise as at best an unfortunate necessity to keep the body in reasonable shape and at worst sheer masochism. The majority of people drive everywhere, walk as little as possible, never cycle or run but perhaps follow the fashion for going to the gym. A small minority of people are really into sport, very competitively. I fall into neither camp – which is perhaps why I'd have been institutionalised long ago if what mattered was the number of times people have said to me: 'You must be mad!' Mad to cycle, especially to work? It keeps you fit, gives you space and time to think, costs very little, lets you enjoy the scenery and the weather, the birdsong and the wild flowers in summer, the dawn and sunset in spring and autumn, the starlight and moonlight in winter. In wild weather it brings a bit of challenge and adventure into an otherwise routine day. It's only the car manufacturers who have conned you through endless adverts, motoring magazines and TV programmes into thinking that driving in a stream of traffic is enjoyable in any way. A car is a bit of metal and rubber, it almost completely insulates you from the natural environment, it gives you a sore back, tired eyes and a headache, it's dangerous, pollutes the environment, costs a fortune to buy, run and insure... hours of precious time is wasted in washing, cleaning, maintaining... you've got to park the thing, garage the thing, worry about breakdowns and accidents and garage bills and thieves. Advertisers have done a remarkable mass brainwashing job in conning people into thinking that there is something glamorous about cars. Anybody who buys a Porsche or a Ferrari is simply that much more gullible than anyone who owns an old van. I've got a car, it's useful if someone needs to get from place to place quickly, I think it's a blue one.

'Did I see you RUNNING? You must be very fit...' Jogging is just another good way of seeing and appreciating this wonderful world in which we live. It can be more exhilarating than walking which is sometimes tedious on roads and tracks. My reaction would like to be (but I'm too polite) 'Did I see you DRIVING? You must be very unfit...' In fact I'm not very fit. I've always been utterly useless at team sports or anything involving catching, kicking or hitting bouncy objects. If I take part in any real athletic event like the Wick Triathlon or the Caithness Half Marathon I finish last or near the back of the field. Almost everybody else who cycled to work would overtake me. The one occasion I attempted a ten-mile time trial on the bike I finished in a state of exhaustion in over 30 minutes; youngsters on mountain-bikes manage 27 minutes whereas any half-decent racing cyclist will do under 25. I was the PE teacher's despair at school. I've no natural aptitudes for sporty things at all, so anything I can do anyone can do – and probably better – unless they have some medical problem. Obviously you'll need to spend some months building up stamina and fitness if you've only ever driven a car – but most people could easily do more than me.

Swimming – that's another area where people sometimes question my sanity. I simply like outdoor swimming, in the lochs and the sea, when the weather isn't too cold. I've no layers of fat to provide insulation so can't stay in for long, but again, swimming outdoors is another way of appreciating this amazing creation we are part of. Clearly you shouldn't swim in cold unsupervised waters (and most certainly not out of your depth) unless you are a strong swimmer and know your capabilities. But if you practice in the swimming pool until you can manage half a mile, you'll be safe enough doing a few strokes in a loch. My swimming is slow and inelegant, less than half the speed of the keen members of the Swimming Club, but so what – its another nice way of getting about. I envy the few people in Caithness who can manage a dip in the sea, every day, all year round – and even more those who perform impossible feats like swimming the 27 mile length of Loch Ness, as a lady did recently in about nine hours.

Surely if anybody is mad it's those who ruin their health through lack of exercise, overeating, smoking, alcohol or drugs. Surely those who tour by car, totally insulated from the environment, are deluded when they think they've seen the countryside. Surely it's mad to sit watching soap operas or drinking in a pub when you could be out watching the sunset, or fishing the loch, or listening to the greenshanks over the moor. Surely those fortunate enough to have the full use of their arms and legs and eyes are mad not to use them walking, running, cycling, swimming instead of adopting a lifestyle which could be lived by the disabled or a man or woman in their eighties.

Somehow, I don't think many people will agree with me...

April hills

Oh for the wings of an eagle! It was 7.15pm and I was nearly 3000 feet up on the easternmost summit of Slioch, in Wester Ross. The setting sun glowed on the snows of Beinn Eighe and turned the cliffs blood-red on the other side of the deep glen. Below me was Loch Maree, strewn with innumerable islands, stretching in its entire length to the shining Atlantic. The magnificent scenes all around had however begun to lose their appeal after a day which had begun before six in the morning. I was more interested in the fact that, just half a mile away, I could see my tent with its promise of a brew, and food, and a sleeping bag. It was, though, 2500 feet lower down a mountainside which, while possessing no real difficulties, was not going to be much fun with my legs feeling like jelly.

The thermometer had been reading -5C when I'd set off south on a clear April morning. On a last minute impulse I'd put skis in the car and, on encountering Alpine scenes of snowy peaks and blue skies, determined to try them out. The gentle slopes of Fhionn Bheinn, above Achnasheen, looked about my standard and so shortly after nine I was climbing the slopes above the village with the skis and poles strapped to my rucsac. The morning was truly superb, the kind of rare perfection of weather that leaves you blinking and dazed, wondering whether the previous months of storms have been a dream. I crunched over partly frozen peathags in a dip then climbed up to where there seemed to be enough snow for the skis. Cross-country skis are supposed to make the going easier on snowy hills, a fish-scale pattern on the base allowing one to ski uphill without sliding back. Unfortunately it didn't seem to be working, an icy crust giving so little friction that anything other than the slightest climb,either up or down, was almost impossible. After an hour's valiant struggle I took the things off and, unencumbered, soon gained the summit ridge at 3000 feet. Below lay Loch Fannich, on all sides snowy mountains marched to the horizon. The wind was still bitter, I lingered as long as I could then set off down, intending to have another go with the skis on the gentler slopes. They certainly didn't save any time or energy, but did add some amusement to the descent. The sun had now softened the snow and by dint of linking gentle traverses I managed to get down a fair way, even with a non-existent technique which relied heavily upon the flying buttock arrest! I was back at the car in hot sunshine which had taken the day straight from winter into a summer afternoon. The legs were already feeling a bit stiff after that unaccustomed exercise with the skis but such weather was not be wasted. I drove the few miles on to Kinlochewe, packed the rucsac with camping gear and set off walking towards Slioch. Pottering along the path towards Loch Maree was very pleasant in the warm sun, with the river below and all the birds singing. After three or four miles a little bridge took me across a gorge down which a river, swollen with melted snow, was thundering. Here the climbing began – and the less with a full pack the better! After half a mile I was hot and jaded and with relief found a reasonably flat, if wet, spot to pitch the tent. It was half past four and the temptation was just to sit and enjoy the sun for the rest of the day.

Hillwalkers must have a masochistic streak. Why set off late on a fine afternoon for a second 3000-foot climb? Why indeed. But then why do anything! The path didn't prevaricate but climbed upwards steadily, steeply, purposefully. Up into a high, open corrie where it vanished under slushy snow, leaving me to pick my way up steep slopes between snow fields to gain a rocky ridge by a small lochan. And the top was still nearly 1000 feet higher. I was decidedly tired, with that jellyfish feeling growing in the legs, as I surmounted the last rocks to see the top still another quarter of a mile off across snowfields. With great relief I reached the trig point at last, to survey the tremendous scene of mountain and loch, my only concern now being whether my legs would last the descent. I thought longingly of the quiet evening sun I could have been enjoying instead of forcing myself up and down 3000 feet of rugged mountain. Back in the tent, drinking tea by candlelight, the regrets had gone; the effort had, as always, been worth it. Even if I was stiff for the next five days!

Highland hazards

It was probably a split second subconscious reaction that turned my foot sideways before it touched the ground. That way I just gave the coiled adder a nudge with my toe instead of landing right on top of it. I leapt another two yards and carried on running without looking back!

When crossing open moorland country it's advisable to keep at the back of your mind the fact that there might be snakes. I'd completely forgotten about them, the ground was ordinary wet peaty moorland with patchy heather and rush, it was only about nine in the morning and cold, with the sun not yet shining strongly. One tends to think of adders as liking drier, stonier country, and sunbathing on gravel or rocks. I was jogging in light trainers, about seven miles from the road, heading for the Scaraben ridge, having run up the long estate track from Berriedale nearly as far as Wag. I'm told that adder bites are unpleasant but not particularly dangerous for a healthy adult, but was glad not to have to spend the seven miles back to Berriedale finding out.

Every year I see a few adders which means that they must be pretty common. I've never seen so many however as near Abriachan, above Loch Ness. We've often walked along the track which runs southwards from the village, high along the hillside. On a sunny summer day the views of the loch are magnificent, the trackside thick with wild flowers, the birches green, the heather coming into bloom. Rocky outcrops give excellent spots for picnicking and admiring the views. It's advisable though to look carefully before you sit down. I don't think we've ever walked there without seeing at least one snake, usually sunning itself on the track. A number of years ago my young son was about to sit down at one of the outcrops with a glorious view down Loch Ness. There was a largish stone lying there. 'Be careful,' I said, 'there may be a snake under it.' He picked up the stone to look. 'Yes there is, dad,' he said in a matter-of-fact voice, as a young adder slithered away into the heather. Once, a few miles from Tongue, we came across a young adder, not much bigger than a large worm, trying to swallow whole a small mouse. It heard us coming and reared up to defend its prey before escaping into the heather. Adders are however the least of the hazards in the Highlands, much smaller beasties being far more pernicious.

I continued on my run, which soon turned into a walk up the steep heathery flanks of West Scaraben. Higher up were patches of snow, left over from the 'May gobs' of a few days earlier. The morning was fast turning into the best day of the week, clear sky and sun, views for many miles across the emptiness of Sutherland to snow streaked hills, a day with more of the feel of March than of May. The end-to-end traverse of Scaraben is a grand little hill-walk on a fine day, though in bad weather the peak is one of the most wind-scoured places in the north. The ridge of bare frost-shattered rocks and moss resembles more southern summits over 1000 feet higher. There are three main tops and a subsidiary further east, over these I jogged, walking the steeper sections and stopping at each for a bite to eat and a gaze at the views. From the last top it was a long jog down through rough heather and wet moor towards the Berriedale water and an old broch which occupies a high eminence above the valley. The descent from the broch to the river is awkward – brochs were usually defensively sited! The slopes are steep and covered in rough heather and gorse, but were now basking in the warm sunshine. I pushed my way down through the undergrowth, stopping down by the river on the green grassy flats. Fortunately I was wearing tracksuit trousers not shorts – the ticks were out in force! The warm sun must have wakened these worst of Highland insect pests, my trousers were crawling in them, all sizes and shapes. I spent about ten minutes flicking the bigger ones off so that I'd get back to my change of clothes before they'd managed to crawl anywhere that mattered. Now that we know ticks can carry the rather nasty 'Lymes Disease' they are more than just unpleasant. Most hillgoers must however have been bitten so many times that they're probably immune.

The lower stretch of the Berriedale water deserves to be much better known, though within sight of the A9 virtually nobody goes there or knows of the secret path into the valley which winds below the cliff from Berriedale village. Although it had been snowing just two days earlier, the warm late-morning sun in this sheltered valley had already brought the white stitchwort into flower, as well as violets and the first of the bluebells. (In June you can look up this valley from the A9 to see the blue sheen. Best stop the car first...) Large patches of primrose were now past their best and the birches were almost fully in leaf. Chaffinches were singing but no cuckoo as yet – and there were lots and lots more ticks in the grass. No midges at any rate...

Back at the car I quickly changed and removed a few biters which had already fastened on around the ankles. Oh the joys of the Highlands! But the insects and the adders and the weather are all part of this country, part of what makes it one of the finest places on this planet. If the sun always shone and nothing ever bit or buzzed you might be wearing a virtual reality headset but you wouldn't be in the real world. I know which I prefer.

May runs

Normally, on a clear moorland evening in May, the snipe would have been drumming, the golden plovers calling, the larks singing. Insects would be starting to gather in small clouds, even the first midgies. That evening, when I stopped to listen, just silence. The browns and yellows were the colours of winter. Cloud was clearing a whitened Morven, a shower had left snow lying down to 1000 feet. In the bitter wind it could have been a day in February. I left the track to jog up to the top of Beinn Nam Bad Mor as a shower swept in over Loch Scye, rain turning to sleet then snow. The top of the hill was not a place to linger in shorts! For once I was glad of my light cagoule and woolly hat which I usually just carry as a precaution when out running on the moors. Rarely have I completed the ten-mile round run from Shurrery without even raising a sweat! Snow in May is not unusual, but by the middle of the month it's definitely getting unseasonal. I've seen snow on low ground in early June though, and one of the coldest days I've ever experienced on the hills was a 31st May.

Nevertheless it has often been bright and clear, excellent weather for outdoor activities. On one of the calmer days, with the sun hot, we walked round the Duncansby clifftops. This is always the best place to see the great vertical colonies of kittiwakes and guillemots, the shags were already on nests at the bottom of the geos and fulmars on nests at the top, with large rafts of birds on the sea. Clear cold air, sudden warmth in sheltered sun, long views to distant islands and mountains, the constant ark-ark-ark and kitt-eee-wake, kitt-eee-wake calls echoing up from dark cold geos, the smell of ammonia, the yellow primroses and red campions and white scurvy grass on sunny clifftops, the tide-race roaring past below – that's Duncansby in late spring.

Another 'training' run was to circuit Dunnet Head, again on a bright clear day but with a very cold wind. Walking in Caithness seems to be gradually getting more popular and the Dunnet Head circuit – as fine a clifftop walk as any – is certainly seeing a few more people. There are no major obstacles or difficulties and treated sensibly it's perfectly safe, just the outing for a good day. Such days are greatly at a premium however, and more often when I've been running along those clifftops it's been in at least half a gale and driving rain. From Brough it's easy, just follow the cliffs, up and down, to arrive at the lighthouse much sooner than expected. You have, however, only covered about a quarter of the distance. I can never resist keeping along the cliff-edge round the back of the lighthouse buildings so as to be the most northerly person on the British mainland – don't try it unless you've a very good head for heights, and keep away from the edge! There are colonies of kittiwakes and guillemots here, too – but not as easy or safe to watch as those on Duncansby. The western clifftops, back towards Dunnet, are my favourites, an easy run for an initial two or three miles along sheep tracks with the high cliffs to the right and the moors and lochs of Dunnet Head to the left. You'll get wet feet and in wild conditions I've been drenched by waterfalls blowing backwards. Part of the clifftop has recently collapsed in a spectacular rockfall, a warning (if any were needed) not to go too near the edge. After rounding several deep geos the cliff turns the corner and Dunnet Bay appears in the distance ahead. The next mile or two are along the remotest part of the headland, some very attractive bracken-covered slopes give sheltered sunny spots to sit and watch the Orkney ferry sailing past. On the left, Loch Bushta (when low) has a lovely little sandy beach at its southern end, just the place for a swim on a warm day. It must be a good five miles from the lighthouse to Peedie Bay below the Northern Gatehouse, it certainly always turns out further than expected. I nipped down to look at the sands, then jogged slowly up the track to the top of the hill and the road.

The trouble with Dunnet Head lies in getting back to one's starting point; I always seem to end up struggling through deep heather, bogs and extremely rough old peat diggings. It's easiest just to go round the road, but that's a bit tame. Between Dunnet and Brough is a scruffy area of moor, a place where old bicycles and prams come to die and dismembered cars lie rusting, a place I've yet to find a really good route across. Eventually I came out at an old crofthouse, still much the same as it was 20 years ago, and probably for the 30 years before that. An old lady must have died suddenly, leaving the house stuffed with all her possessions. The garden is now an overgrown thicket of Japanese Knotweed. It's rather sad to push through to the flagstones by the front door and peer in the windows at the mouldering furnishings piled high; an open cupboard door still bears pinned-up notes, and maybe unpaid bills, while a tattered hymnbook lies open at one we had to sing only last Sunday.

People often complain these days about the difficulty of escaping noise, or at any rate the sound of man's activities, anywhere on this planet. In most places there is at least a constant traffic hum, or at the minimum the regular roar of passenger jets high above. Perhaps we take our Caithness silences too much for granted. Early on a calm, grey Sunday morning I took another of my favourite routes, from Dorrery to Loch Caluim and back, a nice round jog of ten miles. Once past the lodge, over the hill, past the forestry plantation and down to the river Forss you reach a little gate set in the middle of a wooden bridge over the river. This, two miles from the lodge, is for me 'the gateway to the flow country'. The track is a bit tedious to walk; it's easy to cycle but you miss the atmosphere that way. Best is to jog, out into the scented, singing (on this occasion silent!) moors, with the sandy beaches of Loch Caluim, one of the finest in the county, an incentive to keep going for the full five miles. The last mile, along the river with low broken cliffs above, is particularly good and one of the few places I've seen an otter. This time a short-eared owl silently skimmed the rushes. The loch was utterly silent. Lapping water, calm grey skies. No planes, no traffic hum. A ringed plover, running along the beach, started calling, almost piercing in the quiet air. I stood, and looked, and listened for a few minutes. Then turned and started jogging down the track, to be back in civilisation before the morning had hardly begun.

From Inverness to Braemar

The modern A9 takes you through the high Grampian mountains almost as if they weren't there – except, that is, in snow. People have been known to drive from Inverness to Perth in an hour before the days of speed cameras and unmarked police cars! Most have no idea what a barrier to travel the mountains used to be, and indeed are still, away from the A9.

There is no tarred road across the Monadhliath mountains for the 40 miles between the Slochd and Spean Bridge, or across the Cairngorms between Drumochter and the Lecht. There are though many hill passes which were used in the past, and these still provide good routes for the walker or cyclist. To begin a week's mountain-bike tour I decided to take a couple of these through routes which had always intrigued me on the map. From the upper reaches of the Findhorn I'd cross the remotest part of the Monadhliath, by the headwaters of the Dulnain, and descend to Kingussie. I'd then take the bike through Glen Feshie and Glen Geldie to Braemar. That would be just the start... my mountain bike was going to climb above 2000 feet many times and cross the 3000-foot contour at least twice during the week.

The start was benign enough, cycling out of a bustling Inverness on a hot sunny Bank Holiday Saturday with a full load of camping gear. You don't have to get far out of the city, however, to reach quiet roads, and soon I was enjoying (if that's the right word) the steep climb up the B861 across to Strath Nairn. Bike-camping is a strenuous activity, bike-packing across mountains even more so. The important thing is to take it slowly, allowing plenty of time, and not to try to cover the distances you would on a lightly laden bike. Camping gear gives the freedom to stop the night where you like, when you like, high in the hills or even on mountain tops, at no cost. A week's holiday cost me less than £20 – the train fare to Inverness and back – apart from food which I'd have had to buy anyway.

From Strath Nairn a single-track road climbs to over 1500 feet across the moors to the Findhorn valley – this is a well-known cycling route avoiding the main road from Inverness to Tomatin. Still stretching the legs after the train journey I managed to cycle up all the hills in spite of the load and the heat, and greatly enjoyed bowling along across the top and down to the Findhorn, already feeling I was back in real country. I turned up the river, following the road for another few miles to Coignafearn. On a fine day this valley is very attractive, but it can be bleak indeed when the wind is howling down. There's a very select estate feel to the place, with strategically situated farms and fine houses every mile or so and you always feel you're being watched – which perhaps I was; at the end of the road were a number of parked cars with a gaggle of birdwatchers equipped with telescopes, tripods and binoculars. This is a good spot for seeing eagles without having to walk. At last on a track, I cycled on up the glen for another three miles to the huge, unlikely rambling building of Coignafearn Lodge. A track led up the side valley of the Elrick Burn, I then wheeled the bike up steep zigzags to reach the 2500-foot plateau. It was less than two miles to where I planned to camp but, as is the way with bike-packing, it took the best part of two hours. The Monadhliath are notorious for their rough peat-hag country and it is slow going indeed with a laden bike. It's great country for wildlife though, with lots of birds, arctic hares and deer. Green stream valleys give easier going and eventually I found my way to one, only to encounter steep broken ground and little waterfalls which took over half an hour to negotiate.

I'd always much rather camp high in the hills than stay in any hotel or B&B – it is indeed true that the best things in life are free! Often the best part of the day is the evening camp, cooking and eating tea (again much preferable to any restaurant meal), pottering around, perhaps wandering up some low neighbouring hill. I found myself on top of 2800-foot Carn an Fhreicaidain, high above Kingussie, looking across Speyside to the evening light on the Cairngorms, far removed from the rush of the A9.

The weather had turned a bit drizzly by the next morning but no matter, ahead lay a long trek through Glen Feshie. First, however, to get down to Kingussie. After a short climb back up to the watershed, a good track led down, down for nearly 2000 feet all the way to the valley; mostly bikeable and a great descent. Golfers were out and Kingussie was busy with holidaymakers, I pedalled through without stopping and soon was riding along friendly forestry tracks from Tromie Bridge to Glen Feshie. I remembered tramping this way a few years earlier at night, in snow – it's amazing how time, season and weather can change the aspect of a place! Once past Glen Feshie Lodge you realise how this glen has achieved its reputation of being the jewel of the Cairngorms. Magnificent scots pine and birch woods adorn the valley and hillsides, with the high rounded hills above cut off by steep crags and waterfalls. You can also see the problems of bad management and far too many deer, with erosion and no regeneration of trees. Fencing is one solution but the only real answer is to abandon deer-stalking as a sport and keep the deer population at a much lower level.

A lovely grassy track led through the stately pines – too good to be true? It was, a landslip had taken the path with it and getting the bike and pack through proved both tricky and strenuous. Half a mile on the same again – so to avoid it I forded the river twice, not easy with boulders and quite a flow of icy water. Four lightly laden mountain bikers had already passed me ('Rather you than me,' had been the comment on seeing my load!) But, like the tortoise, I was carrying my house with me and didn't need to hurry to reach Braemar that night. For the next few miles I mostly wheeled the bike, still climbing out of birch woods, past fine waterfalls in a gleam of sun, then into bleak moorland in the remote heart of the Cairngorms. A route-finding error left me floundering through desperate peat hags – enough was enough and I camped by the upper Geldie at 1750 feet. A road was very nearly driven through Glen Feshie a number of years ago and I was only a couple of miles from the end of a good track which would take met to Linn of Dee and Braemar the next morning. Remoteness in Scotland is always something of an illusion. Yet every time I wander off the beaten track in the Highlands I'm amazed at just how empty the country is, how few people actually live in or even visit anything other than a tiny fraction of the region.

Drizzle and rain were sweeping in, nevertheless there was just time to nip up the remote top of An Sgarsoch (a name which sounds like a female munro-bagger) – a hill I hadn't visited for 25 years and one of the remotest in Scotland. The rounded, stony summit overlooked hundreds of square miles of empty moorland, the grey mist came and went – and there was a cosy tent just three miles away!

The cool of the evening

Perhaps my favourite verse in the Bible story of the Garden of Eden is the one which describes the Lord God as walking in the Garden in the cool of the evening. I like the implication that even God, after a hard day's work, relaxes in the evening beauty of his creation before taking up again the daily battle against chaos and evil. For most people, most of the time, most of the day is taken up with work, responsibilities and rushing around. Any time to spare is likely to be in the evening when the day's work is done. It's great if you can manage a whole day out in peaceful and beautiful countryside such as you find throughout rural Scotland and northern England. Usually, though, duties dictate otherwise. Early morning, when many are still in bed, is a grand time to be abroad but is tempered by knowledge that the main part of the day, with all its problems, still lies ahead – and how many actually manage to do anything other gobble a rushed breakfast and leap into the car?

It really is amazing how sheep-like most folk are. Take the English Lake District which has the busiest and most-walked mountains in Britain, if not in the world. On a fine summer day there will be a steady stream of walkers across all the tops, maybe even several thousand over the most popular hills. Yet before eight in the morning or after seven in the evening the high mountains will be empty. One of the great benefits of staying in mountain areas is that it is easy to take an early morning or evening wander across the high tops without having to plan it carefully beforehand.

An early May heatwave brought temperatures in the upper seventies to the north of England, quite a change after weeks of cold and rain. The drive south was long and hot and it was good to relax early the following morning by climbing high then jogging across tops of 2500-2800 feet in the calm sunshine. There's a great freedom on any high mountains in fine weather but especially so when running across the plateaux wearing hardly anything in the clear air of a fine morning. You think of all those rushing to work, of the four lanes of fast moving traffic on city motorways, you think of those still asleep in bed. You have even these busiest of hills to yourself till, on the descent, you start meeting the first well-equipped fell-walkers sweating up the steep stony track.

Later in the week, after a hot, busy day, I set off on a fine evening to potter up a moorland hill which rises to just over 2000 feet. The most popular long distance path in Britain crosses this top which must see hundreds of people a day during the summer. At seven I met the last two walkers heading down to the valley and after that the hill was mine. At 8-30 on this most visited of summits I could have been the only man in the world. The evening was perfect, unbroken sunshine, shadows lengthening, all the moorland and mountain tops bright and clear, the green Vale of Eden (aptly named) stretching out far below. Most of the day's hillwalkers would be sitting indoors, in pubs or hotels or hostels. Most ordinary people would be watching television. You truly felt that the Lord God was walking the hilltops in the cool of the evening but that very few were there to keep him company.

The following evening, after another hot day, I set out for a gentle bike ride – another good way of appreciating the beauty of the countryside at one of the best times of day. Indeed the weather was so good that the ride turned into something a bit less gentle, up long hills (walking the steep bits, there was no hurry so why not enjoy the gradually changing landscape as the road climbed up past 1500 feet?) to reach again high moorland country of peewit and drumming snipe. The road wound in and out, up and down, passing England's highest inn where, from the number of cars parked, quite a few folk were spending this most perfect of late evenings indoors. A long, steep descent took me into the evening shadows of another valley, followed by a steady climb towards the setting sun to gain the cool of a 1700-foot pass, fresh with the scent of the moors and the call of the golden plover as the dim red sun disappeared on the horizon behind gathering heat-haze. So steep was the next descent that it took me little more than ten minutes to cover the five miles to what was one of the nicest of country towns but still worlds away from the magic of those evening uplands.

Gardeners, too, know that the evening is the time to wander round enjoying the flowers and the scents and the evening birdsong after a day of digging, planting, mowing and weeding. Why not switch off the telly on the next fine evening and go out and enjoy the garden or the river or the sea even if you can't get to the hills. You never know who else you might meet enjoying the cool of the evening!

Cairngorm spring

The Highland camping season usually lasts about a fortnight. Sometime around the end of May comes that brief interlude between the last of the winter and the first of the midges, with the best chance of getting good weather on the hills. That's when I like to have my annual 'walkabout'. The worst part of a camping trip is the evening before setting off, trying to fit tent, stove, sleeping bag, spare clothes, waterproofs and a mountain of food into the rucsac. Eventually it's all in somehow – and then the thing seems so heavy that I can hardly lift it. My plan to climb to 3600 feet and walk about 15 miles on the morrow seems impossible. Then there is the minor problem of getting four miles from home to the station for the early morning train – and I'm not yet old and decrepit enough for a taxi!

This year the Cairngorms were my venue – not the skiing area above Aviemore, but further west and south. Aviemore is, at least, a place you can get out of quickly and it was with considerable relief that, an hour's walk from the station, I turned off the Cairngorm motorway into the singing Inchriach woods. It was to be just about the only fine, warm day – much too warm to be struggling up steep heather slopes from the Spey valley onto one of the dullest of all munros called, of course, Geal Charn. My old map showed a path that no longer existed and after searching around in thick pine-clad slopes covered in ants I gave up and headed straight upwards. Pints of sweat later the summit was eventually reached, with a raging thirst – and this was meant to be a holiday! It was now, though, pleasantly cool. A glider made me jump, circling noiselessly a few hundred yards away. Eastward, gentle slopes led to the higher tops of the Sgorans. A snack lightened the pack a little (psychologically at any rate) and a deliciously cool spring slaked my thirst a mile further on. At last I was beginning to enjoy the day. From the top of 3600-foot Sgor Gaoth steep crags fell for 2000 feet to Loch Einich, looking a very long way down. It was a boost to morale to realise that I'd lugged the heaviest pack of the week up more height than that and was still on my feet!

A couple of hours later and still above 3000 feet – eight o'clock on a fine evening and not a minute too early to camp. A fine spot in the high hills, just above the rim of the steep corrie dropping away into Glen Feshie, with the wind carrying the scent of the trees up from far below. A warm night, but with mist and drizzle rolling in to clear slowly the next morning. As the sun gradually won I resorted to 'munro bagging', visiting two tops on the plateau to the south. A Landrover track climbs onto these hills from Glen Feshie, ending at the last summit. Here, to my great surprise, a white van was parked with a man asleep in the back. I wrote out a parking ticket, left it on his windscreen and would have liked to be there when he woke up! The rest of the day was fine and warm for crossing remote Monadh Mor and Beinn Bhrotain before descending to the Geldie, west of Braemar for another comfortable night's camp near the ruin of Bynack Lodge. It was to be the last mild night of the week.

I had a shock the next day when it started snowing hard on 3400-foot Glas Tulaichen, near Glenshee. I was camping high that night, at 2600 feet by Loch nan Eun (The loch of the birds – black-headed gulls nesting on a grassy island). It snowed, it froze, it blew and on the morning of 30th May the ground was white and the tent covered in frost. I nipped up another remote munro (Carn an Righ) in a snow-shower then packed up the tent in a brief interlude of sun and headed for An Socach. This peak has a mile-long curving summit ridge and though the sun was bright the temperature was well below freezing and the northerly gale bitter. In spite of walking fast with full pack and wearing all my warm and windproof clothes I was getting colder and colder – enough was enough and instead of following the ridge north to Morrone, above Braemar, descended into the welcome shelter of Glen Ey. This turned out to be surprisingly attractive, with an enjoyable walk in the sunshine down to the Linn of Dee. Two miles of less attractive road-walking followed, before a path took me up onto the hillside below Morrone, for a camp in sheltered woodland a couple of miles from Braemar. Snow-showers enveloped all the high hills to the north and even here a few sleety flakes fell, though it felt positively warm out of the wind. I'd missed the midges but not the winter!

May clifftops

Now is the time of year for the coasts, or the hills, or the moors, or indeed just about anywhere in the Far North! There is simply so much going on in the natural world, everything is rushing to nest, breed, flower or set seed before the first snow comes to the hilltops in September. The cliffs and rocky shores which surround the county are particularly fine at this time of year on a good day. We've had some grand weather, bracing days of bright clear skies with passing showers, days of warm sunshine. In such conditions there's nowhere better to be than a Caithness clifftop, even if you've only an hour or two to spare.

Perhaps I'd better not be too specific about my route in case someone falls off when trying to follow it. Common-sense is however all that's really needed to be safe on the cliffs. From the bay I jogged up over the headland, the sun already warm in a hazy sky, though it was only just after seven in the morning. The yellowish grass was spotted with Scottish Primrose, the flowers wide open and a brilliant purple in the sunshine. A little further on, across the other side of a geo, a bank of ordinary primroses was almost dazzling in its brightness. Is it imagination or are all the flowers brighter and more colourful than usual this spring? The white flowers of scurvy grass were also profuse along the clifftops while red campion adorned the tops of some of the geos. Kittiwakes were wheeling in clouds like snowflakes, the air full of their calls. Guillemots sat in black-and-white rows on the lower ledges while a few fulmars wheeled silently overhead. The sea was almost calm, and a creel boat pottered westward below the cliffs. Now I cut down steep grass slopes, scrambling over rocks to a stony bay where rusting plates from an ancient shipwreck lie and the waves wash in and out of a cave through the headland. A pair of eider-duck swam silently out to sea through a narrow passage between a sea-stack and the mainland. A long steep climb and a short narrow ridge took me to a conical grassy top, much liked by gulls and sheep; indeed a group of four sheep with lambs were precariously threading a narrow trod half way down a 60-degree slope which steepened into vertical cliffs below. From my eyrie I looked across a deep channel to a stack whose earth and grass slopes were dotted with hundreds of puffin burrows. Already considerable numbers of the birds were in residence, sitting outside their homes or emerging into the sunshine, while groups of a dozen or more were flying to and fro, circling my top in an anticlockwise direction. Nowhere is better for watching puffins! I sat for some ten minutes in the sunshine then resumed my jog along the rough clifftops.

A small, narrow stream valley interrupted the moor just inland of another cliff of kittiwakes, here the birds were flying back and forth below me, gathering beakfuls of moss and mud to take to their nesting sites on the cliff ledges. The birds were silent – was it too important a job to waste energy in calling? Leaving the cliffs, I headed inland, climbing gently across rough moorland then through heather to reach a small loch inhabited by four greylag geese. I'd been getting pretty hot in the warm, windless conditions – so why not have my first outdoor dip of the year? The water was cold, but not too cold, and most refreshing, much needed before a half-mile slog through heather to reach the road. After the rough moorland it was nice just to jog along a smooth easy highway, up over the moor with the curlews. People were out cutting peat, making the most of the excellent conditions. I came down through woodland, the trees now almost fully into pale green leaf with bluebells (and some pink) in the verges and chaffinches singing.

The grassy slopes above the sand-dunes were bright with cowslips, some of the individual flowers as much as a half an inch across. Oystercatchers and ringed plovers took off from the beach, a sandpiper was calling and a tern, the first I'd heard this year, screeched overhead. The waves were lapping rather than breaking, the harbour basked in sunshine. Just three hours out – and so much to see.

Short-cut to Inverness

How long does it take you to travel from Drumochter to Inverness. An hour maybe? I had two whole days for the journey – but then I wasn't quite following the A9. On a typical Drumochter morning of low cloud and drizzle I packed up my tent from a heathery glen above the pass and made my way down the path to where I'd left the bike. The three miles of main road were cycled as fast as possible, before turning off onto the quiet road through Dalwhinnie. The weather seemed to be following the pattern of the previous days, a grey start soon brightening but with heavy showers and downpours later on. You take what you get on these trips. There is now a small shop in Dalwhinnie, well stocked with groceries and general supplies, providing a much-needed service both to the local community and to passing campers like me. Long may it survive! I'd dined in luxury the previous two nights with a few extra tins and fresh bakery items; of necessity the back- or bike-packer can't carry many such things.

The road to Laggan passed quickly in the warm sunshine with the greenery around the village a welcome change from the bleak Drumochter moorlands. It was morning break at the local primary school and children were shooing cows off the playing field by the river. White, towering clouds were building over the snow-streaked corries and peaks of the Ardverikie hills. Just another mile along the green strath – then up, up into the Monadhliath. It used to be, I believe, a well-known route over the mountains from Glen Markie to the Fechlin and Foyers, possibly the shortest route from Dalwhinnie to Inverness. I'm sure that many of the old-style 'rough-stuff' cyclists passed this way. Does anybody nowadays? The route had intrigued me on the map for a long time and now there was plenty of time to drag the bike up to nearly 3000 feet and down the other side. An increasingly rough track was just about rideable for a couple of miles, with a succession of about eight gates to open. Then came the first big obstacle. The River Markie was high, bouldery and without a bridge. I had to leave the pack, manhandle the bike through the water then return for the pack – three river crossings in all. Shouldering the pack I wheeled the bike for another mile up a faint path to where my route turned steeply uphill. A patch of grass by a small waterfall gave a good spot for a late lunch, to enjoy the peace and freedom of the high hills which only come to the cross-country traveller. With tent and food for two days, there was no hurry, I could stop when and where I liked. It was indeed as well there was no hurry. The slopes were too steep to climb with both bike and pack, I would slowly push the bike up a couple of hundred feet, jog back down and return with the pack. The going was not difficult though, deep heather had been burnt and the grassy banks of a burn gave an easy, meandering route through a corrie of peathags. A final steep climb took me up onto the plateau after wheeling the bike across a small snow-field (I do hope somebody saw the tracks!)

The sky to the west was black, and the wind cold, the cloud would soon be rolling in. An easy route down gentle slopes led to a high loch, followed by good progress along the grassy banks of a stream wending through the high, remote moors of the Monadhliath. The feel was of being a long way from anywhere, this was golden plover and deer country. Little eel-like creatures make their way up here from Loch Ness, growing to several feet before returning to the loch and growing into something much bigger. (Maybe!) Showery rain became heavier. A faint path appeared and the going turned much rougher. It was more the probability amplitude of a path, in other words it came and went and gave a higher chance of finding slightly easier going among saturated peatbogs, hags, moss and swollen burns. Hard work wheeling a bike, it was. After another two miles an estate track could be seen in the distance, contouring the hillside and indicating that the main difficulties were over. It was now about six in the evening and pouring with rain – time to camp. Two hundred feet lower down, two hill rivers tumbled over waterfalls and joined to make the River Killin which subsequently becomes the Fechlin. Here was a small area of grass next to the river with a view of the falls, an ideal campsite. Soon I was in the tent, enjoying a big meal as the rain bucketed down. The rain eased off later on and I ventured out for a short walk up the hill. The falls were now beginning to thunder rather than roar, and the river was not that far below the tent. An hour later the water was a foot higher and still rising... at nine I took the decision to move the tent rather than risk being flooded out in the night. A wet, miserable procedure, with nowhere else to camp other than boggy ground covered in deep heather. The falls were now really thundering, amid clouds of spray. Whether I'd have been flooded or not I don't know, but there were at most a couple of inches to spare.

The last day of the trek dawned grey, more of the same. Soon I reached the estate track, it was nice to actually be able to ride the bike. The track steepened to plunge down the hillside amid birchwoods in a succession of zigzags. I walked again. Far below, at the end of the glen, there suddenly came into view a huge, square, shooting lodge, a great surprise in such an out-of-the-way spot. On approaching it became apparent that the windows were out, the walls just a shell. A huge gaunt ruin, everyone's idea of a haunted mansion.

The glen was friendly enough though in the warm sun, a fine ride down the track to a road-end, then past Loch Killin, deep in its bowl of hills, and on, coasting down long hills through greenery and birches to Strath Errick. The rest of the journey was straightforward, by Foyers and the quiet eastern shore of Loch Ness, as showers turned into heavy downpours. It had been a mountain crossing to recall every time I travel from Drumochter to Inverness!

Ben Loyal the hard way

Two cuckoos were calling to each other from the scattered birches beside Loch Loyal; simultaneously the wailing of several red-throated divers drifted across the water. The area around Tongue is indeed a very special part of the Highlands.

I'd driven out from home, seeing little other than the road. Now, with the bike unladen from the roof, things were completely transformed. First there was a hill to cycle up, not even noticed in the car, with a growing view across Loch Craggie to the sunlit slopes of Beinn Stumanadh. Next, spectacular views back to Ben Loyal as I cycled the road past lochans and over the Sutherland flow country. Those travelling this way emerge, high above Tongue, to a sudden view, one of the best in the Highlands. There really should be a small carpark and viewpoint to encourage tourists to stop. Below is the whole of the Kyle of Tongue, the sun often gleaming on large expanses of wet sand, with the distant line of the causeway road curving across then climbing up the vast Moin moors to the white dot of the Moin house. Further to the left rise the steep slopes and crags of Ben Hope contrasting with the green fields and woods fringing the Kyle.

I freewheeled down between the hedges and walls of the narrow lane leading into Tongue, where the children were just going into school. Tongue always seems a village straight out of heaven, though no doubt it has its problems, like everywhere else. Memories are of walking through on a hot sunny Good Friday many years ago, nobody about, total peace except for some lively Scottish dance music drifting out of the door of one of the slumbering cottages. On the Kinloch road is a monument to the 'bard of the clearances' reminding that even Tongue has seen evil times, passing this I turned down through Ribigill farm and began bumping along the rough track leading towards Ben Loyal. A herd of Highland cattle watched, with a mean-looking bull fortunately on the other side of a strong fence. A couple of walkers were no doubt wondering why anyone would want to take a bike this way, the cycling was getting rougher but I was determined to ride as much as possible. There certainly wouldn't be much riding in the next couple of miles. Trying to cycle through the Rhian Burn ended up with getting both feet soaked, I managed a few yards further and that was that. Now it was a question of wheeling, then carrying.

Ben Loyal isn't a particularly easy mountain across which to cycle. Indeed it would never have occurred to me to try, especially not via the steepest route, except that... the cover picture of my previous anthology, 'Ralph's Far North', shows a man carrying a bike up a very steep mountain with a loch far below in the background. The picture fits in quite well with an article in the middle of the book about a bike-camping expedition across the Grampians. The loch however is drawn with a faint line linking shore to shore and those who know their Sutherland will immediately identify it as the Tongue Causeway. The mountain is Ben Loyal. I'd never taken a bike over Ben Loyal. I had to make sure to do it before the publication date of the book in mid-July 2000! The weather was bright and very cool, indeed almost cold, with a few showers, good conditions for hard labour. The first few hundred feet weren't too bad, the bike could be wheeled up the path without much difficulty. In order to fit that cover picture I would, though, have to tackle the 45-degree slopes leading straight up to the north top of Sgor Chaonsaid. With the bike over my back I started the slow, steep climb, the main risk being one of toppling over backwards. I kept my cycle helmet on just in case. Slowly I gained height, stopping for frequent rests. A grassy gully split the crags ahead, very steep but feasible. Not many bikes come this way. It wasn't really that difficult, just slow and requiring great care. The gully was steeper than it looked. There was no way I could scramble up rock and had to carefully pick a route up the steep grass and moss. Slowly the lip of the steep slopes drew nearer; at long last I reached easier ground and could put the bike down, I'd be able to wheel it the rest of the way. I was now at the high rocks at the end of the ridge which give a tremendous view out over the Kyle, the ground to the west falling away almost vertically for 2000 feet. There's good scrambling on the rocky tors but not with a bike!

In spite of the bright weather the wind on the top was bitter and eventually I gave in and pulled on long trousers, cagoule and gloves. A short stretch down to a dip could be cycled before wheeling up to just below the summit rocks. There really wasn't much point, but just to be able to say that I'd cycled up Ben Loyal I dragged the bike to the very top. All around were those superb views you always see from an isolated peak in the north. Out over the lochans and flows of Sutherland to the Caithness moors and the white dot of Dounreay, across the sea to Hoy, round to Scaraben and Maiden Pap and Morven and Ben Armine and Klibreck, the big lochs to the left, south to the distant snow-flecked Fannichs, west to Ben More Assynt still bearing large snow patches, on round to Ben Hee and the Westminster Estate hills and Ben Hope, also with a dirty-white patch of snow.

The only easy way off the summit rocks of Ben Loyal is the way you came up, I carefully lowered the bike down then wheeled it to easier ground which gave a steep ride down over moss. Any lingering conscience about riding a bike over such 'fragile' ground was soon dispelled, the bike left hardly a mark whereas somebody had actually been driving quad bikes up here, their tracks plain to see. Very few people will take the effort to drag bikes up steep mountains, any damage or disturbance will be minimal. One quad bike probably does more damage than 100 bicycles. Once over the next top, cycling was possible again, down into the dip, quite an experience to be riding a bike so much on top of the world! From the last summit, Carn an Tionail, I managed to zigzag down some of the way, wheeling steeper and rougher sections, to the shore of Loch Na Beiste where an angler was out in a rowing boat. Two walkers were descending the steep Cnoc nan Cuilean, on such a fine afternoon I couldn't resist leaving the bike and climbing the 700 feet to the top for another fine view over the emptinesses of Sutherland. Not that Ben Loyal was quiet, there were more people about than I'd ever seen before on the mountain. The last slopes down to the road were easy, mostly rideable through heather and bog, then four miles of smooth tarmac along the loch shore took me back to my starting point. Cycle over Ben Loyal? Much more sensible just to take a gentle walk across the mountain and enjoy at leisure the very special country around Tongue!

Twenty-four stolen hours

It's a wet morning in Crianlarich with a bad forecast and you have to be in Edinburgh the following day. Would you drive there for lunch, spend the afternoon shopping and the night in a hotel? You're not Ralph! I had 24 whole hours and was not going to waste them, weather or no! It was simply a question of which mountains to climb. I'd visited none of the most southern munros and this was an opportunity not to be missed. I decided on two peaks above Lochearnhead which were not far out of my way and drove the 20 miles there through the steady rain.

A farm track led up Glen Ample, then a path climbed the hillside through forestry plantings into the corrie below Ben Vorlich and Stuc a Chroin. It was, simply, wet. The rain became heavier and heavier as I climbed, the wind gradually picking up, but it wasn't that cold. Streams and rivers were rising, cloud covered the tops. I crossed the burn and headed up steep slopes into the cloud, sheltering behind a rock to remove my cagoule and put a pullover on underneath. During this manoeuvre I managed to rip off my watch, a pin from the strap disappearing between boulders... Soon I gained a ridge which led on up to piled boulders topped by a summit cairn and a memorial. Cold, wild and wet, no place to hang about – I set the compass and turned north. The path immediately began a steep, rocky, descent, which was odd as the map had suggested a quarter of a mile of gentle ridge first. It was an old map and presumably wrong, the direction was certainly correct and as expected the slopes eventually eased off and the path began a steep climb up Ben Vorlich. The hoses turned full stream onto me on the summit ridge and with relief I hurried down the gentler western slopes to emerge from the cloud above the valley where I'd set off. The rivers and streams had risen, hillsides were seamed in white and the Burn of Ample was roaring over the rapids at the Falls of Edinample. The rain was lighter in the valley but no less persistent. There was a new map posted up at the entrance to Glen Ample, I checked to see if my old one was indeed wrong. Funny, the new map also marked a long gentle ridge leading north from the summit of Stuc a Chroin. Oh no... the cairn I'd climbed up to was actually a couple of hundred feet lower than the true summit, which I'd managed to miss. I'd have to climb the peak again sometime. (Which I did, two years later, once again in heavy driving rain. Funny how these two hills always seem to gleam, beckoning, in clear sunny air when I'm making a long drive south with no opportunity to stop!)

For some reason I'd taken my camera with me, there weren't going to be any photos but one is always told not to leave such things in the car. It had been well wrapped up in polythene bags but in the hosepipe conditions water had found its way in, and the case was wet... I removed the camera and water dripped out from the shutter mechanism. It was completely dead. Not a very expensive model but a nice modern one, all automatic with a good zoom lens. What with missing the summit of Stuc a Chroin, a soaked camera and a broken watch-strap it hadn't been quite my day. (I took the batteries out of the camera and hung it over the car's hot-air vent for the next 400 miles, driving with the heating full on and the windows wide open. Amazingly, it recovered.)

Now for a night in Edinburgh? No way! The Pentland Hills are another fine part of Scotland and I had a perfectly good tent in the car. So on down through Callander and onto the motorway as the weather, at last, began to clear. Hills don't change much, so I often keep using my old maps. I had a 'one-inch' sheet of Edinburgh and the Pentlands, last revised in 1953-4, which while perfectly accurate for the hill slopes gave little help in finding my way off the motorway and up through Ratho and Kirknewton. The small roads were, however, much as on my map and I drove through narrow lanes past Cockburnhall to eventually emerge at Threipmuir reservoir and a convenient carpark. Even here there were a few midges as I set off again at around six into an improving evening. The road up to Bravelaw and the path towards the Logan Burn and Habbie's Howe were just as on my old map. A couple of miles further on was an ideal campsite just below a little rocky ravine where the Logan Burn tumbled down waterfalls. Cuckoos and curlews were calling and here, only ten miles from Edinburgh Castle, a pair of ring ouzels was in residence. The three-note call echoed throughout the evening and began the dawn chorus at 3.30 the next morning! Several times I saw the birds, like slim athletic blackbirds, the male with a prominent white collar.

The highest Pentland top of Scald Law was only a mile away and made a good objective for an evening walk after I'd cooked my tea. The Pentlands are real wild hills in spite of being so near the big city, the higher slopes have peatbogs and rough heather, cloudberry was growing near the top of Scald Law, there were grouse and larks and pipits. I looked out across Edinburgh to the islands of the Forth and the hills of Fife, Penicuik lay to the south with beyond the Moorfoots and Tweedsmuirs. Nobody in Scotland has any excuse for feeling trapped in a town or city; there is glorious unspoilt countryside within easy walking or cycling distance of any centre of population. In England (apart from the most northern counties) towns and cities sprawl for ever, countryside is commuterland and there really is no escape without long journeys on busy roads or crowded trains.

A few joggers and mountain bikers came past in the late evening making the most of the fine end to the day, otherwise it could have been some remote part of the Highlands. I drifted to sleep listening to the ripple of the burn and the song of wrens, cuckoos and moorland birds. In the morning the sun really did warm the tent out of a clear blue sky, the site was far more idyllic than any of the previous few days in Highland rain, midges and even sleet. It was hard to believe, as I packed up and walked out across the heather slopes of Hare Hill, that the Edinburgh rush hour would be in full swing. Yet once I'd started the car it was just five minutes drive into Balermo and another 15 into the city.

It always pays off to be a bit more adventurous. Two (nearly) munros, a walk over the highest tops of the Pentland Hills and a good night's sleep in a tent amid the ring-ouzels and curlews, had been far more rewarding than a wander round the shops and an expensive night under the tame roof of some luxurious guest house or hotel!

What makes Caithness?

(This piece was written in 1993, I've left it almost unchanged, you can judge for yourself if, and how much, the county has changed since then!)

WHAT is it that makes Caithness? No sooner do I seem to be getting a feel for it than it slips out of my grasp. There are so many different strands to the county, more separate than interwoven, yet crossing here and there.

There is the farming. The cool, damp summers and long hours of daylight lead, on the clay lands of Caithness, to some of the best grass-growing conditions in Britain. Caithness is the fields of sheep, the mixed herds of beef cattle, the April lambing, the market sales. It is the summer sound of tractors and balers and roller makers, working in any dry slot in the weather, day or night. It is the fields dotted with hundreds of straw and silage rollers, glowing in evening sun. It is the lights of the combine salvaging the oats on a frosty November night in a bitter wind. The Caithness farmer, in the tradition of the shift-working and seafaring aspects of the county, will work all night to make the most of a dry interlude. Caithness is the slab fences, patched with corrugated iron and car-bonnets, it is the gable-ends of abandoned crofts, it is the prize-winning herds, the crofts with 40 acres, the Dounreay worker with a couple of goats and a few sheep.

There is the sea. The trawlers unloading in Scrabster and Wick, the fish markets, the Orkney ferries, the creel boats, the tankers and cargo boats heading through the most difficult waters in the British Isles. It is watching the St Ola, a dot in the distance, disappear behind the cliffs of Hoy on a fine evening. It is the surfers at Thurso East. It is the 30-foot waves rolling in at Dounreay on a north-westerly gale. It is salmon netting boats in the early morning at Thurso harbour. It is the Grey Coast of Neil Gunn, the dozens of small harbours down the east coast, the old herring-fishing buildings, rusting rings set in the rock down remote geos. It is the sand blowing on Sinclair's Bay, it is seven lighthouses seen blinking from the top of Olrig Hill on a dark night. It is salt-haze in the air and salt crusted on the windows, stunted trees and flying spume, rock-pools and tangle.

There are the estates. Lodges and keepers and private roads. Red deer stags roaring to each other on the slopes of Scaraben on a clear September morning, grasses red, heather dying, frost in the valley bottom, the tang of autumn. Grouse rising. The lights of an Argocat on the moors on a late October afternoon, bringing the stag back to Dalnawhillan after stalking. Tweedy fishermen studying the Thurso from Halkirk bridge. The keeper out setting snares for foxes, culling the hinds in December, feeding the stags in February. Green estate Range Rovers negotiating bumpy tracks. Hawking with peregrines below Dorrery.

There is industry. For nearly two centuries there's been an industrial strand to Caithness – first the flagstone industry, then the herring industry, now the nuclear industry, and freezers, and glass, and electronics. There is a large group of people who have little connection with the land or sea, who live in the towns, who travel daily to work like anyone in the cities. There are the housing estates of Thurso and Wick, the stream of traffic to and from Dounreay, the familiar outlines of the nuclear plant.

There are the shops and banks and offices, and all those aspects of town life that go with them. There are the coffee mornings and jumble sales and musical evenings, the shopping trips to Inverness. There is the plethora of clubs and societies meeting on the long, dark winter evenings. Caithness is a hard-drinking place, with more drunks per square mile than almost anywhere else in Britain.

There are tourists. Tourists see the gift shops at John O'Groats, the glass factory, the inside of many hotels. Few realise that the 1:50000 Ordnance Survey map is the best guidebook of all and venture off the main roads. Caithness is the traffic jams in Thurso with coaches unloading at the Royal Hotel at 5pm. It is bemused tourists wandering the early-morning streets trying to buy a newspaper. It is camper-vans with foreign registrations overnighting in laybys, it is a packed campsite swept by driving August drizzle. It is golfing and trout-fishing and sailing.

There is history. Men have lived here for thousands of years; the chambered cairns erected 5000 years ago remain, the brochs and castles, sites of war and battle, are everywhere. Standing stones and stone circles and stone rows are so common as to be overgrown and unvisited. Yet man has made little real impact on the county, save perhaps by the recent devastating plantations on large areas of the flow country.

There is nature. Caithness is the county of the cliffs and the moors, the great seabird colonies, the sanctuaries for flora and fauna on the steep broken slopes of the east coast, blue butterflies over banks of flowers. It is that great sense of space, emptiness and light of the flow country, the dark-blue water of a remote loch rippling onto sand. It's the wail of the red-throated diver, the mournful golden plover, the musical greenshank. It is the utter silence of the Knockfin Heights under deep January snow.

There is weather. Caithness is the wind, never still, fresh summer breezes, 100 mph squalls of hail blasting across on a January night. It is air semi-liquid with mist and drizzle for days on end in July. It is the mud and darkness and storms of December. It is the absolute clarity of air on a May evening, skylines sharp as far as Birsay, Morven, Foinaven and Cape Wrath. It is the welcome evening sea-breeze after a rare hot summer day, it is the whiteout blizzard and blocked roads with a complete thaw three days later. It is all four seasons in a day, any time of the year, and the weather-forecaster's despair.

Caithness is the people. It is the place. It is much more than both.

Blackmount

Just south of Glencoe lies a range of ten munro peaks which I'd seen from a distance many times but somehow never managed to visit. I reckoned I could cross the entire range of mountains, known as the Blackmount, in a single walk of two to three days; enough of a challenge for me but pretty slow given that a fit fell runner could probably manage the lot in five hours.

The weather was fine for the drive south but the forecast was indecisive, rain over Central Scotland might or might not move north. By ten in the morning, after four hours drive, I'd had enough, the traffic was building up and Ben Vair, above Loch Leven, looked fantastic. It was another of those popular peaks a long way from home which I'd never climbed; the Blackmount would have to wait. Five hours later I was back at the car after a circuit of the high ridges in glorious sunshine and a cold wind. Two munros, tremendous views across a vast sea of mountains and lochs as far as Skye, Mull and Rhum, the weather looking set fair for weeks. The sky to the south was indeed white with ominous high cloud but it didn't seem to be getting any nearer.

An unpleasant hour's drive up Glencoe and down Glen Etive followed in the heat and traffic. Glen Etive is great to walk but terrible to drive, the road is busy and single track with many blind bends and few passing places. Eventually I had the car safely parked near Loch Etive, the pack on the back and set off thankfully into the hills again on a fine late afternoon. I forded the river Etive – waist deep but warm after the day's sunshine – then climbed up past the 'Robbers' Waterfall' towards the high corries below spectacular Ben Starav. It would have been wise just to carry on until dusk, it was early June and wouldn't be dark until 11pm. But I was tired after driving 250 miles and climbing two mountains and at 7.30 decided to stop and camp just below the main ridge. It did, after all, look as if the next day would also be fine.

The evening was indeed beautiful, soon the sun went behind Ben Starav but a short walk onto a nearby ridge brought me back into the late evening sunshine, the hills around glowing red with shadowed Glen Etive far below. A ring ouzel sung in the distance, its characteristic triple call a feature of all the high corries. Patches of cloud were forming and evaporating but there was no sign of any major change in the weather... till the first patter of rain on the tent at two the next morning. Any hopes of being woken by the early morning sun faded as the rain started in earnest at six. Not that the weather was going to stop me. First there were two munros to climb before packing up and heading east along the ridge for the rest of the Blackmount. It was however remarkably cold for early June, even at 2000 feet. Almost cold enough for snow, indeed that grey haze below the cloudbase at around 3000 feet looked suspicious... A quick ascent of 500 feet took me to a stony col, then on up the steep ridge leading to Ben Starav. Sure enough it started to sleet, then snow as I gained height. The ground had been well warmed by the previous day's sun and the snow was melting from the rocks but the grass and moss were white. In the mist I gained one false top then scrambled up a narrow ridge to a higher point with another quarter of a mile along a line of old cornices to the true summit. There was no dramatic view down to Loch Etive, 3500 feet below, and the blowing snow was turning to fine drift, stinging my eyes. I hadn't thought of taking snow goggles in June! The second peak, Ben nan Aighenan needed a big detour, down to a 2000-foot col then back up 1000 feet into the cloud and snow before returning up and down the whole way to the tent – where it was still raining.

For the rest of that long day I climbed steadily up and down, into cloud and snow above 3000 feet, into clearer air and mostly light rain on the lower slopes. Three more munro tops were crossed, there were misty views out to unidentified grey hills, there were Alpine flowers including large clumps of cushion pink, there was a mother ptarmigan fluttering along the ground to draw me away from her fluffy chicks, there were even a few other walkers braving the sleet and rain. At 7pm and just below the 3000-foot contour I'd had enough, it was time to camp again, in a high corrie looking out through the haze of rain and sleet to Rannoch Moor. High camping has the romantic appeal of sunsets and dawns from the summits but is more often just cold, damp and uncomfortable. Ever so often the patter of rain on the tent would change to the rattle of snow, eventually it died out but the hoped-for early morning sun never arrived. Instead another grey morning, fingers of cold wet mist reaching down to the tent. By the time I was only half packed-up I was shivering and my fingers were numb, there was nothing else to do though but struggle on; striking camp in cold wet conditions is one of the miseries of hill camping.

The effort of crossing the next peak warmed me up, but the continued grey cold was depressing and I was on the point of retreating to the valley when a brightening of the sky encouraged me to press on. So I turned off the descending ridge to gain a high col, put the tent up to dry, then set off up long scree slopes leading back into the mist for the last three peaks (remembering the motto: 'Tomorrow may be worse.' It was.) Those mountains proved a bit nerve wracking; unknown peaks in poor weather with just a cagoule, map and compass and most of my gear miles away. The final peak, Meall a Bhuiridh, required careful route-finding and another big detour, down a steep rocky ridge to a col then a long climb up boulder slopes to 3600 feet. There are ski-tows from the Glencoe ski-centre right to the summit but fortunately all the mess was hidden by the thick cloud. Although normally very accessible, this peak was right out on a limb for me and I was glad to regain the main ridge an hour later. It was with considerable relief that I emerged from the cloud to pick my way down the boulder and scree to my tent and a well-earned brew of tea. Then to pack up again and, at 4pm, head down the valley towards Glen Etive. I'd camp near sea-level that night, midges being preferable to sleet!

Five hours later and I was still on the move. I'd put the tent up just below the steeps of Buachaille Etive Beag, cooked a meal and was now walking down the road for six miles to retrieve the car. With the tension of the long mountain crossing over I could actually relax and enjoy the scenery, tired or no! At almost every step the views of the steep mountains around changed, vistas of long valleys opening up and closing, sudden cliffs and high corries coming into view. Cuckoos were calling, snipe were drumming. I can't think of any other road which is such purgatory to drive and such a delight to walk! Why, you may ask, bother climbing bleak misty munros when it's so much more enjoyable to walk down Glen Etive on a quiet evening? Why indeed...

The Caithness coastal walk

Someone recently asked me about the possibility of walking right round the Caithness coast. It's certainly well worth doing, I've walked it all, much of it many times – but never as a single walk. All the coastline is spectacular, especially in early summer with cliff-nesting birds crowding the ledges and the clifftops and steep slopes natural gardens of primroses, squill and campion. May and June are also however the best months to visit everywhere else and there is danger of disturbance to nesting birds – so perhaps winter is a better season for the walk; the wild seascapes then make up for the lack of birds and flowers. It would take at least a week to follow the whole Caithness coast from the Ord to Drumholiston – doing it properly, not cutting off all the corners or simply walking the roads. Even I tend to forget just how contorted and indented the east coast, in particular, is.

A couple of weeks ago I set out to follow the coast north from Sarclet towards Wick, one of my favourite stretches (like most others!) but one which I hadn't visited for a few years. The morning was grey with light rain, weather conditions which I simply didn't notice when following such a fascinating stretch of cliffs. It took me three hours to reach Girston Bay, below Hempriggs, just two and a half miles in a straight line from my starting point at Sarclet, but a walk of at least three times that distance. Five long geos, one after another, cut back south in the first mile of clifftop – Riera Geo, Broad Geo, Tods geo, Ashy Geo and Ires Geo – and it takes lots of time to walk round all of them without shortcuts. Either you're walking the coast or you're not – and if you are, you may as well do it properly and not miss all the scenery.

First came Riera Geo, almost cutting back to Sarclet. A waterfall tumbled some 100 feet into its depths – well worth looking at – but it was quite difficult to get through the deep mud around the head of the geo. Back onto the coast again – then two detours inland, first the little Corbiegeo then the main Broad Geo which came almost all the way back to a prominent new house dominating these clifftops. A few hundred yards on and again I was diverted inland, this time by Tods Geo, from where a short-cut to the top of Ashy geo would cut the distance by a factor of four but miss the sight of a fine natural arch (known as 'The Needle') only visible from the headland to the south-east of Ashy Geo. (Did sea-eagles, which were known as 'assa', ever nest at Ashy Geo?) Half a mile on – about 100 yards in a straight line from the end of Tods Geo – and you can walk across this natural bridge to a headland without realising that the wild sea is under your feet! Ires Geo, the next, is the biggest, almost worthy of being called a bay. A ruined croft house, on a dry patch of grass surrounded by a sea of mud, sits almost at the head of the geo but nobody comes here now. The geo is relatively easy to descend to a bouldery beach with a stream coming in down a ravine to the south, it is hard to believe that this spot, with such a remote feel to it, is only a mile from the main road and three miles from Wick. Dozens of grey seals now come here to breed in the autumn.

North of Ires Geo, moorland comes right down to the coast and the walking is more straightforward until the geos start again at Craig Hammel. Helman Head calls for a visit, jutting out more eastward than anywhere else along here, you can scramble down towards the sea as far as you dare... The South Stack and Dunbar Stack now come into view above the deep Girston Bay – and it was time for me to turn back. The coast onwards from here to Wick is equally good and slightly better known, by the Brig o' Tram and the Tail o' Brough and the Old Man of Wick – and it would take at least another two hours to reach the town centre. It didn't take much more than an hour to get back to Sarclet. It was still raining (I now noticed) as I cut across soaking moors to the hill of Toftcarl with its trig. point, then made my way back towards that prominent new house. A path marked on the map had completely gone to seed, lost in the bogs and never walked for years. A pity. Farmland, as everywhere else in the county, was saturated and some of the mud was too deep even for wellies. Sarclet Bay with its gaunt building and rusting winches was grey and quiet. The coast south of Sarclet is, if anything, even more contorted and it would certainly take a full day to do justice to the stretch from here to Lybster.

No, on thinking, it would take me nine long days, covering an average of 20 miles a day, to walk the coast properly, without taking shortcuts. Suitable stretches might be:-

Day 1:- Ord Point to Dunbeath, by Ceann Ousdale, Badbea and the fine cliffs north of Berriedale. The first stretch is possibly the roughest and most difficult part of the whole walk. A big detour is needed round the grounds of Dunbeath Castle (or does the new access legislation allow one to walk through?)

Day 2:- Dunbeath to Clyth, visiting many fine little harbours and secluded bays such as Achastle and Forss. Ideal for a hot sunny day!

Day 3:- Clyth to Wick via Whaligoe and Sarclet, incorporating the walk described above.

Day 4:- Wick to Keiss, taking in Noss Head and a walk along the full length of Sinclairs Bay.

Day 5:- Keiss to John O' Groats via Skirza and Duncansby Head. Highlights are Freswick Bay, Wife Geo and the Duncansby Stacks.

Day 6:- John-O-Groats to Ham (including Scotlands Haven and St John's Point).

Day 7:- Ham to Castletown, a superb walk including the entire circuit of Dunnet Head and a walk right along Dunnet Beach. An incentive to put your boots on, this one!

Day 8:- Castletown to Crosskirk via Murkle Bay, Thurso, Scrabster, Holburn Head and Brims. A fine walk along shores and low broken cliffs, a bustling town and harbour then back to the high clifftops.

Day 9:- Crosskirk to Drumholiston via Dounreay and Sandside Bay. Take the adventurous route along the Dounreay foreshore, swimming the two deep inlets forming the old intakes to DFR and PFR. This is perfectly legal! Otherwise you have to walk right round the outside of the Dounreay and Vulcan fences to the south. Enjoy the walk. There is far more risk of being washed away by a freak wave, or of contracting skin cancer from sunburn, than from radioactive pollution! There is more fine cliff scenery again west of Reay. Best carry on to Melvich and a good finish at the golden sands of Melvich Bay.

June walkabout

As I write, a man is completing a trek, by foot and by bike, across all the Scottish hills above 2000 feet. It will have taken him a year to climb nearly 1000 mountains. There can be few of us with either the opportunity or the stamina for such an expedition! What is more feasible is to take Scotland in bite-sized chunks, wending one's way across the hills for a week or two at a time – and that's what I've been doing for nearly 30 years. Munros and other high mountains are an objective on such trips but not the main one, the real aim is simply to spend some time alone in one of the remoter and most beautiful, if harsh, environments of Europe. This year, after the usual dithering and indecision I finally chose a trek on foot across the west, from Lochcarron through Glenshiel and Knoydart, then over the hills by a roundabout route from Glenfinnan to Fort William.

It's difficult to get the balance right between either carrying too much or being poorly equipped. A good tent, warm sleeping bag and Primus are the main essentials. Dehydrated food is a waste of time and money, I end up half-starved and feeling ravenous all the time. I can just manage to carry a week's decent food but it's better to be able to restock part way through. Once the weight of the pack increases above 30 pounds I start to suffer and that means carrying nothing more than is really needed! To actually set off on a solo trek across the Highlands takes a lot of determination – it's so completely different from normal life – you just have to go ahead and do it. The worst is always packing up the day before, picking up a rucsac you can seemingly hardly lift (and plan to carry over the mountains), listening to doubtful weather forecasts, remembering all the things you should be doing. It's only when you actually start walking up into the hills that you're suddenly glad you made the big effort to break out of the rut.

Eight hours after leaving home I alighted from the Kyle train in sunshine at the tiny Attadale request stop, the train pulled out and the rattle subsided into the distance leaving only the sound of the wind in the trees with the song of chaffinches and a distant cuckoo. It was to be the warmest, sunniest day of the whole trip and clad in T-shirt and shorts I began my walk up the road past the brilliant splashes of colour from the rhododendrons in the Attadale gardens. Across the loch, the big Applecross mountains basked in the sunshine behind Lochcarron. I planned to walk till late, crossing some high mountains before camping that night.

The estate road led past holiday cottages and a big house, turning into a track zigzagging up into forestry plantations. A path turned off, leading steeply up a grassy ride then in and out of over knobbly hillocks to emerge clear of the trees at the crest of a 1000-foot pass. Below lay the deep valley of the river Ling, beyond rose the high peaks I was to cross. While gazing at the scene a 'hello' from behind made me jump – a couple were sitting in the sun above the path, also admiring the view. I cut down across dry moorland to the river, aiming to ford it at a big hairpin loop; fording rivers is one of the features of these cross-country treks! The water was low so I balanced across the slippery underwater rocks in bare feet then, with boots on again, picked up a prominent path zigzagging up into the corrie.

Now the views improved, especially towards the Bearnais loch and its surrounding steep hills with the cone of Sheasgaich prominent (a remote mountain I once climbed many years ago on a hot day wearing nothing but boots and a smile...) The path petered out in the corrie and it was a slow pull up very steep slopes to the south to reach the main ridge at 2500 feet as views opened out across to Lochcarron and all the rugged Torridon peaks beyond. It was after six but all the hills for a hundred miles were basking in the late sunshine and for the next couple of hours the high tops were mine as I ambled along the ridges. Most of my memories of this part of the world are of mist, drizzle and grey gloom and it was a nice change to see a sunlit landscape of friendly mountain and sea-loch. A cold wind and perhaps a hint of cloud descending on peaks to the north prompted me to descend into the Coire Domhain before making camp below the 2800-foot peak of Faochag.

I slept the sleep of the proverbial log and waited, in the morning, for the sun to strike the tent – and waited – and eventually looked out to see grey, mist enshrouded hills with a veil of drizzle just beginning to descend. The weather had changed, and it would be another four days before I saw anything other than the briefest gleam of sun. Not to be defeated, I raced up and down Faochag, mostly in cloud and driving drizzle. The hills were back to form. A few hours later saw me wending my way up a narrow path across a steep hillside above the gorge of the River Glomach. The Falls of Glomach are rightly famous, most people approach from Morvich and miss this more spectacular approach where the scenery is more like the Alps (or Norway, I'm told). Almost vertical crags, partly covered in birch and rowan, soared up for hundreds of feet on the other side of the gorge, even here the cuckoo was calling. My hillside was coloured with acres of bluebells, also white wood-anemone and wood-sorrel, but few trees. A steep path winds down from the top of the falls to a precarious viewpoint which must give an amazing spectacle when the river is in spate. As it was, the white cascade tumbling several hundred feet into the deep gorge was still quite a sight. It was 25 years since my last visit but it was most encouraging to meet a man who'd first visited the falls in 1948! I must go back in the 2020's. The path climbed on over a bleak, grey col, the round trek to the falls is a full day's hill walk for the ordinary tourist. Once again it was too cold and windy for high camping so I went down 500 feet to pitch the tent in a steep-sided valley below more waterfalls. Deer and wild goats were grazing just above; I could watch them from the tent entrance. Before retiring for the night there was however some unfinished business – my only unclimbed munro in the area, A Ghlas Bheinn, was just 2000 feet above. The long grass was saturated but the drizzle stopped as I clambered up steep hillsides and, amazingly, the cloud lifted as I climbed higher. For once the best part of the day coincided with my visit to the top, the sun came out briefly as I descended the northern ridge with views down to Morvich and east to the Affric peaks which looked as if they'd been basking in the sun for weeks. Back at the tent the midges were starting and the drizzle soon came on again – a good tent inside which you can safely cook is essential in the Highlands.

The following day began with a descent to the valley, walking out through Morvich – a familiar spot as the starting point of many 'Highland Cross' events – then along the road to Shiel shop, one of those vital staging posts for cross-country walkers. Then followed that grind along four miles of main road through Glen Shiel which I never seem to be able to avoid! Low cloud and occasional drizzle were welcome for once, it wasn't a good day for the tops but nevertheless at least 30 cars were parked at the foot of the latest 'new' munro on the Five Sisters ridge. After turning off the main road at last, a climb of nearly 3000 feet loomed ahead to cross the mountain barrier to the south. Fuelled with calorie-rich fresh food from the shop it wasn't as bad as expected, up through birch woods into the corrie then slowly up steep grass into the cloud. A woman coming down, said it was very thick on top and that she'd had some difficulty finding the way. I didn't expect any such difficulties, and indeed easily found the 2800-foot Corbett summit, it was just a bit dreich. I set the compass for the south-east ridge, clearly marked on the map, but encountered very steep slopes, with, far below, the sound of running water. I turned back, and tried again. Same problem. For ten minutes I wandered back and forth in the mist before at last discovering that the ridge was a couple of hundred yards east of the summit. My old map was wrong.

Knoydart didn't look very welcoming as I emerged from the cloud. A bleak valley stretched south, disappearing into a haze of drizzle and midges below lowering skies. The path had gone to seed and I squelched through endless bogs looking for a good campsite, hard to find as always in the wet west. The drier spots had long grass infested with ticks, these wee beasties are everywhere in Knoydart. Yet the weather brightened in the evening, cloud began to lift and by morning it looked quite promising with even a few patches of blue sky. I left the tent and climbed up past slabby waterfalls into a high corrie, gaining the ridge and scrambling up another 1000 feet to reach the summit of Sgurr a Mhaoraich. Miraculously, the cloud was blowing clear, giving spectacular views down to Loch Quoich and Loch Hourn, the hills to the west were still covered in thick cloud while sunshine and shadows chased across the mountains to the east. Below lay a great mass of tumbled rock where half a mountainside must have collapsed – these places seem to be a feature of hills west of the Great Glen – perhaps minor earthquakes from the fault are to blame. I raced down after detouring up a subsidiary rocky top (just in case it was a munro!) to be back at the tent by 9-30 for a second breakfast.

A well-made path led down to the main glen, contouring above a steep gorge through surprisingly fine oak and birch woods. Kinlochourn is an out-of-the-way spot at the head of fiord-like Loch Hourn, reached by car via 20 miles of twisty single-track road. I was amazed to see over 50 vehicles parked at the end of the road, but then it was a holiday weekend. For those munro-climbers who like to drive their car from a hotel to the foot of a mountain and then climb it, the Knoydart hills must come as a shock. Only the very fit can reach them in a day from the nearest road, otherwise a night in a tent or bothy is obligatory, unless one is organised enough to hire a private boat from Arnisdale, or book B&B well in advance at Inverie, the only village in Knoydart. An amazing path wends its way for seven miles from Kinlochourn to Barrisdale, a path the like of which must have been common in the days before General Wade. You follow, approximately, the loch shore, sometimes on a stone causeway built out from the rock-face into the loch, sometimes climbing up to 400 feet then dipping right down to the water again. You walk through woods of birch, willow, rowan, even Scots Pine, some trees overhanging the sea. Bluebells, stitchwort, campion, thrift grow profusely. It is not a route to walk in a hurry; it is one of the classic Highland walks to carry on through to Inverie, as I was doing. Cuckoos called non-stop, sometimes several at once. Across the loch, steep slopes rose into the cloud.

Two walkers were picking up a boat back to Arnisdale from the point; Barrisdale was half a mile further on, with a big house and garden which could have been plucked from Halkirk. Here was a miniature tented city with dozens of lightweight tents pitched on the 'official' site. Munro-baggers, all! I carried on for another mile to put the tent up on a rise below the Mam Barrisdale. Only once in Britain have I ever stayed on an official campsite; in my opinion such campsites have all the disadvantages of camping with none of the advantages of more substantial accommodation! Once again, the weather started improving as evening came on. It was calm and midgey and I had the choice of either sealing myself into the tent or climbing a mountain. Just above rose the very fine peak of Sgor a Choire Bheith, not often climbed as it only manages a height of 2999 feet and so isn't a munro. My legs were tired but it was worth the effort, a long slow climb up a fine ridge as Barrisdale and its wooded slopes sunk below. There was even a pair of soaring golden eagles. Banks of cloud rolled in over the summit before I reached it, the climb took nearly two hours but the best thing was running back down, through the tearing mist, to emerge into the evening gloaming, high above Barrisdale and be back at the tent by nine, in little over half an hour from the top. This was real Knoydart, a spectacular landscape of steep mountains, oak, pine and birch woods, water and rain and mist, cuckoos calling non-stop, bluebell hillsides, midges, ticks, ants and other insect life worthy of a tropical rain forest.

It rained overnight and for much of the next day, though with some dry interludes between the showers. A good day for walking out across the Mam

Barrisdale, a bleak hill pass contrasting with the lushness of lower levels. From the top, the path led down across hillsides covered in bluebells to a loch where it joined a good track to Inverie. Here, on a steep knoll, is a monument erected by the late Lord Brockett, infamous for his feudal treatment of the Knoydart residents. It is about time things changed in the way estate land is bought and sold in Scotland. At least the future of this area looks brighter now as, at long last, it's under the control of the residents. The tiny village of Inverie (population 50) can be reached by boat from Mallaig and I met a few day-trippers, including a couple of toddlers in carriers, going down to the river for a picnic. One of them had lost a red wellie and mum was running back to look for it... Before the boat arrived there was time for a meal of fish and chips at the little Knoydart Foundation restaurant in Inverie, a meal which turned out to be the most delicious I've ever eaten anywhere. Then a two-hour ride up the loch and across to Mallaig, with all the other backpackers and tourists, as shower after cold shower lashed the Knoydart hills.

Dear Sir or Madam,

Regarding _ _ _ _ _ _ 's Strawberry Trifle 'six servings' packet. On a recent solo backpacking/camping trip across north-west Scotland I purchased a packet of same in the Spar shop in Mallaig. There was little time to spare twixt boat and train and restocking for four more nights in the hills had to be done in a hurry. I grabbed the packet thinking it was Angel Delight or some such which makes a useful camping dessert (three servings does me nicely for one meal). A six-serving packet would do two nights.

Come my camp, halfway up some bleak munro, miles north of Glenfinnan. What was this? The box held three packets – or was it four? Jelly powder, custard powder, synthetic topping, decorations, dried biscuity things... and instructions that would involve about an hour's work preparing the stuff. Does anyone really do all that for a synthetic trifle? At home I'd use real cream, Swiss roll, tinned fruit – not a lot of synthetic powders! Oh well, either use it or miss half my meal. So – tip the jelly into water in my wee pan, start brewing up. Add custard powder and some dried milk powder. When boiling, take pan off heat and stir topping and decorations into the Macbethian red brew. Add a couple of those desiccated sponge fingers and a few dried dates to give some body.

The resultant hot gooey concoction went down quite well (and stayed down, too). The rest of the packet will do for tomorrow. Can I suggest this for your recipe book? Seriously your instant desserts are good for camping but not for real food for real people at home – does anyone actually buy them for that – and with such tiny individual portions? Perhaps you should target the camping market instead!

Yours sincerely,

Ralph

Assynt in June

After two hours hard going I was only a mile, in a straight line, from where I'd started – I know of nowhere in Scotland more rugged and rough than north-west Sutherland. From the end of Loch Glencoul I planned to climb up onto the peaks of Glas Bheinn and Beinn Uidhe, then cross Ben More Assynt, the highest peak in the area. It doesn't look all that far on the map, but the difficult, tangled country comes right down to sea-level.

The first problem was to find a route up from the sea through the crags, I tried one route beside a waterfall and had to retreat, then eventually managed to zigzag my way up through tiers of broken rock to reach a lochan on a high shelf. Scrambling up these steep hillsides above the fiord-like sea-loch you realise why the birches are stunted and scattered – every inch of accessible ground, even on 60-degree slopes, is pockmarked with deer hoof-prints. The deer are everywhere, far too many, and it's amazing that any soil manages to cling to the slopes at all. It's fashionable to complain about erosion caused by people on popular mountains; such damage is however confined to very narrow corridors and is negligible in the larger scheme of things. A far greater problem is this gross overgrazing and erosion caused throughout the Highlands by both deer and sheep – as anyone climbing these supposedly wild Sutherland hillsides can immediately see.

Broken heathery country with scattered lochans led on upwards, it seemed that I'd been climbing for hours but had still only reached about 1500 feet. An easier ridge finally led for another 1000 feet up to the bare stony top of Glas Bheinn. I'd certainly taken the most difficult route up the peak, most people will climb it easily from the road between Assynt and Kylesku with the benefit of a start at an altitude of over 800 feet. The spectacular cliffs and corries of Quinag were just across the pass with the isolated peaks of Suilven and Canisp beyond. Southwards stretched the long rugged ridge leading to a very distant-looking Conival and Ben More Assynt. The day was turning into one of rare clarity and perfection. I had lots of time, which was as well given the slow going over miles of boulders and bare rock. Beinn Uidhe was not only deserted but showed no sign that anyone ever went there, though it's only a few miles from Inchnadamph. Ahead, like an oasis, could be seen a large, gently sloping grassy corrie to the north of Conival, a strange contrast to the extremely rough lower slopes and barren rocky landscape above. During the second world war a plane crashed here and the wreckage – broken metal, engines and undercarriage – looks remarkably fresh. A cairn commemorates the crew.

This range of hills is perhaps the most magnificent as well as the highest in Sutherland and catches the most extreme of weathers; I was lucky to get such a clear settled day. The views, on gaining height, were amazing. To the west, beyond the sea, were the islands – Harris, Lewis, and a long line stretching all the way down to the Uists. Further south – the Trotternish ridge on north Skye. Indeed I could see right across the top part of Scotland – the Affric mountains formed the southern horizon, sweeping round to the Fannichs, the Deargs and Ben Wyvis; the sea was visible past Inverness with still more distant hills beyond – probably Ben Rinnes. North – the neighbouring ranges of Foinaven and Ben Hee, then east across Sutherland to Ben Armine, the Griams, Morven – even the little pimples of Dorrery and the Shurrery Hills. Eighty miles to the north-east, were the hazy hills of Hoy. Simply by turning my head I could see from Orkney, to the Uists, to Skye. The nearer landscape, too, was most spectacular, isolated peaks rising steeply out of a landscape of rock, moor and loch with the contorted cliffs of Breabag just to the south.

It was late afternoon when I began the final steep climb up the boulder and scree slopes of Conival. I'd had the hills to myself but now saw that the ridges ahead were alive with people. Conival and Ben More Assynt are 'munros'... most people bag both peaks in a day from Inchnadamph. It's a long mile between the two tops, an undulating rocky ridge with quite a bit of climbing – and you have to return all the way to Conival after visiting Ben More Assynt. There is a still further 'top' reached by a scramble along a narrow airy ridge, the sort of place that only the keen hillwalker used to visit. Unless you are fit, it's a tough assignment to do the lot in a day. There must have been 30 people between Conival and Ben More Assynt, this was rush hour and all were heading back towards Inchnadamph. Men and women in equal numbers, quite a few couples, mostly but not all English. Most didn't seem to be particularly enjoying themselves. I would greet people with 'fantastic day,' or 'grand day,' or something similar – and tended to get a funny look in reply. Few seemed even to notice the incredible scenery, to be appreciating their good fortune to be in such a place on one of the best days of the year. They picked their way over the rocks or strode out with walking poles, hot and tired, another couple of munros in the bag, only looking forward to getting down. Some, doing the tops as well the main munros, had dragged themselves out to the furthest top and then all the way back again... Most would have been much happier on Stac Polly or Suilven or Cul Mor, or just doing Conival on its own. The ridge is mostly bare shattered rock, yet somebody had brought a dog. Here was a young lady, grim-faced, striding out and followed by her husband (sorry, it's partner these days) with a high-tech rucsac/carrier containing a sleeping baby. Perhaps this was its last munro. The mountain could do nothing but endure patiently, awaiting the next storm.

At around six in the evening, as the last of the stragglers headed back west, I reached the top of Ben More Assynt and scrambled out along the ridge to the far top. I had the hill to myself and could sit enjoying the vista, until it became too cold to linger in the wind. I'd been heavily laden but this had given me the freedom to cross the mountain from end to end, now I picked my way down the east ridge and found a sheltered spot a couple of thousand feet below to brew up tea and soup and lay out my sleeping bag. I dosed off watching the evening light fade over Ben Klibreck while pools of mist gathered round Ben Armine and the stars appeared faintly in the never-dark sky of early June.

The Grampian mountains

Every year – and getting older doesn't make it any easier – I pack rucsac, tent and sleeping-bag for a week or so in the hills. My objective on this occasion was to wander over a dozen out-of-the-way munro peaks in the Grampians and Monadhliath. It's an excuse, as with many who fish or stalk, to spend some time in the mountains. Hamish Brown walked all the munros in three months and I kid myself I'm following in his footsteps for a week. He wandered up Glen Tilt and Glen Fender from Blair Atholl reading a book, before strolling across Beinn a Ghlo (carrying tent and all gear). Pouring with sweat and with aching shoulders I plod uphill out of Blair on a fine afternoon, trying to shake of the daze of six hours in crowded trains. Plans of camping on the tops soon evaporate and after five miles I put the tent up at the end of Glen Fender. Beinn a Ghlo is better without the pack, it's five before I reach the main ridge but there's no hurry on a fine evening. Most other walkers are already down, I could see the glittering sea of cars parked at the start of the usual approach. 'Late start?' asks the last homeward-bound walker. Cheek! I'd set off from home at five in the morning. I sleep well, that night.

The rest of the week? Perhaps some scattered impressions give a flavour.

Buzzards soaring, soaring. A whole Bank Holiday Monday, and the Tuesday, without meeting or seeing anyone else. The endless rolling hills of the Grampians, still yellow, brown and white after the hard winter. Although often derided as boring hills, I wouldn't be anywhere else but striding for miles across these high plateaux on a fine clear day.

Nests, stumbled across by accident. Nearly a dozen grouse eggs. Four golden plover eggs, arranged in beautiful symmetry in a soft hollow. Tiny eggs of a meadow pipit, in a little hole in a clump of rushes. I never stop, just glance and keep on walking, and the bird will return.

Opening the tent flap to see an eagle coasting out of sight round a distant mountain slope. Brewing tea in the tent while watching a herd of deer on the hillside. No radio. No mobile phones. No TV. No distractions.

Hills of the North, Rejoice!

Huge patches of snow remaining after months of drift. Some must be over 100 feet deep, completely filling burn valleys on the plateau. Crevasses?? Rivers, swollen with melting snow, icy to cross and icy for washing! It's June.

Waterfalls tumbling into narrow river valleys above the deep Gaick Pass. A glimpse of civilisation – the A9, and the metropolis of Dalwhinnie, four miles away and 2000 feet below.

Ten minutes of hot sun on the tops, flies rising – then the wind again. No midges. Not one all week. Is that a record? Clear views to higher peaks of Cairngorms and Nevis, still even whiter. Must be skiing still! Very very dry, peat bogs dusty, bogs crunchy. Great care with a camp fire, right next to an icy river but one mistake and the whole hillside would go up.

Meall Chuaich, kicking steps up several hundred feet of snow slope, snow which was visible at a distance of 20 miles. An eagle-eye's view of most of Strath Spey and the distant A9 traffic, worlds away. A seemingly endless slog over miles of featureless and desolate grouse-moor south of Kingussie, grey skies, heavy pack, great to camp at last. A fire to cheer up the grey, drizzly evening. Usually I'm camped too high to find any wood.

Restocking at Newtonmore, the contrast between the town-life and the empty, harsh environment of the hills. Struggling up the track towards the Monadhliath heights, tired, hot, pack weighing a ton, what's the point of such self-inflicted purgatory – why am I here? But at last, camp in a high upland corrie. Must try and be more lightweight in future. But official campsites don't bear thinking about. It's an old shieling area, with at least a dozen ruins on grassy riverside slopes below the craggy hills. It must have been well known that the glen has its own 'goddess' – the hills above, seen from the tent, look just like a naked woman.

I meet the first walker I've seen for two days. 'No a bad dae,' I say, forgetting it's not Caithness. He replies, 'pardon?'

Geal Carn, outlier of the Monadhliath, taken at a run – leaving the pack to jog three miles across the rolling plateau, and back, just beating black thunderclouds approaching from the Ardverikie hills. A long tiring walk back over the tops in heavy rain – but at least no lightning. Rosemarkie was less lucky, I heard later.

Nine in the morning at 3000 feet, an icy wind but bright, far below and miles away the dark line of a train, like a worm, creeping north out of Newtonmore station. In a few hours time I'll be on that train, homeward bound...

MacGregor hills

For the first time in many years I was on my own for a long drive down to the north of England. Ralph is not one to waste such rare opportunities – a night in the hills, with a few munros thrown in, would be the ideal way to break the journey! So, having left a bleak, wet Caithness at six in the morning, I arrived at an only slightly less bleak and wet Crianlarich some five hours later. All the higher hills were enveloped in cloud and although the rain had stopped the cessation looked only temporary. Had the weather been perfect I'd planned to do the five munros south of the village with Ben More thrown in for good measure. Well, I'd miss Ben More but those five munros on which I'd never set foot would just have to be done!

I'd planned for midgey, warm, thundery weather and was still feeling sunburn from the previous week's 'Highland Cross' which had coincided with the only scorching day of the summer. I carried lightweight tent and sleeping bag, waterproofs and cold food, but, to keep down the weight, no change of clothes or stove. It was enough, just. Leaving the car in the Youth Hostel carpark I tramped a mile down the Aberfeldy road then struck up through steep forestry plantations to gain the north ridge of Cruach Ardrain, my first peak. For the only time that day I was too hot and stripped off to T-shirt, I was still stiff after the long drive and the climb seemed very slow with Crianlarich never seeming to get any further below. At 2000 feet came the wind, a cold near gale from the west. Tattered cloud blew across the ridge, there was still a gleam of sun towards Ben Lui but a wall of grey was approaching from Rannoch Moor. The drizzle started, then the rain. Over the next hour all my clothes and waterproofs went back on. I needed them. In mist and horizontal driving rain I scrambled over the subsidiary top of Stob Garbh, then followed the path down through rocky defiles, meeting a few other walkers who were more sensibly heading back down. A steep bouldery scramble led me up to the summit in a brief dry interlude.

Hills of the North, Rejoice!

A ridge led south to my next peak, Beinn Tulaichean, indeed the weather seemed to be improving, with mist blowing clear and gleams of sun. Below was Balquhidder, Rob Roy's glen, beyond were the hills of Loch Lomond and Arrochar, all unknown country to me. The 3100-foot summit was definitely the best of the day, clear of cloud, very windy and briefly dry ahead of the next belt of sheeting rain which hit before I'd left the top. Now came a long 2000-foot descent before climbing up to my next peak, Beinn a Chroin. The rain poured down. I chose a route carefully, contouring below steep crags on the southern flank of Cruach Ardrain to gain the col. It was a bleak spot; I was strongly tempted to give up and go back down to Crianlarich for a night in the Youth Hostel, rather than fight over another couple of mountains and sleep out in a wind- and rain-lashed tent. But then, I thought, Rob Roy was born only a few miles away from here. These were all his local hills, the 'Children of the Mist' would think nothing of crossing the peaks on their way to rustling a few more cattle and would simply wrap themselves in their plaids to sleep out. What was a bit of rain? So I pushed on, a long pull back up to 3000 feet, huge boulders littering the hillside giving some temporary shelter from the elements. The weather was most frustrating in that, although the sun kept shining over Rannoch Moor it only seemed to be evaporating water which then condensed over my mountains in ever heavier downpours leaving the hillsides streaming with white burns.

There were new paths across all these mountains which were not marked on my map, so I still needed the compass to cross the rocky tops of Beinn a Chroin and find my way down to the col below the fourth peak, An Caisteal. Now, at seven in the evening, the rain was at last relenting and the final climb was only in wind and mist. Below was the green valley of Coire a Chuilion where I could camp the night, leaving the final peak for the morrow. By 8-30pm I'd munched my cold sandwiches and drunk my cold water in the tent, regretting not having brought a warmer sleeping bag or a stove to brew hot tea and soup!

The rain and drizzle came on again in the early hours, the wind driving it against the tent fabric, and I looked out at six to a dismal scene with mist right down to port. To put damp clothes on again and climb another peak was not an inviting prospect, yet the summit of Beinn Chabhair was only 1500 feet above and it might be years before I had another opportunity. Don't think about it, just put those wet clothes back on and set out... and once you've actually got going it's never as bad as it looks beforehand. The rain was only light and the climb soon warmed me, only the last bit of ridge to the summit was cold and exposed. I was on top before seven and was back at the tent and packed up by 8-30, with just eight miles to walk back to Crianlarich then another 200 to drive. Curtains of drizzle swept the green hillsides as I made my way down towards the main road, the temperature rising rapidly with gleams of sun appearing as I reached the main valley. The last four miles were along the West Highland Way, first along a new path through birch woods below the main road then across the hillside above it. Soon I was meeting walkers who had just set out from Crianlarich. The whole 98 miles of the route was run in under 19 hours by the winner of a recent West Highland Way race – which puts one's own little outings into perspective.

Huge clouds were building, the respite in the weather wouldn't last long. Midges were out in swarms too, even in the carpark at Crianlarich, and I had to seal myself inside the car before changing into dry clothes. There was still some delicious warm tea to drink from the flask before setting off again for some very different experiences driving through Glasgow and down the A74 in yet more downpours...

One hundred wild flowers

A hundred different birds have been spotted in one day in Perthshire, this would make a good challenge for an ornithologist in Caithness! I fancied a rather easier task.

The best time of year for wild flowers here is normally mid to late July; some of the early-flowering varieties are still in bloom and there are not many more yet to come. I'd try to find over 100 in one day within a radius of five or six miles of home. An advantage of setting my own challenge is that I can make my own rules, I'm no botanist and so the flowers would have to be readily distinguishable, no half-dozen hawkbits or eyebrights. All would have to be either actually in flower or so close to flowering that the colour could be seen. Grasses, rushes and the like would not count (a good excuse as I can't identify any of them). I'd include insignificant weeds that could be easily identified but wouldn't try too hard over tiny white things.

Although the weather had been mostly cold and grey, the Caithness flowers are quite used to such conditions and were as plentiful as ever. Unsurprisingly the first on my list was – daisy, followed by buttercup (though it wasn't till much later that this one flower became two when I convinced myself that there really was a difference between the meadow and the creeping buttercup). The third flower, early purple orchid, showed that Caithness is indeed a special place, there are some very fine spikes that would out-do many hyacinths. Without moving more than a quarter of a mile from home I was soon up to number 22, mostly common things like hogweed and cow parsley which give white banks along our roadsides for miles. There were nettle and dock, which can give surprisingly spectacular displays, there were garden weeds such as bush vetch, cleavers, and mouse-ear chickweed as well as a few nicer plants like the yellow tormentil and meadow vetchling, the aromatic herb robert and the cuckoo plant. A few gorse flowers remained, left over from the brilliant displays of early summer, a thick patch of watercress with dense heads of white flowers filled a well.

Slightly more unusual at number 23 was the green twayblade orchid on a fine patch of roadside verge which also included a single violet, the blue milkwort, pink millfoil, bedstraw and a few spikes of St John's wort. A farm track gave a couple of common weeds, the little scentless mayweed and some fine shepherds purse, as well as a very beautiful early head of spear (Scottish) thistle. Normally blue, a very fine white variety grows near here. The track led to the open hill and boggy ground where the numbers rapidly increased. Here was the purple lousewort in profusion with bell heather and cross-leaved heath. Try as I might I never found any true ling in bloom, it was still too early in the season. Both the insectivorous bog plants, butterwort and sundew, had flowers, the butterwort's purple especially attractive but the tiny white sundew still mostly in bud. A clever trick to use insects for pollination then eat them! The flowers of the bog bean were over but the marsh cinquefoil was out, as was red rattle like a large lousewort. On any damp moorland the white tufts of cotton-grass waved in the cold wind. Two different eyebrights I could recognise, one very common with its relatively conspicuous and very attractive white-and-yellow flowers, the other with tiny blooms on longer stalks. For the sake of argument I called them common eyebright and bog eyebright; the books showing a dozen varieties weren't much help. Here were a few heath orchids which would soon be blooming in much greater numbers, also a yellow spike of bog ashphodel, the first I'd seen this year, later it flowers thickly in suitable locations, a very beautiful sight and with a characteristic honeyed smell.

Hills of the North, Rejoice!

A cornfield had weeds growing almost as thickly as the crop, red dead-nettle, chickweed and water-pepper. Hawthorne was still out by the wood, also a single, very late, red flower of the salmonberry. This plant normally flowers in April, risking late frosts to set fruit early; hedgerows were full of the ripe orange berries which are edible, if a bit woody, and supposedly very good for winemaking. With the list approaching 60 there were still plenty to note down, a wild dog-rose, some tiny blue forget-me-nots, the silvery leaves and yellow flowers of the silverweed which grows everywhere on the very edges of roads, a wild broom, a patch of the pink ragged robin, a single early spike of foxglove. A detour into a small forestry plantation added the nondescript lesser twayblade to the list, with a single little purple flower of fumitory where a roadside had recently been dug to place kerbstones. The verges around Fryster are particularly good, I'd seen most of the flowers already, but added fragrant orchid (yes, it has a lovely perfume) the wild iris (yellow flag) and the lady's mantle which is often grown in gardens. Up to 70 now in barely two hours, the remaining 30 would take a bit longer.

Next I took the bike into Thurso, watching the verges closely; there was the first creeping thistle of the year, a patch of red campion and, at number 74, a dandelion! Honeysuckle was just coming out, the first woundwort of the year was opening near Dixonfield, and in the town along pavement walls, was the first groundsel I'd seen.

The road from Glengolly to Calder, near the top of the hill, is one of the best places for wildflowers, if I'd gone there first I'd probably have noted 50 on a mile of verge. There were superb displays of the nodding heads of water avens and the first creamy-white meadowsweet in flower; summer is really here when miles of these these strongly-scented flowerheads line the Halkirk-Calder road. (The best meadowsweet of all is at Bridge of Forss when mixed with rosebay willowherb in August, an acre of pink and white to inspire all the Dounreay commuters.) A short walk along the ditches at the top of the hill added yellow rattle, speedwell, yellow bedstraw and sneezewort to the list. The following wind, downhill, was unwelcome for once, it was much too fast to see many flowers but there was more dame's violet (flox) here, perhaps a garden escape but naturalised in many places and so added to my list. The ditches beside the Halkirk-Calder road give spectacular displays of yellow balsam and blue water forget-me-not, even more amazing when the meadowsweet is fully in bloom. A single sow-thistle by the A9 brought my total to 89.

In the continuing cold wind my next destination was the Dunnet Links to add a few specialities. First white campion by the roadside and sea-rocket on the beach. Then, crossing the fence south of the road by the mid-beach carpark, I soon found, by the burn, one of my favourites, the superb globe buttercup. Perhaps my favourite of all, wild thyme, was prolific in the short grass, here too was mountain everlasting and the Scottish primrose, flowering as profusely as I've ever seen it. The purple and yellow heartsease, another favourite, took my total to 98. Late afternoon now, time was getting on... Murkle Bay was my next destination; down by the dunes the yellow meddick was growing thickly in the grass, making number 99. I left the bike and jogged along the beach and over the slabby rocks round the point, to find number 100. Yes, the fleshy oyster plant still had some some brilliant blue flowers but not the lovely display of a few weeks earlier. Thrift and scurvy grass were added to my list from the clifftops, I hunted for angelica but could only find leaves and one big bud.

Back home a couple of little garden weeds, thale cress and the moss-like pearlwort, both with the tiniest of white flowers, were noted down, I decided to count another common yellow weed (whether charlock or rape or both I've never sorted out) and discovered a single stitchwort in a wet field. The total? 107. One hundred and seven different wild flowers in a day. I could have added a few more if I'd gone further afield; comfrey at Dounreay, cow-wheat and bladder campion and flowering angelica on the east coast, moorland bilberry and bearberry and cloudberry, rose-root on the cliffs. Some possibles such as blue cranesbill were rejected as likely garden escapes, others such as rosebay willowherb and ling would have been flowering just a few days later. A good botanist would probably double my total. But the list was almost entirely of wild flowers which look very different from each other, which didn't need hours with a flora and a magnifying glass for identification. Most were proper, attractive flowers, most could be found within a few miles of any location near the coast in Caithness.

Now, how about trying to find 100 different birds...

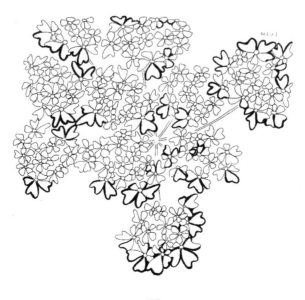

75

The hill of the sheep

Everyone knows that munros are hills higher than 3000 feet. Corbett tabulated the 2500-footers and Donald provided a mammoth list of the 2000-foot hills. Somebody has probably even climbed them all. A list of 1500-foot peaks has been suggested in jest, but anything lower has not even been thought of. It is thus perhaps strange that the peak which has turned me back possibly more than any other is only just over 1400 feet high! Most people, setting out with serious intent of climbing a Scottish hill, reach the top unless beaten by bad weather, exhaustion or encroaching darkness. My record of perhaps one out of five successful ascents of Meall Nan Caorach is thus not good.

You can pretty well guarantee that neither Hamish Brown nor Tom Weir nor Wainwright has set foot on this particular hill. From a distance you don't even notice it, just another swell in rising moorland, a few uninspiring contour rings on the map. There must be thousands of hills like it in Scotland, high moorland viewpoints unclimbed from one year to the next. So why the difficulty? The hill rises steeply out of the far side of Boblainy Forest near Kiltarlity, extensive spruce plantations containing remnants of the woods which grew here for thousands of years. It is the nearest thing possible to Tolkein's 'Old Forest', a cross between a maze and a tropical jungle, swarming with biting insects, alive with deer and pine martens and wildcats. Overgrown paths lead here and there, fading out and usually taking you down to the Bruaich Burn which twists through the steamy heart of the woods. Nowhere in the Highlands is it more true that a mile on the map turns out to be two on the ground. You can't get really lost if you use common sense and keep going up, or down, but you can go badly wrong. It's not a place for the inexperienced walker. Only after many visits do I know my way around well enough to make good speed through the forest taking all the shortcuts.

The main road lies just two miles from Caorach, as the hen-harrier flies, but the ground is very rough with much knee-deep heather. Consequently I've usually attempted the hill from the Kiltarlity side, with all its attendant difficulties.

On the map, the hill looks a good target for an early morning run and this is where the trouble lies. Giving myself an hour and a half I've set off from Kiltarlity, perhaps four or five map miles away. After an hour of tick-infested jungle, wrong paths, swarms of flies, I eventually find the steep forest slopes leading to the open hill. It is then more than time to turn back. A forestry road leads into the heart of the forest, meeting a track coming in from the other side – indeed the through route gives a fine, if strenuous bike ride. Cycling can save some three miles running, however little time is gained as the cycle route involves an 800-foot climb followed by a steep rough descent. Using a car to help is cheating.

Hills of the North, Rejoice!

Only once, years ago, have I actually made it to the top from Kiltarlity by running all the way; it was more than half a marathon and took over two hours on a scorching morning when the flies and ticks were out in force. I must have been mad or very fit, running right round the outside of the forest, up through deep and very rough heather then plunging back through the steamy jungle. My second successful ascent took a whole day, cycling from Muir of Ord station to the end of the forest road, visiting the secret Culnaskiach Falls and defeating all the forest's tricks simply by having lots of time. Other successful attempts have been made on long summer evenings and even then I've ended up running through the forest in wellies to avoid being caught out by nightfall. For its diminutive height the views, if they aren't obscured by the flies, are superb. Caorach is the highest top for miles. Below lies all Boblainy Forest, backed by the fertile land of the Aird. West lies a tangle of rough country and lochans, deep in heather, with the high Farrar and Affric hills beyond. Indeed it's very like the view from the Barrow Downs across the Old Forest to the Shire, with the high mountains rising far in the other direction. The whole of this unvisited area at the back of Boblainy has that sort of atmosphere, as does Boblainy itself. Culloden is only 20 miles away, much history has passed around here.

Munros and Corbetts and Donalds are usually just straightforward walks. Most of them aren't a patch on the ascent of Meall nan Caorach from Kiltarlity via Boblainy Forest!

The Caithness flows

In Thurso, 'you can almost hear the greenshanks and golden plovers calling from the flow country'. This is how many who came to a recent 'Peatlands Conference' saw the town – yet how many townspeople, caught up in the stress, worries and problems of day-to-day existence of work and home, ever think of this? Yes, Thurso is right on the edge of one of the world's unique landscapes, a place where large areas still show little influence of man, a place where you can wander for miles under the huge sky with only the moorland birds and the deer for company and let your problems and worries fall into perspective. The Caithness Flow country is well publicised now, but I've yet to meet anybody when crossing the moors away from the estate roads and river valleys. A recent brochure on the Caithness and Sutherland Flows, issued by the LIFE peatlands people, has some nice pictures but does little other than suggest car drives which are obvious from any map. It's time that we were positively encouraged to walk out along the estate roads and tracks and cross the moors, the area is vast and will never be busy.

It's only human to try and cram as much as possible into a short time so I often find myself rushing through glorious countryside trying to fit a day's outing into a free morning, or a half-day into a couple of hours. It is good for once to spend a whole day out on the moors, without constraints of time. One of my favourite routes is to link up the chain of lochs running from near Altnabreac to Loch Tuim Ghlas and Shurrery. This area was saved from forestry planting in the nick of time, though the new forests – which should never have been allowed – remain obtrusive on skylines. Over many years I've never seen anyone at these lochs, fishing or otherwise.

I set off on the mountain bike at about 6-30, normal going-to-work time, but instead took it easy, pottering out along the roads past Loch Calder to Dorrery Lodge. Low cloud had spread in overnight but already showed signs of clearing to a warm day. Rather than take the forest roads to Altnabreac I'd chosen to cycle the track out to Loch Caluim. For those who want a straightforward, unadventurous introduction to the moors and to a beautiful but rarely visited loch, walk this track and explore a little on either side. From Loch Caluim an old drove route heads up the Forss tributary then over the moor to Skyline Loch, now surrounded by little trees. A bike can be wheeled fairly easily this way, though fording the river is required as a bridge has long since degenerated into two widely spaced rails. For a first moorland crossing with a bike this makes a good route, returning by Altnabreac and Dalnawhillan or the forest roads. Indeed, 20 years ago, this was one of my first through routes. The old drove route hasn't been used for years and is gradually fading into the bogs – a few more visitors wouldn't do any harm! A high stile over the forest fence gives access to Skyline Loch from the north, deep heather along the shore then making for hard going till you reach the forest road.

It had been a good (or bad!) year for clegs on the moors and as the day warmed up there were always a few buzzing around; if you swat them when they land, little harm is done. By the end of my moorland crossing the population was several hundred less. Things get really bad when you're attacked by 20 or 30 at once, as happened to me a few years ago near Forsinard – my attempts to ward them off resembling the dancing of a jig until liberal applications of 'jungle juice' deterred them a little.

To reach my first loch in the chain, Loch na Cloiche, I couldn't avoid a couple of miles of forest road and a section of open forest ride before heaving bike and self across the fence to regain open moorland. Then, slow progress north across the tussocks and peat and along the quiet shores of Lochan Ealach Mor, Lochan Ealach Beag, Loch Torr na Ceardaich. Broken cloud gave way to hot sun. Sandpipers trilled. Dappled deer calves trotted off with their mothers. Clegs buzzed. The warm sun drew out that moorland perfume of bog-myrtle and heather. Distant low cloud still poured, white, over and around Morven. No hurry, time for a dip in the lochs, though only Cloiche proved really deep enough for swimming. No sign of man other than that distant forestry skyline. I followed the western shore of Loch Torr na Ceardaich to avoid an awkward river crossing at its outflow, then forded the inflowing stream to pick up a flattened-grass quad track which gave easier bike wheeling up to Loch Tuim Ghlas. This is one of the finest lochs in Caithness, half its perimeter fringed by sandy beaches, a moorland setting which the tourist literature would describe as 'stunning'. Hot sun, lapping water, thyme, heather and bog-myrtle, deer on distant slopes of rounded moorland... most people don't realise such places exist in the twenty-first century.

For half a mile I rode the bike along the water's edge, then picked up the estate road which climbed northwards to an old stables now used as a boathouse. The last loch of the chain, Lochan Dubh Cul na Beinn, lay a short distance away over the shoulder of Beinn Nam Bad. In spite of its name (Black loch at the back of the hill) this is a most attractive little stretch of water, enticing for a swim and quite deep enough once away from the peaty shore. Swimming alone, in the middle of a remote flow-country loch on a sunny day, is one of the great experiences of this part of the world.

The estate road, east to Shurrery Lodge, is bikeable but the wheel ruts are initially quite deep and pedals tend catch in tussocks of grass and heather. Better to walk the track at a leisurely pace and detour up Beinn Nam Bad Mor for a view across the whole of the area, glittering with lochs and dubh-lochs, then go down to the little sandy beach at the south end of Loch Scye. The track improves after this, giving generally easy cycling back to the road. Once past Shurrery Loch it was just a question of picking up a well-travelled route between home and work, by Brawlbin back to the Dorrery turn and on to Halkirk, a good ride even though taken hundreds of times before. A few weeks earlier I'd counted up to 70 different wild flowers by the roadside verges on a ride home from Dounreay.

Remember that people come from all over the world to visit our local landscapes. Remember how close such beauty is, next time you are queuing (or serving the queue) at the checkout or trying to cope with six different jobs at once. Indeed, why not take a leisurely walk or bike-ride out there yourself?

An Orkney interlude

In just over five summer weeks we've had ten inches of rain, the wettest spell since I started measuring rainfall a number of years ago. That may be pretty dry for the western Highlands but is about three times the normal for Caithness. A few fine interludes have however coincided with weekends allowing some good opportunities for getting out and about.

Taking the bike across to Orkney gives a grand day when the weather is good. In bleak, grey weather, Orkney is just like Caithness only more so – but when the sun shines it can be magical. So, with a good forecast I took my chance and joined the tourists on the Pentland Venture for the morning sailing. Although the wind was light, the tide-race through the Firth was the strongest I've seen and passengers were ordered off the top deck of the boat to stop it wallowing too much in the chaotic seas off Stroma lighthouse. The sea was running east at least as fast as the boat was heading north, giving strange illusions as the distant hills appeared to be moving sideways while we were apparently going straight ahead. The captain seemed to be heading for St Margaret's Hope as we passed just east of Swona but no, the current gripped the boat and swept us precisely into Burwick. Nice bit of sailing!

The sun shone and the wind was from behind, giving a lovely ride up and down the hilly road to Kirkwall, a favourite run when the wind is favourable. Views of the sea come and go all round, you pedal uphill and speed down through the bare but fertile farm landscape of South Ronaldsay. You race over the Churchill Barriers, pass harbours and sandy beaches and blockships, cross bare heathery islands and enter the rolling country of the south Mainland. Kirkwall is not my favourite place on Orkney, and to miss it out I turned down a track to Scapa Bay, pushing through long grass and thistles, ruts, mud and water but managing to stay on the bike.

The road now headed west, climbing in the late morning sunshine over the heathery moors to Orphir. One of my objectives for the day, the 900-foot Ward

Hill rose ahead, this is the highest top on Mainland Orkney yet there is no path and one gets the impression it's almost never climbed. A bumpy track took me up from Swanbister to some peat workings where I left the bike to continue on foot. Many of the Orkney hills have a characteristic growth of tussock and heather, very rough and giving slow and difficult going. So it was here, but only for the half mile up to the summit. The weather was glorious indeed, and the hilltop a grand spot for a leisurely lunch. In the very clear air the view extended across Scapa Flow to the high purple hills of Hoy and through a gap to the Sutherland peaks of Foinaven and Ben Loyal, 70 miles away. Far to the south was the familiar Morven skyline, seen as through binoculars the wrong way round. West lay the grey town of Stromness and the endless Atlantic, while to the north were the lochs of Stenness and Harray and the patchwork fields of Mainland, with the North Isles filling the north-east horizon. Almost all of Orkney was visible. A combine harvester could be heard in the distance; the Swanbister farmer was making the most of the fine day to cut the first spring barley in either Orkney or Caithness.

For ten minutes that day the wind dropped, and that ten minutes coincided with my arrival back at the bike. Midges! Clouds of them! Taking midge repellent to Orkney hadn't occurred to me. I managed to pack up and set off without too many bites, and bumped on along the track to come out on the road near Stenness. Another little road took me up and round farms and over the hill with a steep descent to Finstown, then on, over the side of Wideford hill. With time to spare I turned off up a steep road which climbs right to the top of this 750-foot hill and more fine views. Model gliders were being flown in the strengthening breeze, a breeze which had turned into the inevitable strong south-easterly by the time I reached Kirkwall. It's always worth a trip to Orkney just to visit St Magnus Cathedral, there is nothing like it for hundreds of miles. Pity though that Kirkwall is otherwise much like Thurso!

At least there was plenty of time for the ride down to Burwick – have I ever ridden this way without a strong headwind? Still, with no rush, the journey could be enjoyed, stopping to admire the views, taking side roads wherever possible. Down at Burwick the wind was cold and the sun had gone behind an evil-looking grey sheen of cloud spreading up from the south.

'What do you think it'll do tomorrow?' one of the tourists asked.

'Rain!' I replied.

'You mean because it didn't rain today?'

I didn't like to tell him that the centre of a deep low was heading our way and that I'd be happily sitting by the fireside on the next day while the rain hammered down on an easterly gale (nearly another inch fell). The tourists have had to be hardy this year – but the ones who have persevered will have been rewarded by the occasional really good day!

Summer days

On a long, hot drive north of over 400 miles, tired and with a headache, I turned off the main road for a break. Here was a secret little bay with golden sands, seals sunbathing on rocks, caves, thyme growing in the short grass, a little waterfall. The fresh sea air soon cleared the cobwebs and after half an hour I was revived enough to continue. Three small children were just leaving the beach on their way home for tea. The oldest was a girl of perhaps six, with a boy of four, both with little dogs on leads. Behind trotted a wee boy of at most two. They were talking quietly, happily, along the sunny lane between high banks of July grasses and flowers. Of such is the kingdom of heaven!

Central Sutherland. Here the vast Fountain Forestry plantations finally give out into the high, remote, flow country. August now, most of the birds have flown, the moors are quiet. The wetter areas, with deep peat and dubh-loch, look much as they would at any time in the last few thousand years. Here too is a strange, circular pit in the peat, perhaps ten feet across and as deep, with a stony bottom. Fall in there and you'd never get out again... The drier slopes would naturally be covered in birch and willow, as witnessed by a small wooded island in a loch where the native trees have been protected from browsing deer. An enticing objective for a morning swim! The little island bore a dense undergrowth, completely unlike the bare country around the loch and precluding much exploration. Over the whole vast area, the insects were king. Clegs homed in all the time, flies buzzed, midges gathered downwind. For hour after hour I cycled, long dusty tracks through endless plantations, August sun beating down, insects attacking whenever I stopped. It could have been Finland or Canada.

In the recent days of beating sun, Caithness and Sutherland could rival anywhere in the world for sunbathing. On a hot Bank Holiday, with a breeze to disperse the insects, the sandy beaches of Loch More could not be bettered anywhere, the distant mountains and flow-country horizons sharp under the dark blue sky, the warm peaty water ideal for swimming. Yet there were only a couple of families on the whole beach.

Hills of the North, Rejoice!

The flowers on the Dunnet Links have been particularly spectacular this year. It's not well known that some of the best displays are across the road from the carpark halfway along the beach, just over the fence. A few weeks ago the breeze carried the perfume of thickly growing scented orchids, now the harebells are at their best, a blue haze across the grass. Even the common eyebrights make a fine display, while the area is studded with grass of parnassus like daisies. Look closely at the grass – and it's almost all flowers!

After a sweaty afternoon at work and a hot ride back to Thurso a dip in the sea, off the campsite, seemed a good idea. The tide was a long way out and I paddled across sand below the rocks, noticing the occasional flatfish dart away under the water. Then I trod on something very sharp. I looked, annoyed with myself for not wearing something to protect my feet against broken glass and the like, but couldn't see any damage. After swimming just a few strokes my foot began to hurt, so I retreated to the beach. There was a tiny hole in the sole but it looked nothing, nevertheless it got more and more painful as I hobbled back to the bike and pedalled off. Something had stung me. Within ten minutes it felt like my foot was immersed in boiling water; fortunately the pain then gradually dissipated with no after-effects. A small stingray, lying in the sand below the low-tide mark, perhaps? One should always wear light footwear when swimming out-of-doors!

A lovely clear, early morning at Murkle bay, low tide, creels stranded on the sand with crabs inside. Groatie-buckies in the shell sand, fossil fishes in broken rocks to the east, the blue oyster-plant rambling over slabby rocks to the west. Tiny waves lap onto the beach, the cliffs of Dunnet Head and Hoy glow in the sun. Dense grass grows around the headlands. A bit of scrambling is needed to get along the shore; in one place you can crawl, if you're slim enough, through a hole in the rocks like the eye of a needle. Easy slabby rocks and beaches then lead all the way to Castletown. Rock pools and anemones, a hundred varieties of seaweed. Two very large, and very dead, seals. A tern shrieks. Meanwhile traffic hurtles at 60 mph along the main road to Thurso, just half a mile away.

Another early morning, fog has rolled in from the sea but our hill is an island above it, looking much as it will if and when global warming melts the Antarctic ice-cap. I pedal down into the cold damp fog, a white fog-bow ahead before the sun fades. Further west it's clearing, sun reflects off the windscreen of an oncoming tractor to illuminate intervening mist like a lighthouse beam. It's already clear and sunny; at Dounreay it will be a long, hot day.

Foinaven

The mountains are becoming overcrowded, loved to death – or so we keep hearing. Most such statements issue from journalists who, I suspect, venture little further than the local bars. The plain fact is that much of our Scottish countryside sees virtually no visitors at all. The most popular summits and some narrow routes of ascent can be busy, for a few hours around midday on fine summer days and at weekends, but even there, for most of the day, most of the year, the deer and mountain hares have it to themselves.

Morven now has a faint path at the very top, indicating that a few more people do climb the hill, but nobody walks over neighbouring Scaraben. The spectacular Sutherland peaks such as Foinaven seem to be less climbed than ever. For some reason it's usually August when I visit Foinaven, often around the Bank Holiday. Rarely though have I met anybody on what is the most rugged and spectacular of all the Sutherland peaks. (The mountain's official height is 2999 feet. The small summit cairn takes it to over 3000 but that, apparently, still doesn't make it a munro!) Certainly nobody goes in by my favourite route, from the head of Loch Eriboll across the bare slopes of Cranstackie, down to Strath Dionard then up one of the many corries or ridges.

If there's any weather going, Foinaven will catch it, there's no other peak as steep and high so far north-west. Only in settled high-pressure conditions can the mountain be dry and clear – consequently in August, when there isn't cloud with drizzle or lashing rain, there will probably be a heatwave. At least that's been my experience – either deluges or drought. This day must have been one of the hottest of the year. Early Caithness fog soon cleared as I drove west and even at eight in the morning it was warm and sticky by the Eriboll shore. There was just enough breeze to deter most of the midges but the clegs were a more serious pest. I set off with a litre bottle of water – a bottle which was refilled three times during the course of the day. The sunshine remained unbroken, the temperature soaring so that even on the summit, with a stiff easterly breeze, a T-shirt was only needed as protection from sunburn. The contrast with conditions a few years earlier was complete. Then, the same route up over the bare rock slabs of Cranstackie had been into the teeth of driving rain. After the steep 1200-foot descent and a crossing of the rising river Dionard I'd carried on up by white waterfalls to a bleak rain-lashed corrie below the summit... and turned back. Recrossing the Dionard, even though much further upstream above Loch Dionard, had been difficult and not a little dangerous. By the time I'd made it back to Strath Beag rivers were bursting their banks, water was pouring everywhere and I wallowed waist deep through bogs and tributary streams to regain the road. This time sunburn, dehydration and heat exhaustion were the only hazards. The River Dionard trickled in the sun over stones, I crossed without even taking off my boots. Peat bogs were dry and dusty.

A delight of the hills in August is the wild thyme, there's always some about when scrambling up a steep rocky hillside in the heat and it's most refreshing to rub a leaf or two between the fingers and take a good sniff. I particularly associate wild thyme with Foinaven, this was the first place I came across it, some 30 years ago. That was the only occasion I climbed the hill by the long and brutal western slopes, also during a heatwave. The only occasion too when I had company – in the form of a well-endowed young lady who was also taking a day off from a bothy renovation project near Cape Wrath. You didn't meet many women on the hills in those days and I well remember the envious looks I received from a group of men near the summit! Reminiscing is a sign of old age – but Foinaven holds many memories. Before the new hard road up to Loch Dionard was built, the strath used to be churned into a morass by all-terrain vehicles taking people up to the loch for the fishing. On my first visit I'd walked for nearly a fortnight from Lochcarron, heading for Cape Wrath, and had wallowed knee-deep down the whole six-mile length of the valley in the drizzle. Nowhere else in Scotland, before or since, have I encountered worse bogs.

Now, in friendly sunshine, I followed the stream up to Loch Duail, then carried on up the east ridge of Ganu Mor to the stony summit. I'd expected people on such a fine day but there was nobody at all. Perhaps everyone was sunbathing on the Sutherland beaches. The dry air gave clear views, across the literally countless lochans far below, to the Atlantic, to Kinlochbervie and Cape Wrath, east to Ben Hope, Ben Loyal, Strathy Point and the distant white dot of the Dounreay sphere. Southwards lay the bare, rocky ridge of the mountain, with the neighbouring stony peak of Arkle to the west. There's not much vegetation high on Foinaven, just rock, boulder and scree. I scrambled along the ridge for a mile then took a knife-edge east, leading to the narrow crest of A Ch'eir Gorm – sometimes known as 'the whispering ridge'. The crest is crumbling quartzite above steep broken crags and long screes. W. A. Poucher in his old classic 'The

Hills of the North, Rejoice!

Scottish Peaks' reckons that you can sit here on a calm day and listen to the rocks falling off the crumbling cliffs. In spite of many visits I've never heard this myself and suspect that what the writer heard was a small group of deer crossing the screes below. 'Scree-running' can rarely be indulged in these days, most suitable slopes having long since been scraped bare of small stones – but nobody ever descends from A Ch'eir Gorm so there are plenty of virgin slopes you can quickly descend in the classic manner, dig in the heels and lean back.

Strath Dionard was hot. I'd hoped for a dip in the loch but fishermen were out in a boat, so I had to make do with a small peaty lochan higher up, not deep enough for a good swim but at least enough for cooling off. Strath Beag was stifling, the temperature certainly in the low eighties, the rough miles out to Eriboll long. I found a river pool and had another dip, the clegs homed in and followed me, waiting to attack even when I surfaced after swimming underwater.

What a contrast with the English Lake District a few weeks earlier! Then, on a long walk on a fine hot day, I must have met some 250 people. On Foinaven during Bank Holiday week, not one other walker. Let nobody tell me that the Scottish hills are becoming overcrowded.

Changeable

That best describes the weather over the past few weeks. Changeable. There's no real cause for complaint though, quite a few days have been fine or bright and it hasn't stuck in an endless rut of low cloud and drizzle as sometimes happens in August. I've always found the weather hard to predict in this part of the world but the professional forecasts seem to have been worse than ever lately and there is no hope of looking beyond the next 24 hours. What definitely doesn't help is that Caithness can be lumped in with north-west Scotland, north-east Scotland, northern Scotland or even 'The Northern Isles' depending on the whim of the forecaster. Sometimes I suspect they just don't want to admit they've no idea at all. My approach is to listen to the forecasts, watch the sky and the wind direction, use all the clues I can and then make a judgement based on the lot. And I'll still get it wrong. Perhaps the best thing is just to go out when there are no big black clouds immediately looming!

Saturday looked fine and bright early, the forecast was good but with a possibility of showers later. It would be a nice morning for a walk/jog across Scaraben, one of my favourite short expeditions. By 8-30 I was already crossing the old suspension bridge across the gorge of the Berriedale water, a mile below Braemore – the bridge which surely inspired Neil Gunn in 'The Well at the World's End'. The heather is good this year, miles of it, the shortbread tins and the like not illustrating the wide range of colours to be found within a few dozen square yards. About one in a million is white. A steady climb up through the heather took me to the main ridge and a jog/walk across bare quartzite slopes to the east top. My forecast was already wrong, the wind was bitterly cold for August, perhaps only four degrees Celsius, I was glad not to be in shorts, a precaution against ticks, not cold! It was gloriously clear though, across all the rolling Caithness flow country past Ben Alisky and the Beinn nam Bads to the distant hills of Hoy. Cloud was lifting off the Sutherland mountains, the sea to the east sparkling to the Moray coast with the Beatrice Field oil rigs prominent.

Hills of the North, Rejoice!

The occasional white dot of a lorry wound over the Ord. Gobernuisgeach house, five miles away, was just visible, nicely framed between Maiden Pap and Morven, while Glutt Lodge basked in the sun at the end of the long straight estate track from Braemore.

Here and there on the ridge were the scattered raspberry-like berries of the cloudberry plant, red ripening into soft orange. It's always a surprise to find these in such bleak exposed places and I've picked them at above 3000 feet. They are perfectly edible, though with a slightly medicinal taste. Hurrying, just keeping warm, I jogged down to the col and up to the main summit in the middle of the ridge, then turned and headed back the way I'd come. Just below the east top a pair of ptarmigan scuttled away, these birds always seem very tame and you can get quite close to them. They looked like young birds, quite small and grey/white, not the normal adult summer plumage. There were lots of deer (far too many in fact) but I don't think I saw one grouse… The most eastern bump on the ridge, a 1600-foot heathery top with a very fine view out over the sea, had a small summit cairn which sheltered a dwarf rowan, about a foot high, presumably seeded from a bird which had perched there after eating berries from trees lower down. The lower hillsides would be covered with birch and rowan if it wasn't for the deer. A light shower swept across as I struggled back up from the bridge through deep heather towards the car. I'd seen no sign of the rain coming and the skies looked distinctly grey to the north as I drove homewards. Now the forecast ominously mentioned that the showers could be heavy in north-east Scotland. For once it was right; by 2-30pm the heavens had opened into a downpour which lasted the rest of the afternoon.

A few days later, after a fine morning, an afternoon jog round Beinn Ratha (roughly following the hill race route) seemed a nice idea. Although a bit cloudier at Reay than it had been at home, it still looked fine so I set off in shorts and a T-shirt, jogging up the track past Helshetter woods. The sun was warm, soon I was hot and sweating, fortunately there was enough breeze to keep most of the flies away. At the end of the track I took the usual route, straight up across rough wet heather and grass slopes, passing below the middle top of the hill to climb onto the ridge just north of the main top (you now have to climb a new forest fence if you go this way). The view on a clear day is always better than remembered and certainly comparable to that from tops thousands of feet higher. Even Ben More Assynt in Sutherland could be seen, with all those bare peaks marching along the horizon from Ben Hee through Foinaven to the Parph country of Cape Wrath. Rural Caithness stretched eastwards with the lochan-strewn flow country south to the Morven hills and Ben Uarie between Kildonan and Loth. Out to the west a change seemed to be coming in, drizzle and low cloud hid Strathy Point and Ben Hutig. The wind was stronger and it had suddenly turned cold.

It was another rough, pathless mile from Ben Ratha to my next objective, Loch Garbh, and a quick swim (planned on the assumption that it would be warm and sticky) – just 50 yards across to the other side of the narrow loch and then back. The water was cold but probably warmer than the air, however there would be several miles of rough going to warm me up again. The old path to Sandside House is now so overgrown that it's often easier to take to the open moor, but still gives a quick route down. A little cairn, half a mile from the loch, is a good viewpoint and prominently seen from Dounreay and the Drumholiston road. I wonder how many people who've noticed this little top from afar have actually visited it! Drizzle suddenly swept across, patches of low cloud obscuring the hilltops I'd just visited. A sudden change in the weather indeed, once again I'd nearly been caught out. The air had turned even colder, more like October.

The tide was out at Sandside Bay, the wide sands empty and beautiful. I jogged along the beach, splashing through the waves to wash the peat off my legs. I'd thought that the weather had set in for the rest of the day but now it was clearing. Wrong again.

Hoy cliffs

'Wilderness walks' are all the fashion nowadays, particularly in exotic locations such as the Californian Sierra or the South Island of New Zealand. Many such places are much less wild than we're led to believe, with organised campsites, way-marked trails, rangers, wardens and suchlike. What I do know is that some superb, real, wilderness walking can be had within sight of Thurso.

My visits to the Isle of Hoy have tended to be rushed affairs, a day trip from Caithness used to be possible, allowing seven hours on the island, if you took the Monday 6am sailing on the *St.Ola* and returned on the 8pm from Stromness. For a while though I'd planned a more leisurely excursion, with tent, taking two or three days to walk the entire line of cliffs from Moaness on North Hoy, past St John's Head and the Old Man to Rackwick Bay then on, by the Candle of the Sneuk and the Berry, to Melsetter Bay, South Walls and Lyness. The walk from Moaness to Rackwick is quite well known, but nobody carries on along the south-western cliffs to Melsetter. The whole route, through country as empty, wild and spectacular as you'll find anywhere in Britain, is indeed a great wilderness walk. On a very fine clear evening I cycled up to the Sibmister viewpoint and gazed across the Pentland Firth to that long line of cliffs, their red rocks glowing even redder in the evening sun. Within 24 hours I hoped to be camped on one of those higher clifftops, looking back across to Caithness. August is a midgey month for camping in Hoy, or indeed anywhere in the Highlands. A strong north-westerly wind was blowing though and should, I hoped, keep the beasties at bay...

The sea was choppy and the ferry was moving up and down just nicely on the early-morning crossing from Scrabster. There was a two-hour wait in Stromness before a much smaller boat took a few of us tourists across to Moaness, all holding on tight in the rough waters around Graemsay. A minibus, a taxi and the RSPB warden were all there to greet the half-dozen or so visitors on this English Bank Holiday Monday! I decided to follow the coast and climb up the steep slopes of the spectacular Kame of Hoy, rather than take an easier route inland. This proved something of a mistake; I must have had to cross every fence on North Hoy, tricky with a full camping pack. Eventually, leaving the farmland behind, I followed the faintest of paths above rising cliffs towards the eroded slopes of the Kame. The path soon vanished completely leaving me struggling up very steep slopes thickly grown with rush. Few had ever come this way. At last, soaked in sweat, I reached the 900-foot top of the Kame, with an easier undulating route ahead to the highest point of St John's Head. This (the third-highest sea-cliff in Britain) is relatively well known, a short but very airy scramble, with a 1000-foot drop to the side, takes you onto the rush-covered tabletop of the Head itself with little then to show that you are surrounded by such immense cliffs. The *St Ola* was coming north on its third crossing of the choppy waters, looking like a toy boat far below. A squall was getting up, rain drove in and curtains of mist appeared, tearing upwards across the top of the 1200-foot cliffs; all you needed to complete the scene was some Valkyrie music. A flash from far below indicated a tourist's camera – but from the boat you just don't get a true impression of the scale of these cliffs.

A well-trodden path led down towards the diminutive looking Old Man of Hoy. I'd forgotten just how spectacular is the scene from the clifftop opposite, a little grassy table juts out to give one of the most amazing views in Scotland of this highest sea-stack in Britain. I was tiring a little now, unused to carrying a heavy load, but the scenery more than made up for it. Next on the agenda was Rackwick Bay, a very special place indeed and probably my favourite spot on the whole of Orkney. I've visited less than a dozen times this great beach of giant pebbles and sand, opening between high cliffs and always misted by sea-spray. You need to approach, and leave, Rackwick Bay slowly. It always feels to me like coming home when I make my way down the steep slopes from the clifftops to the bay, I hope I shall never travel there by car. Almost on the beach, in what must be one of the world's top locations, is a modern architect-designed house with features such as a grass-covered roof and a balcony on stilts. There were children's toys in the garden. But whoever lives there will, like everyone else, have illness, sick children, worries over distant aged relatives, blocked drains, broken-down cars... perhaps, as Gavin Maxwell eventually found at Camusfearna, some places are best just visited so that the vision of earthly paradise is not lost in earthly concerns.

I wandered along to the far end of the beach, enjoying a bit of Rackwick boulder hopping, then dozed in the sun until the notorious midges attacked and drove me onwards up very steep slopes towards Sneuk Head. The high clifftops are broken here so I cut inland over moors inhabited by skuas – fortunately the chicks had fledged or I'd have suffered vicious assault. The birds attack vigorously, coming in low and fast with a great whoosh; on a previous occasion I found that waving a red sweatshirt as they made the final low-level approach was some deterrent (until I lost the sweatshirt off the back of the rucsac and had to go back to look for it, unprotected!) The occasional Hoy mountain hare raced off. Below was the green valley of the 'summer of Hoy' – a corruption of old Norse which simply referred to the burn as a boundary marker – I scrambled down, collected drinking water for the night then climbed up to the edge of the 600-foot cliffs to look for a camping site. The wind was strong, shelter was desirable for camping – but not too much, the midges would be just waiting. A level piece of stony ground just inland from the clifftop proved ideal where the wind was deflected by the updraft from the cliffs.

It was one of the most stunning spots in which I have ever camped. From far below came the roar of the waves against the foot of the cliffs while the wind carried upwards the scent of bearberry and heather. A short scramble took me to the top of the Candle of the Sneuk, possibly the best viewpoint on the whole of Hoy, a sentinel high above the Pentland Firth. I could see right along the north coast of Scotland from Cape Wrath through Whiten Head, Strathy point, Dounreay and Dunnet Head to Duncansby Head with, beyond, the mountains of Foinaven, Ben Hope, Loyal, Armine, the Griams, Morven and Scaraben. Above Dunnet Bay were the masts on Olrig Hill, from where, 24 hours earlier, I'd gazed the other way across the Firth. Eastward the red cliffs fell to the Green Heads then rose again to the 600-foot crest of The Berry. Northwards the moors of Hoy glowed yellow in the evening sun. Fulmars hovered below in the updrafts and circled above, with the occasional 'whoosh' as a bird turned on a particularly strong gust of wind. There were still some well-grown chicks, cackling at their parents for food, on ledges near the clifftops.

As dusk fell I climbed up again onto the Candle, watching the *St Ola* heading back to Scrabster on its sixth crossing that day of the Pentland Firth. Straight across were the brilliant orange lights of Thurso, only about 15 miles away; also the sky was strangely illuminated by a flickering yellow light from the east – the Flotta flare, hidden from direct sight by hills. These signs of civilisation apart, this was indeed one of the remoter spots in Scotland. The next stage of my wilderness walk would take me along even less-frequented clifftops, via the Berry, to Melsetter Bay.

I hadn't expected a calm night on top of an exposed Hoy clifftop over 600 feet above the sea. Yet the wind fell away, with a faint pattering of what sounded like drizzle on the tent in the early morning. It wasn't drizzle. A breeze sprung up again shortly after dawn and I looked out to a clear day below a grey, dappled sky. Fortunately I'd eaten breakfast and was well on my way to packing up before the breeze faded to flat calm. I now fully appreciated that my tent was on the edge of many square miles of ideal midge habitat. They attacked. When midgies really swarm it's as impossible to keep them off with repellent as it is to keep dry by donning a waterproof jacket when jumping in the river. Stay in one spot for more than a few seconds and even your eyes are full of them. George Mackay-Brown considered the Rackwick midgies the most ferocious in Scotland with teeth like sharks. The fact is that everywhere in the Highlands and Islands has the worst midgies!

With gear and tent hurriedly and untidily rammed into the sack I was soon making my way eastward along the cliffs at a good speed, there was no chance of stopping to admire the tremendous views as little swarms were making the most of the rare calm conditions. A mile on, the Burn of Forse tumbles over the clifftop in a vertical fall of three hundred feet, the cliffs then rise before falling again to the rocky cove of Little Rackwick. Next, long geos bite inland between a succession of grassy headlands aptly called the 'Green Heads'. You feel they should be patted, like dogs. Steep slopes lead on to the top of the vertical red cliffs of the Berry, 600 feet high and gashed by a great geo. The combination of a light breeze and increasing amounts of warm sun were now keeping the insects at bay and I could enjoy the views again. It was only the second time I'd stood on these clifftops looking across to Dunnet Head, less than ten miles away – how many dozen times have I looked the other way across the Pentland Firth!

I picked my way through rough heather past a couple of small lochs to the highest point of the Berry with a very fine view over the flat peninsular of South Walls. Returning to the clifftops I strode briskly down an easy grassy slope, aiming for lower ground ahead. Fortunately I noticed a line of rocks crossing the slopes ahead, possibly indicating a geo below. I detoured round to be on the safe side... and indeed, one of the most evil-looking slots I've seen interrupted the smooth grassy descent like a trap designed to catch the unwary walker! Ahead was Ha Wick, a mostly rocky bay, sandy at its southern end and with heaps of ancient driftwood piled above highest water. In the warm sunshine this made an ideal spot for lunch as seals mooed and whooshed off the rocks. I carried on round the point, marked by a small lighthouse, then a rough walk along low cliffs fringing wet moorland led to one of my main objectives – Melsetter Bay. On any fine clear day this sandy beach is tantalisingly visible from all the higher parts of Thurso, some 15 miles away. Many people can even see it from their houses – but few have been there! I was as guilty as anyone in not having visited the place before, but was going to make amends by spending the night there. Having walked right round the wildest part of Hoy I was indeed now almost back to civilisation with Melsetter farm and house less than a mile away and grazed fields running down to the beach from the east. I put the tent up by a small burn (but would have to boil the water which ran through pastures) and then set off to explore further.

A lady was making her way slowly along the track, she stopped to talk. She was English (like most who live on South Walls), had lived on Hoy for 20 years, and was a very young-looking 71. Her husband had died fairly recently and she had chosen a fine afternoon for a first return visit to Ha Wick, one of their favourite spots where they had liked to watch the seals. I remarked that it was pretty rough going and the midgies might be bad, but she was quite determined and well equipped with citronella repellent (not much good that, I thought, but said nothing...)

There was still a whole afternoon in which to explore. From the top of the sand-dunes I could easily see Thurso – and Olrig Hill – with Scarfskerry directly across the Firth. I followed the track for a mile to the road, then crossed the narrow spit of The Ayre which leads to South Walls, carrying on for another mile to reach the highest point (less than two hundred feet above sea level) of this green 'almost' island. Melsetter itself was very attractive with hills and trees by the road along the inlet of North Bay but South Walls seemed the dullest of the Orkney Isles.

Back at Melsetter bay I met the lady walking slowly up the track. She'd made it to Ha Wick but it had been a long way and she'd got her feet wet trying to take a shortcut back over the moor. Good for her. Many people half her age would not have attempted the rough five-mile round walk.

'The midgies were terrible,' she said. 'They were all over me. They were eating my eyeballs!'

Very fortunately a gentle onshore breeze kept the biters away that evening and I could even cook outside the tent, sitting on the shore looking across the Pentland Firth to the Caithness coast. Grand to spend a few hours at a spot I'd seen so often but never managed before to visit! Unfortunately, at around five the next morning, a few dozen sheep came past the tent, bringing with them a big cloud of midgies... I had to be away at six in order to catch a ferry from Lyness. It was a lovely seven mile walk along the road in the quiet early morning, the sea almost mirror calm under a grey sky. Lyness itself is such a mess of derelict buildings and rusting machinery that it's almost a work of art; it's about time the detritus washed up by the high tide of two world wars was removed. I'd walked three-quarters the way round the coast of Hoy.

The crossing to Houton was smooth, first passing Fara, now uninhabited and looking an enticing isle to visit. To complete my circuit to Stromness there remained ten miles or so along the shore from Houton. I'd hoped to follow field edges but found the way barred by many fences, crops and cows... fortunately the actual seashore gave reasonable walking, mostly small stones and shingle, even some sand and just a few rough rocky or bouldery sections. It was a pleasant walk under grey skies which threatened but never produced rain, just across the Sound were the Hoy Hills and Graemsay with grey seals lying in numbers on the Skerries of Clestrain. I picked up the road for the last few miles, it made a nice change to be able to look at the views without watching my feet.

Hills of the North, Rejoice!

Stromness is far and away the most attractive town within easy reach of Caithness and it's never a hardship to spend an hour or two there waiting for the ferry. This time the crossing was almost calm. I watched the cliffs of Hoy slide past with more than usual interest and noticed that heavy showers were building over South Walls. The rain came down that night, and the next day; my short wilderness walk round Hoy had coincided with the last fine weather of the summer.

An Alpine saunter

Just north of Grenoble, a city the size of Edinburgh, rise the craggy limestone peaks of the Chartreuse Alps. It's a remarkably unspoilt, beautiful and little-known area in spite of being so close to a large city, with steep wooded mountainsides, little villages, high cliffs and bare hilltops and is threaded by a maze of roads and paths. I'd planned to extend a rare foreign business trip by an extra two days for some walking in a part of the world I'd never before visited; after 15 hours of travel and two days in meetings, I felt in urgent need of a bit exercise.

I set my sights on a 6000-foot peak called La Grande Sure, some 12 miles away. An early-morning train took me a few miles to St Egreve, from where a path climbed from the valley floor towards the village of Mont St Martin some 3000 feet higher. The path was nicely graded but went on up, and up, and up, all the time through dense deciduous woodland. After the equivalent of climbing a munro, I emerged in a little village with farms, houses, and cars. The equivalent of another munro lay ahead. The woods were beautiful, stretching for mile after mile, carpeting the steep hillsides. However, after several hours of climbing, the novelty of walking through steep woodland began to wear off; I started longing for some open country with views. On up, and up. The vegetation hardly changed with height, though at 5000 feet there was a nice autumn tint to the trees. The treeline was sudden. Unlike the Scottish hills, where trees slowly thin and die out, I abruptly emerged from dense, damp woodland to warm sunshine and an open country of grass and juniper bushes.

A little sign directed me to detour to the top of La Grande Vache which, at just under 6000 feet, was the highest point on a broken limestone scarp, rising out of the forests, with clear views as far as Mont Blanc, some 50 miles away. Across the plains towards Lyon stretched a sea of cloud. All around rose the other limestone peaks of the Chartreuse country. For the next couple of hours I followed paths across high open country. Here and there the ground was carpeted with Mountain Avens, with the occasional blue gentian still in flower. In the hot sun I stripped off to shorts and T-shirt, not realising that sunburn was still possible in October… A final steep climb took me to the top of La Grande Sure, to eat lunch in the sunshine at the top of high cliffs overlooking the cloud-sea.

It was with some regret that I descended back into the forests to walk through the shady woodlands for several hours – not, by any means, easy walking. Paths were mostly faint, with confusing false trails branching off. Waymarking by red or white paint was common, but only for some reason where the path was already clear. After twice taking wrong turnings which faded out into virgin woodland I learnt the necessity of closely following the map and frequently consulting the compass. My legs and feet were now feeling the effects of nine hours of rough walking and countless thousands of feet of climbing, yet there were many miles still to go. Another wrong turning added one mile more, and several planned shortcuts proved impossible. Every village house seemed to have one or two huge dogs, Alsatians, Dobermans and the like, and I didn't fancy squeezing past them. I began to regret that I'd refused a lift offered by some chanterelle gatherers!

Dusk was falling, warm, scented, with crickets singing everywhere. Now I tramped for mile after mile down the road towards the city. I had, however, one further diversion in mind, if I could make it before dark fell. From Grenoble a cable car climbs 800 feet to a restaurant and cafe high above the city, the terminus of many paths. By leaving the road and taking more forest paths I could come out there, have a meal, and save my poor knees some of the long descent. It was only just light enough to read the map but I found the path, climbing (to my dismay) steeply from a small hamlet. Owls hooted, night-jars jarred, bats fluttered. In fading light I stumbled up the path till it joined a wide, easy track heading south. I could see the lights of the city far below; soon I'd be at the cafe. But where was it? The path seemed to have come to a sudden end. Steep broken crags fell below. The moon was out now but there was no way I could see to scramble down.

Be prepared! Fortunately I was; there was a torch at the bottom of my rucsac. The map now showed that the path doubled back on itself; I must have carried on to a viewpoint. All that was needed was to retrace my steps till, a quarter of mile back, the correct path headed off. It zigzagged down, interminably. I couldn't risk taking short cuts in the dark. Twelve hours after setting out, the path suddenly emerged at a road-end with lights and a house. Not realising it was the restaurant, I walked straight past. And so the long day ended with a leisurely meal overlooking the lights of the city and a ride down in a glass bubble through the night, with only another half mile to hobble back to the hotel!

On my second day, I was stiff and tired after the previous day's strenuous walk but nevertheless determined to have another long day out. The following day would give a rest on the journey home! An early bus from Grenoble would take me up into the mountains. Not knowing where any of the villages were I couldn't however tell which bus to catch from the bus-station. Then I noticed on one of the timetables the little word in brackets 'funicular'. A glance at the map showed that this should give me a ride up 3000 feet of mountain and a flying start on the 7000-foot Dent de Croles. The bus dropped me off 45 minutes later at De Montford, some ten miles up the valley. The sight that met my eyes was nothing like I'd ever seen before. Above the town rose extremely steep wooded slopes, culminating in a line of limestone cliffs down which a waterfall tumbled. I'd expected to see a cable-car climbing the 3000 feet to the top. Yet up the mountain, straight as a ruler, ran a railway. A coach party had arrived as I walked up to the little station – this was as well, as it turned out that the funicular was officially closed that day. A special trip had however been organised and I'd turned up at just the right time.

The wagons had seats which were designed to be horizontal when climbing at 45 degrees. One wagon ran up the slope counterbalanced by one running down and joined by a very long cable. One hoped it didn't break halfway up. The view back was like looking down a cliff – except that a railway track ran down it. A short tunnel, at an angle of about 60 degrees, ran through the final cliffs, below the upper station. This sat at the very lip of the steep slopes and a few yards' walk led into a village in a grassy Alpine basin. Yes, here was a quiet, ordinary, mid-morning village with roads, houses, a school and even a little supermarket. Not quite believing my eyes any more I wandered in and bought a baguette and some cheese for my lunch.

A steep path headed up through woods towards the next tier of high mountain. Now I was really on my way – or so I thought. Instead, after a stiff 400-foot climb came another road, a park, and then a huge hospital. It had once been a TB sanatorium and was the raison d'être for the funicular which had been built in the 1920's. The wards would have a tremendous view, right across the main valley to the high snowy peaks of the Belladonna massif. There were hundreds of parked cars and a man with an arm in a sling crossed the road in front of me. Doing my best to remember that I was already 4000 feet up a mountain, I set about trying to find where the path left the maze of buildings. I failed, of course, and instead set myself to grind slowly up the 30-45 degree wooded slopes, to intersect the path much higher up. At 5000 feet, grass and scree rose another few hundred feet to the foot of vertical limestone cliffs which went straight up for another thousand. Below the cliffs various steel barriers had been erected as avalanche protection and, scrambling up an open gully in the woods, I came across the twisted remains of some of them which had been brought down while doing their duty. Eventually I found the path which climbed up to the very foot of the cliffs. Indeed much too close to the cliffs for comfort. Rockfall is a very real danger in the Alps and for half a mile the path was totally exposed to anything falling from above. Stones and boulders of various sizes littering the ground did little to inspire confidence; there was nothing to do but hurry along as fast as possible. The path sidled round the corner of the mountain and crossed scree to emerge, to my great relief, on steep grassy slopes. A flock of sheep were grazing a couple of thousand feet lower down and the musical tinkle of their sheep-bells floated upwards.

The rest of the climb was steep, but easy. A large metal cross was fixed in place on the summit with an untidy cairn. The wind was strong and cold, but less so than is normal in Caithness. Although slopes on one side were relatively gentle the top had a very exposed feel to it; the cross was perched on the very top of those vertical cliffs and you looked down over a little limestone bulge to nothing until the village, 3500 feet below.

My legs by now were complaining badly but they would just have to put up with the steep descent. My plan was to pick up a long-distance path – a sort of Alpine Pennine Way – through the forest and then cut down another path which descended 3500 feet from a col to St Ismier. Here I could get a bus back to Grenoble. The path was rough, slippery and slow, up and down over boulders and fallen trees. Time was getting on. At the col I couldn't find the path, scrambled down a few hundred feet to try to intersect it – an orienteering ploy which failed – and had to climb all the way back up again. Instead I had to carry on for another two miles along the ridge to where there should be another way down. A little path wandered along the ridge, a woodland walk, except that sometimes it crept close to the edge from where you looked down steep cliffs and forest slopes to towns 3000 feet below. There should be just enough daylight to make it down. This time though the beginning of the descent was well marked by three or four different notices – and even my French was good enough to get the message 'Dangereux chutes de pierres'. 'Chemin interdit!' I had a 'look' by going down 50 feet or so – and thought better of it.

There was only one thing left to do. A path on the other side of the col would take me quickly down to the high village of Le Sappey, only some 1500 feet below. From there it was six or seven miles down roads to Grenoble, and I might manage to hitch a lift. Slithering and sliding down the muddy path through the woods, I reached Le Sappey in 45 minutes, with plenty of daylight left. And luck was on my side, for the second time that day. There was a bus-shelter – and a timetable – and lo, the only bus of the day was due in about 25 minutes. It was a school bus, taking children home from Grenoble and it first passed going the other way, looking just like any Caithness school bus except that it was rather more modern. It had to be, to safely negotiate the mountain roads. I didn't begrudge the 35 francs (over four pounds) it cost me to ride down the 2500 feet to the lights of the city, far below. A tram-ride back to the hotel finished off the day's round of unusual experiences!

Twenty minutes from home

Early one morning I drove for just 20 minutes, a journey taking me from home into the heart of the Flow Country. The forecast rain was further away than suggested, with just thin high cloud and a freshening south-east wind. People would never believe me when I told them that the Caithness moors, between the Causewaymire and Strath Halladale, ranked among the wildest and remotest parts of Britain. 'What about the Cairngorms, or Knoydart?' they would say. But such popular mountain areas are criss-crossed by paths and tracks and you're never far from people.

At Achavanich I climbed over the fence, straight into the rough, wet and pathless moorland so characteristic of the Far North. The terrain puts people off but there is no problem if you take it slowly and don't try walking through the dubh-lochs or the few patches of deep green mossy bog. First I had to circuit the end of Loch Rangag, then pick up the edge of a small drainage ditch which made a beeline south-west through very rough heather. The practice of driving quads across these moors has reduced their remoteness, one track made by these vehicles came up from the north, probably linking up with the Smerral or Mulbuie road. I crossed another low ridge to a shallow valley of grass and rushes, perhaps once partly cultivated, then climbed more steeply up to the 700-foot hilltop of Coire na Beinn. The sound of traffic on the road had already faded into the distance. A herd of deer grazed half a mile to the north-east. The view was over endless moors and lochs, with the sea to the south. Had anybody been here since my last visit, probably over ten years earlier? Just below the top of the hill is the small Lochan Coire na Beinn; in spite of the cold wind I couldn't resist the chance of a dip in such an out-of-the-way spot. The water wasn't as cold as feared and was amply deep enough for a swim out to the middle of the loch under the bright early-morning sun. When did someone last swim in this little loch? Had anyone ever swum there before? I soon warmed up again by jogging along the ridge westwards, really more of a gentle moorland crest but with the fine views all round which you see from any watershed. A ring-tailed hen-harrier wheeled ahead then disappeared, it's very unusual to see these birds now. Three miles north, in a shallow valley, could be seen Loch Ruard, an attractive dark blue in the morning sunshine and one of the larger of our moorland lochs. Only the occasional trout-fisherman visits its grassy shores. Loch a Cheracher (the shepherd's loch) is another small and attractive lochan on the skyline, right in the heart of this area of empty country, I had to try a dip here also, the floor of the loch was a bit soft but the water deep enough for swimming. Very boggy country with dubh-lochs lay just to the west, tracks showed that the all-terrain quads had been even here.

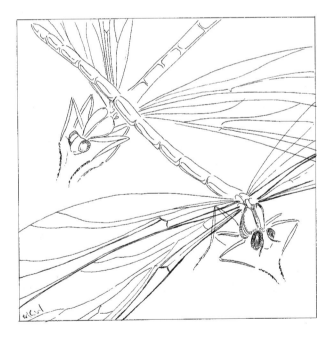

Hills of the North, Rejoice!

The land slopes gently down to the north-west, I could see Loch More some five miles away but the nearer Lochan Thulachan and Loch Sand were hidden in shallow hollows. Another couple of very rough and wet miles led north-eastwards, gently down to a ruined croft at the southern end of Loch Ruard. Once again quad tracks were in evidence, rounding the loch then heading north. There is even a fine fishing hut on the shore – locked – presumably against the hordes of thieves who travel this way. A grassy valley led east, back toward the main road, overgrown lazybeds indicating former cultivation where the valley opened out. Acharaskil, a building prominently seen in the distance from the road, is ruinous, half-full of manure and pigeons. A surprised peregrine shot off from the chimney stack and a big herd of deer moved away, only half a mile from the A9. The sun had now mostly vanished behind thickening cloud, but it wasn't cold, a couple of blue damselflies darted in a brief gleam of sun. There was no respite now from rough boggy country, all the way back to the car except for the last, grassy, 50 yards. Suddenly rain was spotting and within ten minutes the friendly, sunny moors had become their bleak, grey, normal selves.

Just 20 minutes drive from home and you can step straight into country which is probably less travelled than almost anywhere else in Britain, if not the world. It surely does the soul good to know that such places are so near at hand!

Bike south

Someday I must cycle all the way to Land's End on quiet roads and cycle-ways. Almost as ambitious, though, was a 500-mile, week-long mountain-bike trek down to the Yorkshire Dales. Sixty or seventy miles a day would, I thought, be fairly leisurely and, by taking lots of cross-country routes like the Corrieyairack Pass, almost all the busy main roads could be avoided. Having many times hurtled up and down the country in a day by car or train, it would be nice to see the country at a more sedate pace. Given the hard work of riding a laden mountain bike, and never having done a long cycle tour before, the itinerary was, in retrospect, perhaps a trifle ambitious...

Day 1.

I couldn't have set out any earlier as my legs had only just stopped feeling like jelly after a bout of flu that had put me off work earlier in the week. Fortunately the weather was flat calm, even so I decided to scrap my first 'cross-country' plans and instead take the shortest and easiest route down to Bonar Bridge and Carbisdale Castle Youth Hostel. An early start gave a deserted ride over the CausewayMire, taking the back road, as always, by Smerral to Latheronwheel. Sweating up the Ord finally drove away the last remnants of the flu! By Brora the rain had set in for the day, I sat in a cafe for an hour over two cups of tea hoping it would clear, but to no avail. At the Mound I left the main road for the cyclists route by Loch Buidhe to Bonar Bridge, now flagging considerably but still enjoying the quiet single-track road up through the dripping birchwoods. The last few miles from Ardgay to the hostel were slow ones. It was great to arrive, Carbisdale is always a fantastic place to stay, even if pricey by Youth Hostel standards. A real castle, grand views from the windows over the Kyle of Sutherland, lovely woods hung with mist. Highlight of the day was definitely the meal of vegetables and rhubarb carried from the garden at home!

Day 2.

To Cannich, but not by the direct route. Another calm day, the last one. Over the Struie in glorious sunshine, already enjoying that great sense of freedom you get on a bike in the Highlands with no tight timescales to meet. The Struie is now a good quiet road to cycle and there was plenty of time to enjoy the views on the long slow climb. From Evanton the old high-level route led on to Dingwall then, in warm sunshine, through Conon Bridge to Muir of Ord. Then up into the hills. Has any other 'long distance' cyclist chosen such a crazy route? Steeply up a track climbing to 1000 feet at Loch Nam Bonnach, mostly wheeling the bike. Then two miles of rough heather, bog and tussock to pick up the track from Glen Orrin which twists down to Erchless and Struy. The first real hard work, struggling across country with the laden bike followed by a very rough descent on the stony track, passing through old settlements high above Strath Glass, climbing again before a steep descent through forests to the valley, warm in the late afternoon September sunshine An easy ride along the narrow road on the south side of Strathglass took me to Cannich and the Youth Hostel. It was a fine evening for a potter along the river watching the shadows grow on the hills as the dusk descended; nice not to be hurtling through as usual when doing the 'Highland Cross'!

Day 3.

A real tough one this, yet finishing only 30 miles further south. Two big cross-country routes, first from Cannich over the top to Invermoriston and Fort Augustus then on across the Corrieyairack Pass. Open any map (1:50000) of any hilly part of Scotland and all sorts of possible mountain bike routes leap out at you. One such is a track from Corrimony, a few miles east of Cannich, climbing right up the River Enrick to Loch Na Stac. There is no path marked along the loch but the map shows a track leading from the far end of the loch all the way down to the Invermoriston road, a descent of some 1500 feet.

The morning was again calm, with drifting low valley fog and a promise of hours of sun. An initial long climb out of Cannich surprised me, I hadn't studied the map carefully enough and wasn't quite prepared for the 500-foot pull out of Strath Glass. From Corrimony the track proved elusive, obviously few other people had come this way, but with careful map reading I found the route and was soon pedalling – or more often pushing – up an improving track heading into heather hills. The sun shone, it was a lovely morning, if the track continued like this all the way across it would be almost too easy. The good track turned off towards the right, climbing steeply. I had my suspicions and checked the map – yes, the correct way was straight on, along an overgrown trod which was more like a path. For the next three or four miles I had to wheel the bike almost all the way, up steep stony slopes, through bogs and deep heather. It would have made a pleasant walk. The sun climbed higher in the sky. Already I was having doubts about getting over Corrieyairack by nightfall, especially if the track down to Invermoriston was as bad as the one up from Corrimony.

Eventually the high loch came into view, and a weird, gaunt shell of a building, three-stories high, looking every bit a haunted house, on what would normally be a small island if the loch were not low. Somebody had painted graffiti on the inside roof sarking, 30 feet up and only accessible by rope or supernatural means. The loch shore was mostly large boulders, no place to wheel a bike, the alternative deep heather little better. Time was passing. Some considerable amount of sweat later I reached the far end of the loch and, wonder of wonders, an excellent 'hydro' track curving off down to the valleys far below. For a mountain bike as good as a tarred road. An exhilarating four miles followed, like coming down the Alps, down, down, past reservoirs, in and out of forests, down to the main road and then still down, all the way to Invermoriston. I'd still reach Fort Augustus by early afternoon. I gave the Great Glen Cycle Way a miss, preferring to get five main road miles over quickly rather than take another couple of hours going up and down twice that distance of steep forest tracks. Indeed the road wasn't that busy and the woods and loch made it quite a pleasant ride. Fort Augustus, never my favourite spot, was hot and full of tourists, I had to stop to stock up food for the next two days in the wilds but was out again as fast as possible. At 2pm, much too late in the day for such a long route when I'd already had one tough hill crossing, I started wheeling the bike up the bumpy remains of 'Wades Road' – now a scheduled ancient monument – which would take me up to 2500 feet.

From its construction in around 1730 this route was, for 100 years, the main road from the Great Glen to Laggan. It's still in remarkably good shape but in many places the surface has gone and only the rough bouldery foundations remain. The road is a well-known challenge for 4x4 vehicles which cause further erosion. It's passable on a mountain bike but, as I found, you have to wheel the thing almost all of the long climb. At least there were no weather worries, all I had to do was get to the other side before dark. After losing several pints of sweat in the first 1000-foot climb the route levelled out a bit, I could cycle some of it though it was very rough. A line of pylons follows the road and rounding a corner I could see, far, away, pylons on the skyline of a high and distant mountain ridge. A long way to go... The road goes ever on. Not alone though, along came a landrover, bouncing across the boulders, the driver and passenger delighted at having made it this far. Then a tipper truck laden with sand and cement passed and stopped a mile further on where a bridge was under repair. The climb proper resumed, several miles of steadily wheeling the bike uphill. The sun sank in the sky, the air grew cooler. The road went ever on, now high in the mountains. A last climb and the track levelled out at a locked and rusty hut marking the summit.

When planning the trip, in my armchair at home, I'd thought of leaving the bike at the summit and climbing the mountains on either side... Had anyone made the suggestion now there would have been a few rude words at the least. It was 6pm. Steep bouldery zigzags led down, mostly rideable but hard on both bike and rider. Here and there I just had to walk. Once out of the corrie the gradient eased, the track carried on round the corner and a long straight appeared leading down to Melgarve bothy, my destination that night and now visible a couple of miles ahead. Frustratingly much of this last section was nothing but boulders and impossible to cycle. When at last reached, the bothy proved a pleasant surprise, recently renovated and painted, very spick and span. There was even time to sit out in the last of the day's sunshine, drinking a well-earned mug of sweet tea, looking across the wide green strath to the shadowed slopes of the massive Creag Meagaidh hills. I could feel the sun after ten hours of continuous sunshine on bare arms and legs, a tendon in my calf was getting a bit sore, and both bike and body had taken something of a battering. Nothing seriously wrong though, so another long cross-country day to come on the morrow!

Day 4.

A fresh south-east wind had picked up overnight and there was more cloud. Ahead was another ambitious route from Laggan via Strath Ossian to Rannoch Station. That way I'd avoid both Drumochter and the A82 through Glencoe, but would finish the day only another 30 miles further south. Although Loch Laggan was only ten miles due south of the bothy, a range of 3000-foot peaks lay in the way and even I wasn't going to attempt a direct route. So, a 20 mile detour it was, due east into the wind to Laggan village, almost onto the A9, then back west past InverPattack and Loch Laggan.

The day's journey took me through the heart of the Highlands. In all directions the skylines were high, more rounded to the east, more jagged to the west, range beyond range, wide empty straths, forested hillsides. Stag-stalking was in full swing. Landrovers, all-terrain quads on trailers behind, were parked outside the big lodge waiting to take the stalking guests to the hill. Further on a quad was parked at the foot of a hill track, ready to bring back the stag. From Moy Lodge, one of the longest of estate tracks winds for miles through the mountains to the Corrour Shooting Lodge on Loch Ossian, here I met two ladies in a large car driving slowly down to the road, heading probably for Fort William while the husbands took to the hills with the rifles. The Corrour track led for miles up through forests then out into the bare, high glens, exposed to the strengthening wind, through ranges of remote mountains which only the stalker or the munro-bagger ever visits or even sees. Ben Alder. Aonach Beag, Beinn a Chlachair. Sgor Gaibhre. Westward, the Grey corries, the Mamores, Ben Nevis. The skyline changed every mile as new glens opened out and fresh ranges of peaks appeared. The plantations and woods around Loch Ossian came as a pleasant surprise in such a bare landscape, suddenly it was lush again and woodland birds were singing. Two locked deer gates were a less pleasant surprise. Unload the bike. Lift all the gear over. Lift the bike up over my head and hook it onto the top of the gate. Climb over. Lift the bike down. Load it up again. Loch Ossian Youth Hostel has a magnificent setting at the western end of the loch, a mile from Corrour station on the Glasgow to Fort William line. It would have been nice to stop the night there but it was only mid afternoon and I wanted to get a bit further south. I expected the next section, the old 'Road to the Isles' from Corrour to Rannoch, to be slow.

Slow it was, but not difficult. The weather in this normally wet area had been dry for weeks and the path proved generally good for wheeling the bike, though not good enough for riding with frequent ruts, bogs and deep ditches to cross. From Strath Ossian, already nearly 1500 feet up, the path climbs slowly across the side of Carn Dearg, reaching an altitude of 1750 feet at the ruins of the old Corrour shooting lodge, with spectacular views west across sunlit Rannoch Moor to the high peaks of Glencoe and the Black Mount. I was quite content to walk, a change from pedalling for hour after hour! With no accommodation planned, the weather looked fine for a night in the open, dry and with a breeze to keep the midges way. A rare thing in the Highlands! A couple of miles from Rannoch station a large pile of rotting railway sleepers had been dumped, and tinder-dry bogwood roots poked out of ditches. A fire, carefully laid in the middle of a large stony area, blazed with the first match. It felt like being a character in a Western, lying in my sleeping bag looking at the stars with the firelight still flickering and the first rutting stags roaring from the hills above. It was my last night in the Highlands.

Day 5.

This was to prove the most exhausting day of all. I was already tired, it was virtually all on roads and there was mostly a stiff headwind. The first stretch proved fine, down the hills to Loch Rannoch then along the southern shore, mostly sheltered from the wind, past Rannoch school. Then came, as expected, a tough climb up the Schiehallion road, into the wind, long slow miles before a steep, exhilarating descent to Keltneyburn and round to Kenmore at the end of Loch Tay. Already the country was softer, the hills gentler, the villages more trippery.

Hills of the North, Rejoice!

On a long trip you have to compromise as to which maps to take. Ideally I'd have taken only one-inch (or 1:50000) maps but the weight would have been too great, so on more straightforward sections such as this I made do with the smaller scale 1:250000. The map showed a little road climbing over to Glen Quaich, joining the Sma Glen road a few miles further on; this obvious route would avoid the main road. What I didn't realise from my small scale map was that the road climbed for 1500 feet, one of the biggest climbs on tarred roads anywhere in Britain... First steep zigzags up through forest, mostly wheeling the bike, then on, up and up, grassland, heather, high into the hills. Over an hour to the top, stopping for lunch on the way to break the climb. Already the Highlands were, sadly, being left behind, this heather moorland country was more like the borders or even the Pennines. A very fast, steep descent took me down two miles then the glen flattened out and instead of the long easy descent I'd anticipated there was a slow, hard grind straight into the wind past Loch Freuchie to Amulree. At long last I reached the main road and a change in direction. The wind funnels in strange ways down the glens, and to my pleasant surprise was mostly from behind down the Sma Glen, giving a fast ride towards Crieff. My map showed a direct route on byroads across Strath Earn, bypassing the town so I sailed on, gently downhill through lush farmlands and past raspberry fields, to suddenly encounter the River Earn at a ford with no bridge. Fortunately, because of the very dry weather, the river though wide was only a foot deep. Next time I'll take decent maps. My small scale map also didn't clearly show that Auchterarder, where I planned to restock food, was on top of a big hill. Running out of food on a bike can be like running out of petrol in a car, suddenly you feel weak, sick, almost unable to pedal.

With a couple of sweets I just made it to the shops and, revived by bananas, set off across the Ochils for the last ten miles to Glendevon Youth Hostel. With failing energy and a sore leg my planned route over the drove road was abandoned and instead, slowly, with several stops, I crept along the main road up Gleneagles into the wind, over the pass, and down the long miles to the hostel. It was fortunately a lovely sunny evening with the Ochils at their most attractive – but was I glad to arrive that night!

Day 6.

A good night's sleep worked wonders and my leg was no worse in the morning, though still swollen. It was going to be another very long day... Much of the route led through the Central Belt, the area I know least, and had been carefully planned to avoid busy roads and towns, passing north of the Cleish Hills (I hadn't before known they existed) then down the old Perth road east of the new motorway. Straggling hilltop towns such as Kelty proved a surprise. I'd been advised to join the Forth Bridge cycleway at Junction One, but found to my horror I was on the main dual carriageway, with no hard shoulder and traffic just off the motorway hurtling past. Fortunately it was downhill with the wind behind and I managed to get up to about 40 mph, more like a slow car in the fast traffic. The correct route was to join a mile further south. The cycleway over the Bridge felt very strange, high above the Forth with a stiff wind from the side. I had to convince myself it was perfectly safe, indeed much safer than an ordinary main road! South of the bridge, after negotiating a mile of cycleway liberally strewn with broken glass swept off the main road, I was soon into Kirkliston and, after a short stretch through industrial estates back onto a winding country road climbing up to East Calder and Kirk Newton. By crossing the grey Pentland Hills I bypassed Edinburgh altogether, taking the old drove road past Harperrig Reservoir then climbing to 1200 feet before descending to West Linton. Again a mile or two to wheel the bike on heather paths but nothing compared to Corrieyairack, then steeply down a good track into the sunshine and then the road into West Linton. Never having set foot in the Pentlands I was surprised how quiet and little-used the paths were.

Approaching Peebles I realised that, imperceptibly I'd entered border country, with rolling hills rising all around. My thoughts were more on a steady knock, knock from the gear block which had been getting worse and was now also accompanied by the occasional screech of jammed bearings. A new block would soon be needed, and there were still many miles to go before I'd sleep that night. Complaints from both the gear block and a tendon in my right leg continued to get louder. It took a while to find the Peebles bike shop, tucked away down an alley off the main street but maybe the best in Scotland.

Hills of the North, Rejoice!

Although it was only 15 minutes before the shop shut, my bike was on the bike stand in a jiffy, the wheel off, the gear block off (no tool to fit? No problem. Just take the cone nuts off!) The verdict, as I'd expected – 'Knackered. Wouldn't last another 100 miles.' By 5pm I was on my way again with new gears and a potentially dangerous brake fault also discovered and repaired. Pity they couldn't do the same with my sore leg.

Traquair, near Innerleithen, 6pm. With time against me I'd already given up the idea of reaching the head of the Ettrick water (my original objective) by dark and instead was aiming for the nearer Broadmeadows Youth Hostel. Now there was a choice, six miles of paths and tracks over the hills or 15 miles round hilly roads. The hill route looked so easy on my 40 year-old map, just a 1000-foot climb to a pass south of Minch Moor then down to a farm at the head of a valley with a track leading to the main road.

The trap was set.

With only 90 minutes of daylight there was no time for luxuries like wheeling the laden bike up the initial steep stony track; lungs, heart and sore leg just had to put up with the struggle up the first 500-foot climb. New forestry plantations not shown on my ancient map complicated things, after checking the compass I took a fainter path marked by occasional white posts. Much was now too steep or rough to ride but wherever remotely possible I ploughed on through heather and low branches. The sun was setting as I neared the crest of the pass, wave upon wave of hills rolling to the horizon above valleys sinking into shadow. Time was against me. The path crossed a main walkers' highway coming south from Minch Moor, I could have followed this but was only a mile from the farm and imagined myself spinning down a good road in just another ten minutes. The path prevaricated, cutting along the hillside instead of descending, riding the bike was desperately difficult with heather concealing deep ruts. Then at last a plunge straight down a forest ride, 25 degree slopes, crashing through deep bracken and undergrowth, hard on the brakes. A fence. An ancient gate, thoroughly wired up. No further trace of the path, no sign of a track. The valley floor was deep in tussocky grass, long since abandoned by farming and extremely hard work for wheeling a bike. The old farmhouse still stood, and with light failing I pushed the bike up to the door in the hope that it might be an open bothy. Although the main building was locked, an attached wood-store was open and an upstairs loft gave just enough room to lay out a sleeping bag and set up the Primus beside firewood logs piled to the roof. An adjacent burn provided a trickle of water, all I needed. My evening meal was well-earned that day!

Day 7.

It took over an hour to reach the road in the morning. The valley hadn't been grazed for years and trees had been planted in places amid the high grass tussocks. Is this to be the fate of many hill farms? A ghost of an old track appeared briefly about a mile down from the old farm. Yet the house was obviously well looked after, had been repaired and painted, looked comfortably furnished and had been stocked with enough wood to last a winter. How had the materials been delivered, how did visitors get there? Was it now a rich man's retreat reached by helicopter? A mystery.

Shortage of time meant taking the direct route through Selkirk, a cheerful, bustling town – with a climb out so steep that I was nearly overtaken by a woman wheeling a pushchair. Then a rare main road stretch, along the A7 to Hawick. These great sweeping new roads aren't meant for cyclists and can be purgatory when wind and weather is against you. Fortunately the road was quiet and the wind from the side. Hawick seemed a most attractive border town, I'd no idea that the population was split, with feelings running very high on both sides, over whether women should be allowed to take part in the Border ridings. The quiet 'B' road signposted 'Newcastleton 20' led out of the town into winding wooded valleys then climbed steadily up into moorland. Hundreds of square miles of country have been afforested around here. Over the top, and a unique experience on the trip, miles of downhill with the wind from behind.

I'd hoped to buy a map in Newcastleton to forestall a repeat of the previous day's experience but to no avail. I've never seen such sleepy shops (it was Friday afternoon). After waiting in the paper shop for five minutes behind a queue of one man, I tried the self-service grocer; this had no baskets and people were queueing with armfuls of items while the proprietor very slowly worked the till. Shopping was evidently a social occasion. I returned to the newsagent. No, they didn't have the map of the local area in stock. 'Anywhere else in the town I might get it?' I asked. 'I wouldn't think so,' came the reply. Oh well. Rather than risk mapless entanglement with miles of new forest I changed plans again, aiming for the Youth Hostel in Carlisle. By following little roads round Bewcastle and Kirklinton I managed to get right into the city without any traffic at all. Just one busy main road to cross, then a quiet route to the hostel, two miles from the city centre. Another cyclist arrived shortly after me, doing Lands-End to John O Groats. He'd cycled up that day from Preston on a mountain bike and looked shattered, just like I felt myself.

Hills of the North, Rejoice!

Day 8.

Just two days left of my trip now and all the hardest over. There was lots of time the next day, a route of only 60 miles, a tour of dozens of little Cumbrian villages lying along the foot of the Pennines. Stone walls and old stone houses, old churches, Baptist and Methodist chapels, dairy cattle and sheep, narrow lanes, woods, lots of steep ups and steep downs. Only a little local farm traffic. It made a nice change to have signposts giving distances such as two or three miles to the next settlement rather than 20 or 30.

Cumwhinton. Armathwaite. Kirkoswald. Glassonby. Gamblesby. Melmerby. Skirwith. Blencarn. Milburn. Long Marton. Great Asby. Crosby Garrett. Smardale. Waitby. Kirkby Stephen. A litany of villages basking in sunshine below the great scarp of the Northern Pennines.

Day 9.

My last day gave a circular route, south into the Dales then back north to Kirkby Stephen. At last beginning to feel reasonably fit I made the most of it by taking the bike over the 2200-foot Howgills (rounded hills much like the Ochils), bouncing down to Sedbergh and continuing up the valley to Dent, my furthest south. Then up past Dent Station, the highest in England, over the old coal road to Garsdale and down beside the famous Settle-Carlisle line below the slopes of Wild Boar Fell. A couple of days later and I'd take the bike back north from Penrith by train, managing in nine hours to cover the distance it had taken me eight days to cycle!

Caithness autumn

Of all the Caithness seasons, autumn is perhaps the most striking. Winter comes and goes between November and July, summer appears in occasional days after March while spring has to be searched for somewhere in between, but autumn cannot be missed.

That first September evening when, after a summery day, the sun is setting surprisingly early, the sky is streaked with high cloud, the wind is suddenly chill from the south-east and, out in the country, there is that ghost of winter stalking, tangible, almost visible. The wild flowers have gone, except for the scabious and fading heather. The garden flowers are still bright but seem out of place, or time. The moorland grasses have turned, from the first yellow tips of August to a deep orange.

The first skein of migrating wild geese – the local breeding flock has already gone south – followed by vee after vee, whenever the wind has a northerly component. Is any sound more evocative of autumn? Yes, maybe, the stags – throughout the Highlands from Reay to Argyll, having broken out from the September herds to hold their own harem of hinds in October, roaring defiance at each other. Walk out into the moors, almost anywhere, on a calm early morning or evening and you will hear them.

The first true gales, a great swell on the sea from a deep depression off Iceland, the first lashing showers of driving rain – and are those blobs of nearly-melted sleet on the window? On the remoter beaches around Orkney and northwest Sutherland, as well as on the east coast of Caithness, the grey seals are hauling out to have their pups and to mate, as the gales and driving rain lash the western coasts. Starlings, lapwings are in flocks, the curlews have gone to the estuaries, the last swallow was seen several weeks ago. The tourists, too, have headed south for warmer climes. Now the huge flocks of rooks wing their evening way back to the roosts in the Olrig woods, after a day of gleaning the stubble fields. With the shortening days the birds of prey have less time for hunting, and there are buzzards, kestrels and the odd hen-harrier every night around the Broubster road.

The barley, which ripens first, has been cut but combines still sit in fields of wet and wind-flattened oats, awaiting the next fine interlude. On a fine night they are out, cutting by headlight, bitter wind or no. In the garden the tatties are dug, the last of the peas and beans are picked before the wind flattens the plants.

The bike lights, forgotten at the bottom of a drawer throughout the summer are pulled out and cleaned, batteries are charged. Now it's pitch black when I get up, and almost dark when setting off to work – and the first hint of the storms to come are here, making the journey harder than it was!

The Forss is high again, the first real spate roars over the falls, the salmon are leaping and the anglers are back. Go high into the hills, up the moorland burns and you may, if you're lucky, see these huge fish splashing their way up to spawn in the gravel beds.

Summer is still beating a retreat and a fine early afternoon might still be August. Yet winter is encroaching, with the first hard frost and early snow seen on the distant Sutherland peaks. At the end of October the clocks go back (Fall back), darkness descends like a curtain on the evenings, and winter is almost here.

A flow country skyline

Forss Falls, on the Caithness east coast

Morven from Corrichoich

Snowdrops at Olrig

Loch Caluim

Peedie Bay

View from Beinn Dearg, between Ullapool and Bonar Bridge

Culmor

The east coast near Latheron

Loch nam Breac, central Sutherland

Frosty morning, Inkstack

Sandwood bay, dusk, mid-December

The east coast near Latheron

Loch nam Breac, central Sutherland

Frosty morning, Inkstack

Sandwood bay, dusk, mid-December

Bruan

Occumster

February view from Ben Nevis

Lothmore beach, between Brora and Helmsdale

Glenelg eagles

For a split second I thought an aeroplane had suddenly appeared over the hill crest just above me – but the huge pair of outstretched wings belonged to a golden eagle.

We were staying at a cottage near Glenelg, over the pass from Glen Shiel and near the Kyle Rhea ferry to Skye. On family holidays my role is principally that of driver, sandwich-maker and guide on little walks – there's never much time to get out on my own to explore. What opportunity there is has to be rushed in the early morning or evening. So that particular October evening I had less than an hour of daylight in which to race up the hillside across the river to a viewpoint before the next squall drove in from the hills of Skye. The eagle soared along the hillside above the glen before, with a single flap of its wings, disappearing back inland. To see one golden eagle was a marvellous sight, to see four in a week was amazing!

There's a grand mountain-bike route from Glenelg, round a low pass below Ben Sgritheall then back down Glen More. It's all on roads and tracks except for half a mile of pathless moor where, if you take the wrong route, you might disappear into the bogs without trace. Half a day is needed to do the route justice; I had perhaps an hour and a half, before nine in the morning, in which to rush round the circuit. On a fine clear morning, before showers moved in, I raced along the seashore and turned up Glen Beg, a lovely narrow glen with riverside hazel and alder woods below high mountains. Caithness is the land of the brochs but you have to go to Glen Beg for the best examples on the mainland. Two of the three brochs in the glen still have some wall surviving to the full height of over 30 feet, you can see the stairways inside and easily imagine what the complete structures would have looked like. I pushed on, leaving a visit for later in the week, and soon was climbing the stony track past Balvraid with the river roaring over hidden waterfalls in woods to the right.

Short of time or no, I had to stop to take in the scene at the top of the low pass. Below me was a small loch. Above were high peaks, the summits grey with a light dusting of snow or hail. To the right, a slabby waterfall. The sound of running water was everywhere,with the scent of dying bracken and wet autumn leaves. Stags were roaring from the hillsides – then an eagle appeared, soaring right cross the glen before circling, never flapping its wings. I watched for a minute or so then had to hurry on, splashing and dragging the bike through the knee-deep bogs to regain a forestry track for a fast ride down past Moyle, to be back at the holiday cottage barely 15 minutes later.

A few days later, on a morning of west coast downpours, my son and I made a more leisurely circuit in the other direction. Real rain is excellent for mountain biking, soaked anyway you just ride regardless through all the rivers and bogs and puddles. Rain was sheeting across the hills in that spectacular gale-driven manner characteristic of the mountains, higher up you could see dense streamers of sleet with blizzards obviously raging above 2500 feet. Waterfalls were spectacular, rivers roaring, water everywhere – as I always say, the best thing to do in such weather is to go out and enjoy it!

On one long afternoon I managed a walk right across Skye – well, right across the easternmost tip of the island. There's an obvious route linking the Skye Bridge to the Kyle Rhea ferry, the two are no more than five miles apart as the eagle flies but the walk is not easy. The 2400-foot peak of Sgurr na Coinnich dominates this area, prominent from Kyle and Glenelg and looking a deceptively easy climb from Kyleakin. Fortunately I knew from past experience that the lower slopes are very rough, difficult and guarded by new forestry plantations.

The Skye Bridge costs nothing for pedestrians even if it is iniquitous for cars. Anyone with time to spare should park and walk across, the views are superb and you can thereby set foot on Skye without charge. After the bridge and a mile along the Uig road (loops of the old road still remained, giving quiet walking between thickets of brambles lush with berries) I turned off onto a forestry track which came to a sudden end leaving me floundering in new plantations not marked on my old map. The weather had turned warm and sticky but fortunately the midge season was over or there would have been billions. I sweated up boggy rides and valley sides, eventually gaining more open hillsides amongst some of the poorest forestry plantings I'd seen anywhere. At great effort the bare hillsides had been ploughed and planted with Lodgepole Pine; now at least half had died and vanished, the remaining half were stunted, wind-blown, sickly, or lacking in leaves on one side. Perhaps one in a hundred might have struggled to make a reasonable Christmas tree. Climbing the deer fence and gratefully leaving the pathetic forest behind, I made better progress up the wet heathery hillsides to the summit of Sgurr Coinnich. Mist blew clear to reveal a fine view across to Kyle and Raasay but with the Cuillin and the north of Skye still enveloped in dense fog. Sun gleamed over towards Plockton, to the east was the narrow Kyle Rhea with Glenelg beyond.

The Kyle Rhea ferry runs from April to October and takes up to six cars, it's only a five-minute crossing and the fare is about the same as the bridge – so there's still a route for romantics to take a car over the sea to Skye without having to go round by Mallaig. We'd already been across earlier in the week so the friendly ferryman didn't even bother to charge me the 60p or so for a foot passenger.

The best sighting of eagles came, however, from the car on the day we were leaving (so you don't have to be a lunatic to see them!) We were driving up the glen towards the pass when we spotted a pair of birds crossing the ridge to the south, from their size it was immediately clear they weren't buzzards. Just one flap of the wings took them right across the glen, we watched for several minutes as they glided back and forth, quartering the hillside above the road. It's a shame eagles are so rare in Caithness, having been persecuted by gamekeepers and egg-collectors alike – it's several years since I last saw one here. You can still find the remains of a nest south of Reay, and another between Dunbeath and Loch More – but the birds haven't been there for at least 20 years. There is plenty of room for a few pairs of these marvellous birds or for sea-eagles on the cliffs. If the persecutors would leave them alone, eagles might yet be seen soaring above Dounreay!

Dufftown country

'Rome is built on seven hills, but Dufftown's built on seven stills!' Yes, I knew that the area around Dufftown and Keith was whisky country but had never envisaged the scale of the industry. There are, I believe, now nine distilleries in Dufftown. The town is indeed built on, or more more correctly floats on, whisky. Half of all Scotland's whisky is produced within a few miles...

There was an old hymn we used to sing very frequently in school assemblies and which nostalgic elderly congregations still like: 'O worship the King'. One of the later verses includes the lines: 'It breathes through the air, it descends to the plain, and sweetly distils in the dew and the rain.' Even if I'm still awake by that verse I've forgotten what 'it' is. Now I know. The scent of whisky pervades the air. The soil must be drenched in it. Miles away, on the top of 1500-foot Ben Aigan in the early morning, I could smell it on the wind. In the half-light could be seen, from the hilltop, an area of orange lights looking like a small town situated a few miles west of Keith – a collection of bonded warehouses occupying the best part of half a square mile. Not being an imbiber myself, the smell of baking shortbread, drifting from the Walkers factory in Aberlour, was much to be preferred. A fisherman on the right beat of the Spey might well be able to enjoy the simultaneous scents of both shortbread and whisky as he hooked his salmon.

The Christmas lights were already in place on the main clock tower in Dufftown – depicting a whisky still. Not even Thurso has considered having an illuminated depiction of the Dounreay high-active shaft in golden and red lights on, say, St Peter's Church. The shaft should bring at least as much money into the area as the whisky does to Dufftown, given the recent estimates of Dounreay decommissioning costs!

As we walked along a path at the back of Dufftown, discovering yet more distilleries, barrels were being loaded into a van by fork-lift from one of the bonded warehouses. The stacked barrels inside looked just like a Dounreay waste store. One thing's for certain though; the product of those bonded ware-houses would cause far more misery, illness and death than all the Dounreay waste ever would, even if the waste were just – heaven forbid – dumped into the sea. Dufftown is a hill town, some 650 feet above sea level, and the cold winds whistle up and down the main street. I don't suppose though that the locals have many problems in keeping themselves warm.

Above Dufftown rises Ben Rinnes, the highest hill in the area at over 2700 feet, it's the prominent high hill you see across the Moray Firth on any clear day from anywhere between Lybster and Golspie. Early one morning I'd cycled up from the delightfully named Maggieknockater, through the whisky fumes of Dufftown, to the foot of the mountain. An easy if badly eroded path then led quickly up to the summit with a trig point on a prominent rock tor. Rain had cleared eastward overnight and a cold, blustery south-west wind was setting in, the air wasn't clear enough for views across to Caithness but the sun could be seen glinting off windows near the Moray coast with the sea just visible beyond. So much higher is this hill than the surroundings that the rolling country around looks almost flat, only to the south-west were the Cairngorms clearly taller, still capped in cloud.

It took less than 30 minutes to jog down to the bike, it was now a lovely bright morning and, although I was aiming to be back in Maggieknockater for lunch, there was just enough time to manage Corriehabbie Hill, another sizeable peak just across the valley. This one however proved tougher than Ben Rinnes, first a hilly cycle up little roads and tracks to a high farm then a steep ascent through very deep heather, straight into a dazzling sun. Grouse butts had clearly not been used for a few years, testifying to the rapid decline in numbers, indeed I only saw a few birds in what should be ideal grouse country. Eventually the steep slopes eased onto a stony plateau of short heather where a track, intriguingly named 'Morton's Way', led up gentle slopes to the summit. The wind was now very strong but the low sun was bright and it was a most exhilarating place to be standing, high above the deep valley of Glen Livet with the Ladder Hills beyond. A fast run down had me back at the bike in 20 minutes, then a quick ride down the lanes to the main road. It was a rare pleasure indeed to enjoy a long downhill cycle back to Dufftown in the sunshine with a strong following wind. A lady on a mountain-bike was sweating up the hill towards me, slowly, probably in bottom gear. She didn't look too happy as I freewheeled past at about 25 mph. It made a nice change, almost invariably it happens the other way round!

The Speyside Way, a 65-mile long distance route, runs through the area. This, unlike may long-distance routes, is designed for gentle walkers or cyclists, with many miles along old railway tracks. Autumn is a lovely time of year to potter along sections of the route with the fine beeches and birches giving the most magnificent of colours. The pace when cycling is however a little too fast to properly appreciate the scenery, indeed riding along the track into Aberlour felt just like being on a train as the woodland scenery suddenly gave way to playing fields and the backs of houses.

Most of us only hear of Dufftown on the early-morning road reports in winter when the road to Rhynie (a nice ordinary farming village some 15 miles away) is blocked. Dufftown's – well – a funny place. The locals in the shops are certainly very friendly people but I was stared at in a way you don't see so much these days – who was I, what did I want? Every household has somebody working at the distilleries, if you lived there you'd just have to do likewise. Reputedly, Dufftown puts more money into the exchequer (through duties) per head of population than anywhere else in Britain. It is truly the whisky capital of the world. Somehow I don't think a teetotaller would be very welcome there...

The Caithness archaeological cycle trail

The bolt of the metal gate screeched as I opened it. But it was not, as I'd expected, answered by a chorus of barking farm dogs. In spite of the electricity poles and a favoured situation on grassy south-eastern facing slopes, the farm of Oliclett, just four miles in a straight line from Wick, had obviously been deserted for years. Rats scuttled in the loft above as I peered in the open door to a droppings-covered floor. Only the distant glitter of the sea and the warm early morning sunshine were the same as the last inhabitants would have enjoyed.

Did you know that Caithness has an official mountain bike route? You cycle up the Mid Clyth road which turns off the old A9 about eight miles south of Wick, passing the Hill O' Many Stanes; the road comes to an end at a farm and continues as a track. Half a mile further on, where the track enters the forest, a sign says 'Forest Enterprise, walkers welcome'. There is a special gate to allow bikes through and a post with a mountain bike symbol. The track climbs through young trees for a couple of miles with increasingly fine views back over the sea to the distant hills of Buchan. At the highest point, the views across the whole of Caithness, between the trees, is exceptionally good – before a fast descent brings you out through another bike gate onto the Camster road just south of the cairns. The official route back is to take the road south then turn off eastwards on the branch crossing the hill to Mid Clyth – however there is a longer and much more interesting alternative which would make an excellent archaeological bike trail, especially if the odd bike-gate was put in place and bit of new path made. To follow it at present you will need a new 1:50000 Ordnance Survey map, and must be prepared to lift a bike over deer gates and fences and push across some very rough ground.

Take the Camster road north, for another two miles, stopping to look at the Grey Cairns. Just at the boundary of the next new forest a track turns off to the east, through a high – and occasionally locked – gate. Once past this obstacle the cycling is easy for four miles through young plantations passing the hidden ruin of Achairn. It was very early in the morning when I went this way, low mist hung in the hollows and an early October frost whitened the ground. The track suddenly climbed into much warmer air where it swings round to the south onto the slopes of Tannach Hill. Just when all is going well the track comes to a sudden dead end. An obvious wide clearing indicates the way on, to the south-east, but for a quarter of a mile to the forest edge the going is extremely rough and slow through deep tussocks of grass and heather – lightweight bikes would be best carried! Fortunately there is just an ordinary low sheep fence along the edge of the forest and the bike can easily be lifted over. A bit more rough going around old peat diggings follows to reach the ruin of a long house just north-east of Oliclett, a lovely spot in the warm morning sun but sad that it has been so long deserted.

A bikeable track leads now to Oliclett, and a good track down to the tarred road at Yarrows. Here is the Yarrows archaeological trail, an excellent walking route around standing stones, chambered cairns and a broch, which will take you an hour or so. Back on the bike, you carry on down the road to Thrumster. For a short-cut, head straight down the old A9 to Clyth. More interesting is to head back towards Wick, then turn off towards Sarclet. After a mile fork right, taking the road above Loch Sarclet which ends at Mains of Ulbster, another fine farm which has long been deserted. There's an interesting old mausoleum here and it's also worth going down to look at the very fine coastal cliff scenery. The track continues past the farm and comes to an end; the map marks a path heading westward towards Ulbster.

I sometimes wonder if anyone goes walking in Caithness other than along roads and the most well-known paths! Certainly this route looks as if it has not been used for years, there is only the trace of a track and you basically have to pick your own route crossing a fence or two and some very rough boggy ground. If you keep on the line of the path you'll eventually emerge onto a tarred road which leads back to the main road. Just a mile down the road is Whaligoe – stop, walk up and down the steps (they're not signposted – they start at the end of the row of cottages on the left). Then pedal up to Loch Watenen and walk up to the iron-age fort. Here too is the line of the old Wick and Lybster railway. All in all there's a lot to see around here. Another mile on is Bruan, again it's worth stopping and looking around. Just below the road is an unexpected and very deep geo, quite a frightening place with overhanging walls on one side and steep convex slopes ending in cliffs on the other. Best to look from the safe side of the fence...

Another mile down the A9 and you are back at your starting point; you can finish with a good look at the best example of 4000 year-old stone rows in the north. If you make all the detours it's a good day's outing, otherwise it could be done in a long morning or afternoon. All we need is the odd bike gate, a short stretch of path from the end of the forest road to Oliclett, and a bit of renovation of the path from Mains of Ulbster. Perhaps the deserted farm of Oliclett could be turned into some kind of small information/heritage centre. It would good too if the old light railway could be converted to a cycle route from Ulbster to Clyth, thus cutting out the main road altogether. Then we would have the first really good archaeological mountain bike trail in Scotland!

High Cairngorms

A skein of wild geese may have seen me, in the half light of dawn, pedalling the Loch Garten road between Nethy Bridge and Coylum Bridge. In the calm, cold air their calls mingled with the roar of the Inverness-bound sleeper train, heading north through Carrbridge across the Spey.

By eight I was cycling up a rough track through the fine native Scots Pine woods of Rothiemurchus, to Loch Einich, nine miles further on. From the craggy, wooded slopes above came the evocative roaring of the stags in rut. A notice at the start of the track had warned:- 'Stalking Today. Please keep to routes shown on the guide.' A small box housed a set of pamphlets delineating permitted routes. That's the way to do things, not a blanket request to report to the keeper like a schoolboy visiting the headmaster! So I kept to the suggested routes. It was a good ride, up by the river, the trees gradually thinning out as the track entered a high open glen below steep crags. Further on I overtook a group of three walkers who had made an early start for Braeriach. The track ends near the loch and a path then climbs up to the 3000-foot plateau. My plan was to visit the high tops on foot then cross the plateau with the bike and descend into Glen Feshie.

The path was built for ponies and, though slow, it was not too difficult to wheel the bike. The walkers overtook me again where the path entered a high corrie below a final steep section. This looked as if it was going to be a wee bit harder. Ahead I could see that the walkers were having some difficulty, scrambling across a steep rocky slope with a drop below. There was no way I'd get the bike across that! Yet ponies had come this way and so there must be an easier route – and there was, a steep zigzag which the others had missed. The bike needed some carrying but it was safe enough, and the others must have wondered how I'd managed when they saw the bike appear on the plateau! For late October the weather was marvellous, light winds, cloud lifting off the tops, just the odd light shower. The Cairngorms are easy hills except when the weather is wild, which it frequently is – then they can be really savage. Now, four hours after setting out, I left bike and pack and set off up grassy slopes towards the 4000-foot tops. Not far above was the freezing line, with hoarfrost above. The odd flurry of snow blew across as I made my way over Einich Cairn to the edge of spectacular cliffs dropping into An Garbh Choire. Although winter was on the way, there was no snow to be seen in the corrie, the normally permanent snow-field having melted in the exceptionally hot summer. Here are the famous Falls of Dee where the infant river plunges 1000 feet into the corrie. Gravelly slopes beyond lead to the 4200-foot top of Braeriach, vertical crags one side, gentle slopes on the other. It's a dangerous place in severe weather when it's easy to walk over the cliff.

A three-mile jog took me back round the edge of the plateau and down to the bike, exhilarating to be running across this high and wild country. A solitary stag had ventured up out of the corries and ran off for just a few hundred yards as I passed. Above the head of Glen Einich is a rough and knobbly maze of rounded hillocks, a trap for the unwary or in mist. Having been caught before I made a wide circuit to the south, easy bike wheeling and even possible to ride the odd few yards. Two miles of downs and ups, lochs and burns and grass and gravelly slopes, took me to the end of a Landrover track, one of the highest in the country and almost the only place where you can cycle above 3000 feet. After an initial climb which was too steep, I could ride most of the way and made good progress across the 'Great Moss' onto the Feshie Hills. Huge mossy plateaux, these, steep slopes falling into Glen Feshie, unvisited other than by munro-baggers and mad cyclists.

Although the track gives mountain-biking at its best, there was no sign that other cyclists had been this way. Few mountain bikes see mountains! The route climbed up to 3200 feet then turned steeply downhill to give a spectacular view of a steep corrie with the track sweeping down over 2000 feet in two miles. I can think of only one other cycling descent (or ascent) as long in Britain. It took about 20 minutes, stopping now and then to let the brakes cool and to look down the cliffs into the next corrie which the track skirted. It was very rough in places but the bike took the strain well; mountain bikes came up in my estimation! The quick descent emphasised the contrast between the bleak plateau and the shelter of the glen, with Scots Pine woods and warm afternoon sunshine. Nethy Bridge was still a long 20 miles away but not an onerous ride on a fine late autumn afternoon. Gliders from the Feshie Bridge centre were circling like giant buzzards in the updrafts above steep slopes warmed by the late afternoon sun. Tired, and taking my time, I pottered back through the scented Speyside woods to reach Nethy Bridge at dusk, 11 hours after setting out.

Ben Hope

Ben Hope is one of the easiest of our local mountains. There is no long walk-in and the 'official' path starts climbing right from the road; one can easily be up and down the hill in under three hours. About eight miles south of Hope Lodge, on the empty road to Altnaharra, is a carpark and a notice 'Ben Hope – way up'. The popularity of 'munro-bagging' in recent years is soon apparent; what used to be the faintest of paths is now a wide eroded trail and wet moorland has been trampled into a peaty morass. Higher up, the path is less distinct but still well defined and marked with cairns. It's just a simple plod straight up and down and another tick off the list. The only difficulty lies in getting to the starting point as it's a tiring round drive of 140 miles from Thurso, mostly on twisty single-track roads. The effort and expense in petrol is hardly justified by such a short time on the hill.

Hamish Brown once likened Ben Hope to a dead sheep, surely the least flattering description ever given to a mountain! The hill really deserves better than that. A much more interesting ascent than the usual tourist route is from the north, with good corrie and loch scenery and a choice of several ridges leading to the summit. The finest and steepest ridge (the most westerly) is abruptly terminated, just below the summit, by a short bit of vertical rock known as the 'bad step' with a fall of nearly 2000 feet possible if you slip – walkers will sensibly detour to a steep gully which gives a safe alternative. On any route from the north you'll constantly hear the croaking of the ptarmigan on the upper part of the mountain and likely see the mountain hares.

Although I can see Ben Hope in the distance from my house, it's a hill I rarely climb because of the long drive needed to get there. Roads that are slow to drive are however delightful to cycle. The circuit from Bettyhill – down StrathNaver to Altnaharra, through to Hope Lodge and back via Tongue makes a grand round route of about 60 miles, all on quiet single-track roads with a lot of historical and natural history interest and some of the finest scenery in

Scotland. I took the bike on the roof of the car to the foot of StrathNaver and set off south on a cool day of northerly winds and occasional showers. StrathNaver is one of the most notorious glens where the 'peasants' were evicted, sometimes violently, in the early nineteenth century, ostensibly for their own good and to make way for the profitable great sheep. I can never travel this glen without mixed feelings – however the past is the past and dwelling on it now does little good. As it stands today, StrathNaver is a quiet and beautiful strath, scattered with birchwoods along its length and with the occasional farm, croft or holiday cottage. The salmon fishing is highly regarded, closely guarded and very expensive. The cycling is free and a much better way (in my opinion) to enjoy the strath. Past Syre, the road runs through plantations by the river, the larches a lovely autumn yellow. It seems to be heading straight for Ben Armine but then turns west, looping up and down little hills though the birches along Loch Naver with Ben Klibreck to the left and the double hump of Ben Hee straight ahead. You pass Drummore, with its broch and clearance remains, now ironically there is a small holiday caravan site here in the summer. I always wonder what the evicted inhabitants would have thought of that!

Altnaharra has the dubious distinction of being one of the coldest spots in Britain in frosty winter weather and has recorded a temperature of around -27C, only 0.1 degrees above the 'lowest ever' record held by Braemar. At the crossroads, just south of the little village, the signpost says 'Hope 21'; all long miles through very empty country with only a couple of habitations. The road is very single track and can be a difficult drive as the passing places are sparse and mostly unmarked and tourists don't always realise this. I once met a driver who had just passed one of these unsigned passing places but insisted that he hadn't seen one for miles and that I should therefore reverse about a half a mile. No such problems on a bike, just the freedom of pedalling through wide expanses of orange-brown moor, the high mountains well set back, the occasional buzzard or small herd of deer. After climbing above Loch Meadie a steep descent took me down to the floor of Strath Hope, passing Dun Dornaig – one of the best surviving brochs – to arrive at the Ben Hope path. Virtually the only traffic I'd seen had been trailers of sheep heading down StrathNaver for the sales and the odd landrover or pickup – so I was surprised to see a couple of parked cars with the occupants obviously off up the Ben.

The weather was deteriorating, cloud was coming down. I just nipped up and down as fast as possible, the views vanished at 2000 feet and I contemplated retreating but decided that having come this far... Near the top it started hailing and sleeting and the summit was covered with thawing hoar-frost and rime. A couple were huddled together under a cape, perhaps eating lunch (or perhaps trying to do something else on top of every munro). I turned round and jogged as quickly as possible down the slippery path and back through the bogs to the bike. It had taken little over two hours – on the balance worth doing; I'd heard ptarmigan and rutting stags, seen snow-buntings and some good views and generally enjoyed the experience of autumn on the high hills. I snatched a quick, late lunch out of the wind then headed down the last eight miles to Hope Lodge; a lovely road below the crags of Ben Hope and through birchwoods above the loch. The cold headwind slowed me but there wasn't any hurry. A Mars bar by Hope Lodge was fuel to take me up the six-hundred foot climb of the Moin, one of my favourite roads crossing a vast moorland expanse, with tremendous views and many memories (I must be getting old...) I hadn't looked forward to the last hilly stretch back to Bettyhill but, whatever one's state of fatigue, the road from the Tongue Causeway through Coldbackie and Borgie is always enjoyable on a bike, bowling over moor, past loch and rocky bay. The weather had improved again with dappled cloud stretching to the far hills of Hoy and a wind that was more from behind than ahead. Indeed, after the last, fast descent back into StrathNaver I was (almost) sorry to see the car waiting there.

The next day, once again, I could see the top of Ben Hope from home – clear all day!

The highest road

Hills in Britain are not very high, and hill passes even less so. There are not many roads which have a climb even as great as 1000 feet; in Sutherland the road from Kildonan to Glen Loth just about scrapes into that category. Ascents of 1500 feet are even rarer, I can think of the steep climb from Loch Tay over to Glen Quaich – which caught me completely unawares with a laden bike – and a few northern English roads such as Hartside Pass and the Fleak route from Askrigg to Swaledale. In the whole of the British Isles I know of only two tarred roads with a climb of more than 2000 feet; the private road up to the top of Great Dun Fell from Knock, in Cumbria and the Bealach Na Ba in Applecross. From the very top of the Bealach Na Ba, an unsurfaced track climbs another 500 feet to a telecommunications mast on top of Sgurr Ghaorachain at an altitude of over 2500 feet. As far as I am aware there is nowhere else in Britain where you can cycle down – or up – a vertical half mile on good tracks and roads.

A fine, clear, sunny day would be ideal for a ride up the mountain but this time my luck with the weather didn't hold. Instead it was the wettest day of the week with low cloud but at least fairly light winds. In the early morning rain of a grey autumn day I cycled slowly up the 500-foot climb to the pass between Lochcarron and Kishorn. The moors and hills had that glorious orange-brown tint of dying heather and deer-grass; trees in the gullies were also starting to show their autumn tints. Everywhere was the scent of wet grass and leaves, dead bracken, or seaweed on the shore. Waterfalls cascaded down above the road and whenever I stopped the only sound was of rushing water. Just here there are no deer; around the Lochcarron to Kishorn road a very large area has been fenced and is being reinstated as mixed woodland which would naturally cover the lower slopes of these bare western hills.

At Rassal, just above Loch Kishorn, is a native ash-wood which has been there for at least 6000 years on a rare outcrop of limestone. It is now a nature reserve and has been fenced from the surrounding sheep and deer pastures.

Hills of the North, Rejoice!

Anyone who doesn't appreciate the damage done by overgrazing should visit this spot. In the main area, fenced about eight years ago, there is a long growth of grass with many wild flowers and a number of healthy saplings. Immediately outside the fence is short-cropped grass, bracken and nothing else. An area which has been fenced for 40 years is a thicket of young trees – willow, hazel, alder, ash, rowan – under the original taller ashes.

Past Rassal I came to the forbidding notices aimed at deterring nervous tourists from attempting the Bealach: 'Two thousand foot climb. Steep hairpins. Not recommended for caravans or learner drivers. Road normally closed in winter conditions.' Of course the locals drive over with no more thought than we give to crossing the Ord of Caithness. It's a steady, six-mile climb and so not all that steep. Perhaps it's the nearest thing in Britain to a small Alpine pass. Initially the road gains height above Loch Kishorn, the remains of the Howard-Doris oil-rig construction site below. Only a wide cleared area and some piers in the sea remain with, in Lochcarron, the workers' estate of Finnish design wooden houses (known locally as the 'Finlogs').

The red deer stags are in control at this time of year, across ten thousand square miles and more, of Highland country, roaring out their challenges to trespassers and interlopers. Go onto any unfenced moor or mountain and you'll hear them. As I cycled up the hill into the gentle rain and drifting cloud the sound mingled with that of running water – one felt the autumn to one's very bones. Overheating is a big problem though when cycling up long hills in waterproofs; I stripped off to shorts and a cagoule, keeping my warmer clothes for the long descent! The single-track road enters a big upland corrie then climbs diagonally across the mountainside, a narrow ledge cut into a 50-degree boulder scree slope. In a car, you really feel that you're driving up a mountain! Round the corner is a second, higher corrie and a steep, steady climb to the final hairpins climbing out to the crest of the pass. A strong headwind drove the rain into my face but I managed to keep going to some shelter where the road was cut into the hillside; here I stopped and put on a few extra clothes

It was just as expected on top of the pass; misty, windy and wet – but not that cold. Having come this far... in another 20 minutes or so I was up at the even bleaker top of the mountain where there is a small building, built like a fortress against the elements. The spectacular views down to the corrie were hidden by the mist; this range of hills has some of the most amazing natural architecture in Scotland on its eastern side, with huge corries as if somebody had taken a giant ice-cream scoop to the mountain and left semicircular tiers of sandstone crags 1500 feet high. Now for the descent, seven miles and 2500 feet down to Applecross. The first stretch on the steep rough track was slow, hard on the brakes. Then, back on tarmac, just a question of freewheeling downhill for mile after mile, not letting myself get too fast! In spite of new crash-barriers there are still some hairy bits where you might go a very long way if you came off the road. Wind and driving rain blew straight into my face; I emerged from the cloud high above a landscape of rock and lochan, rapidly getting colder and colder. Then came the edge of forestry above Applecross – but still a long way to go till, with chattering teeth, the road at last levelled out by the bay. Next time I'll choose a warm day!

Until 20 years ago the pass was the only land route into Applecross; now an alternative but much longer route has been constructed round the coast to Shieldaig. That took me the rest of the day, another 40 miles to get back to Lochcarron. The rain eased for a time, with views across the sound to Raasay and even a glimpse of a sinister-looking submarine cruising south. The road gets increasingly hilly towards Shieldaig with steep climbs up from bays and crofting settlements followed by equally steep descents. All in all there is more climbing involved on this stretch than in crossing the bealach! On a clear day the views of the Torridon Hills are indeed worthy of that overused brochure adjective – stunning. This time however mist and drizzle hid the hills, gentle rain came and went. I pedalled slowly back through the autumn scents and smells, across the orange moors and down to Lochcarron where long bands of cloud clung to the hillsides above the calm waters of the sea-loch and the stags still roared in the mountains above.

Airports

Here I am, sitting in Manchester airport, awaiting a delayed flight to, of all places, Bournemouth. Yet yesterday, I was eating lunch on a sunny hilltop in Cumbria. Fog and flights permitting, I'll be back in Caithness in three days time! 'So they've let you out for a few days!' A comment, not entirely in jest, from colleagues in the Manchester area. My own reply was to state complete incomprehension as to how anyone could choose to live where they did, let alone further south. Just west of Manchester is one of those spaghetti junction interchanges where about four motorways merge and split in a maze of concrete and flyovers. In just normal morning rush-hour traffic, all four lanes of the M-sixty-something were reduced, by nothing other than the sheer volume of traffic, to a slow intermittent crawl. A brown haze of Los-Angeles-like smog hung over the entire area. Yet people drive daily through this mayhem to work and back. I used to cycle to work on 20 miles of empty roads without meeting a car. The whole business of travel and life in England (except for the far north which is really Scotland) would be utterly depressing were it not for that characteristic perspective of the traveller which enjoys watching and looking, knowing that one is only passing through. So I explore the Manchester terminal buildings, marvelling. It is the people that redeem these places.

At Bournemouth airport, with plenty of time, I decide to walk the remaining 12 miles to my destination in Poole. I've had enough of taxis and cars and planes! It's still summer down in the deep south, even though it's mid-October. I wander through miles of genteel housing estates, finally reaching the sea at Southbourne near a place with the odd name of Wick. An eight-mile long beach curves round to the point at Sandbanks, fringed by a promenade and literally thousands of beach huts. It's an unusual experience to walk along eight miles of completely flat promenade with the destination in sight the whole way. Indeed it becomes apparent that the reason the far beaches can't be seen is not because of haze, but the curvature of the earth. As the hours pass and the distant point grows nearer, the beaches of Southbourne sink below the horizon. A large gathering of police around Bournemouth pier and a hovering airship show that something's happening hereabouts. Just the sort of unreal environment for a conference of people completely out of touch with reality (the Tory Party in actuality). Dusk falls.

Three days later and Heathrow airport. Most people hate the place, I rather like it. If you've got to go to an airport, you might as well go to a proper one. The sheer scale of everything about the world's busiest airport is probably not appreciated by most travellers. It's a place I've not yet, in spite of long waits for planes, had the time to explore properly. Treat it as you would some large, unexplored forest, and set out to find, say, the viewing gallery. No signposts – I'll try to get to the bus-station first. I walk out of the terminal, through the carpark, and down various flights of steps linking the several stories. There's the bus-station – but barring the way is a four-lane dual-carriageway, traffic roaring past and as impossible to cross as a big river in spate. There's what looks like a footbridge downstream – if I retrace steps to Terminal One and take another route I might get to it... ten minutes later I reach the bus-station, noticing en-route a little sign towards the viewing area. Following the signs is a bit like following those way-marked forest routes, ever so often you lose the little yellow dots and have to retrace steps to find where you went wrong. Eventually after a couple of false turns I locate the steps (Warning, says the sign, 72 steps) leading up into the diesel-smelling sunlight and a rooftop view over the airport and, wonder of wonders, a map and information board. There's the chapel – at the back of the control tower. The largest duty-free shopping mall in Europe in Terminal Three, and over there, the far outlines of Terminal Four. Plenty to explore but I've used up my time and have to go for my flight north. I take a return route to Terminal One via seemingly miles of underground moving pavements – the conventional route taken by most travellers. I consider a guide book: 'Walks around Heathrow airport'. I doubt that it would sell many copies. Caithness just three hours away – great.

Strathconon

Combine two of the most boring words of the English language – 'committee' and 'meeting' – and you are hardly likely to inspire more than a yawn. Most committee meetings are to be endured, not enjoyed and are at best chores needed to get things done. After over 20 years of (mostly sleeping) membership I found myself on the local committee of a certain outdoor organisation. This body however is a bit more imaginative about its occasional evening meetings, not for them some hotel room or church hall. The November meeting was scheduled for 7pm in a bothy, high in the hills of Wester Ross. The lack of Sunday trains meant spending two nights away from home to attend a Saturday meeting so I decided to take bike and tent and make the most of the opportunity, even if it was November.

Saturday morning saw me lifting the bike, with some relief, out of a very overheated train in Dingwall. I could have saved myself a lot of miles by waiting for the Kyle train but the weather was good, mild with just a bit of drizzle, and I'd always wanted to take the bike right through Strathconon to Achnashellach. Strathconon is still a largely unknown glen, one of the north's secrets. Tourists are not encouraged along the narrow twisting road and the only signpost on the easiest approach from Contin says 'no through road' – the road ends some 20 miles further on. I pedalled past a calm Loch Achilty amid fabulous gold and yellow autumn colours, and on up the hydro road through farmland and woods to Loch Luichart power station. A steep climb through fine woods above the waterfalls led to the hydro dam of Loch Meig, which the road crossed before joining the 'main' route up the strath from Marybank. Drizzle blew down the glen from the high hills, hiding the landmark triangular peak of Bac an Eich which dominates the glen in clear weather. Yet it was still a lovely ride, quiet woods and hillsides, mountains rising ever higher, the glen narrowing and then opening out to green river flats. There is a real community here with a small village, a school, a church, a post-office and children at several of the farms and estate lodges.

Hills of the North, Rejoice!

Many years ago, after a week's hill-camping I'd descended to the head of Strathconon to pick up a post-bus to Dingwall. The time for the bus came, and went; I waited another half hour then gave up and started walking down the strath, not encouraged by a family who had just driven up the glen and seen no sign of the vehicle. I'd eaten all my food and was onto emergency rations, reckoning that one piece of Kendal Mint Cake every hour would keep me going for the next 20 miles. An hour later the car returned, the lady having sat in the back to leave the front passenger seat empty so that they could stop and offer me a lift! They were a missionary family, on home leave from Africa, for whom camping in the Highlands with small children was a life of luxury. We inquired about the non-existent post-bus at the Post Office: 'Oh, he wouldn't have gone up there if there was no mail!'

The tarred road ends by the last loch in the glen just short of the big lodge at Scardroy, however several routes continue for those on foot. I'd take one and return by another the next day. Both routes would, in the past, have been well-known and much used by travellers. The main glen continues west for another seven miles or so, through increasingly spectacular scenery below high mountains. I had to wheel the bike almost all the way, and although there were some easy stretches other sections were anything but. Bogs, boulders, deeply incised burns, rivers, rushes – and no time to linger, it gets dark early in November. I just ploughed on, enjoying the easier stretches, glad to be abroad in the high hills on a darkening November afternoon. A field of boulders, washed down by flash floods, proved a final obstacle before reaching a good track at Glenuig Lodge – a most spectacular setting, at an altitude of over 1000 feet, facing and surrounded by steep mountains on all sides. They certainly knew where to build these old shooting lodges.

There was just half an hour in which to reach the tarred road before dusk; cycling rough tracks in the dark is very slow and to be avoided! So as fast as I dared I bumped and splashed along the stony track as it curved round into another great corrie below mist-capped hills and watching stags. A steep gorge tumbled below to the valley, the track climbed to a lip with a long view down 1000 feet to the woods of Glen Carron with the lights of Lochcarron in the distance. Gripping the brakes hard I began the long descent, the wind rushing past. A locked forestry gate proved the next obstacle, it was frustrating to have to unpack the bike and lift it over, before hurtling down another two miles to the road and yet another locked gate. Not that my journey was over, there were many miles yet to cycle, then a walk up a hill path in the dark to at last see the candles in the bothy windows shining out as the only specks of light in a pitch dark corrie.

The weather had improved by morning and I took the opportunity to nip up a neighbouring peak. It was 25 years since I'd used the map to set a compass bearing from the misty summit and was horrified to find myself on the edge of a very vertical crag dropping to unseen depths. The old 'one-inch' maps were notoriously unreliable in the Highlands and hadn't marked a big scoop taken out of the summit ridge. Now in clear weather I could see the problem easily, and enjoyed an almost calm November morning among the rugged quartzite peaks and rocky hill lochans. Cloud rolled over the hills opposite and a shaft of early sun lit up Sunday morning in Lochcarron.

Later that morning I turned off the main road a couple of miles short of Achnasheen to wheel the bike along an old hill track across to Strathconon. The first stretch was hard with two high stiles over forest fences and a rocky, rough path through an area newly planted with native trees. This 'friendly forestry' is taking place all over the Highlands, a most welcome development which will turn many bleak wet hillsides into fine mixed woodland. The path had been much used, perhaps a hundred years earlier, but now kept disappearing into deep bogs. A few footprints and even faded bicycle tyre marks showed however that people still occasionally came this way. Onward I wheeled the bike, across vast expanses of orange-purple moor, seemingly much remoter than the few miles I was from the main road. Gradually the going improved till a bikeable track led steeply down into pine forests above the end of Strathconon. In fading light I pitched the tent about a mile from the end of the glen, well positioned for a ride back down to Dingwall in the morning to catch the train north. The night was completely calm, and mild – amazing conditions for November – with a stag occasionally roaring nearby.

How about Highland Regional Council meeting in similar locations and insisting on the use of bikes and trains to get there? That would cut down on expenses and make sure they saw something of the country outside Inverness!

Still December

A free day, perfect weather, even a free train ticket from a special offer... what more could anyone ask for! I cycled down to Georgemas on a calm, starry morning of slight frost and lifted the bike onto the morning train. A much harder frost glimmered outside the windows past Forsinard and Kinbrace; between Helmsdale and Brora the almost flat calm sea washed gently onto dark rocks. The Moray Hills stood in sharp silhouette against a red dawn sky, patchy high cloud reflecting a pillar of light from the still-hidden sun.

Just after nine I alighted at Ardgay. The southern side of the Carron valley was still in cold shadow with a temperature well below -5C under a clear blue sky; I cycled the empty roads to the end of the glen then kept on the south side for another mile, crossing a footbridge to regain the main track leading south from the Craigs. This is a little-known area of rich estates with superb stands of native Scots Pine and views up to higher hills bearing a few streaks of snow. Past Amat Lodge I turned down a track forbiddingly signed 'Private. Glencalvie Lodge only' – but knew well that the track went through and on, right over the hills to Ardross. Sure enough, persistence was rewarded by a 'footpath' sign; the keeper, who was making the most of the hard frost to dig his garden, had no objection at all to my carrying on under the windows of the big lodge to the road up Glen Calvie. I stopped for a sandwich while two young men passed in a tractor pulling a trailor-load of neaps; I followed behind. Ahead was Diebiedale Lodge, perched high on a spur of the mountains like some Transylvanian castle. Alladale Lodge stood out to the north, also high on a bluff surrounded by pines. If I were to own a Highland estate it would have to be one of these!

The track steepened. One of the men was now throwing neaps out of the trailer onto the track for the benefit of a herd of several hundred stags; for the next mile I dodged neaps on the track, eyed by hungry deer which moved off and then returned behind me to eat. By 11-30 I'd reached the crest of the pass at nearly 1400 feet; it was warmer up here, sunny, calm and utterly clear. Leaving the bike I walked on upwards across rough moorland, straight towards the low, dazzling, December sun. Steep slopes above Loch Chuinneag took me into shadow again, scrambling over boulders as a pair of white ptarmigan posed for a photo then flew off before I could get the camera out. I sauntered across an area of stones like the South Col of Everest, blasted and scoured by frequent south-easterly and north-westerly gales, then climbed the last bouldery slopes past a few patches of frozen snow to gain the 2700-foot top of Carn Chuinneag.

Conditions were amazing for mid-December, warm sun, a very gentle breeze, and extremely clear air. Carn Chuinneag is one of those hills you see from everywhere, so the view is correspondingly superb. Endless sharp Highland hills and reddish moors, with a few white snowstreaks, were illuminated by the low sun. Northwards were the Sutherland coastal hills leading to Morven, then west to the Griams and all the high peaks of north-west Sutherland from Ben Loyal to Ben More Assynt. Beyond Canisp and Suilven were the hills of Lewis. Southwards a huge area of rolling moor (where I once walked for a week meeting nobody) led to the great bulk of Ben Wyvis and the more distant Conon Hills, the Fannichs, the Torridons, even the distant mountains of Lochaber. South, across the firths, were the Cairngorms and Ben Rinnes above Dufftown.

Already, at one in the afternoon, the sun was going down and there was a long way yet to go. I jogged most of the way back to the bike, now in the shadow of the mountain, and set off again along the track. It must have been 15 years since I last took this route – shame on me! Much of the road was once tarred and the surface is still mostly excellent for cycling. A couple of miles on was a small wood above a quiet loch lightly skinned with ice, the afternoon sun still warm on a grassy glade. Total peace – but the warmth wouldn't last long, not in December. No lingering. The track climbed gently over another low col then began a long descent by a new forestry fence. Further on, a bridge had been removed and huge boulders placed so that it was impossible for vehicles to drive through. No great obstacle for a bike though, soon I was coasting downhill again, mile after mile, through spruce and pine plantations, in and out of frosty shadow and bright sunshine. On reaching the road it was still another four miles down Strath Rusdale to Ardross. To the south, the Novar wind farm was extremely prominent, huge blades slowly turning on top of the high rounded hills, spoiling a beautiful silhouette against a red sky. Each windmill had a light, repeatedly cut-off by rotating blades, so that the hilltop, at night, would appear a mass of flickering lights. Wind farms should never be sited in such wild and largely unspoilt areas; we have industrialised enough of this planet already.

The last of the sun was still glowing on the humped Struie hills as I began the steep climb north of Ardross, a climb followed by a nice long descent through Strathy to gain the main road. Another three miles north led to the start of the

Hills of the North, Rejoice!

Struie cycle trail with a dozen or so miles ahead, over the hills to Tain. So it was already half an hour after sunset with a hard frost setting in as I set off on another long cross-country route. After an initial descent into very cold air settling in Strath Rory, the track climbed steadily, into warmer air, looping back northwards as it did so with growing views over the Struie and out across the Dornoch Firth. Rounded hills, black against a red sky, rose above dark valleys with the occasional headlights of a car on the road far below. I was glad indeed to reach the 1200-foot top of the climb; now it would be mostly downhill. A long way below, to the south, were the lights of Alness and Invergordon with the oil-rigs in the firth illuminated like Christmas decorations. Across the Black Isle was Inverness, while ahead were patches of orange light strung out along the east coast marking Tain, Dornoch, Golspie, Brora. There was still just enough light to steer round the odd stone on the track – I'd recently heard a bit about night mountain-biking on the radio but hadn't expected to be doing it myself only a few days later! For mile after mile I freewheeled down, the dark getting darker, in and out of forests and clearings, before finally emerging into a sea of mud, churned up by logging operations. Straining to see potholes and stones in the bike's front light, checking the map at every track junction, it seemed a long three miles to the road.

An easy two more miles led on down, across the A9 and into Tain – for fish and chips and a lovely mug of tea. Then down to wait on the station platform; a very icy night under the stars, listening to occasional curlews and redshanks calling from the Dornoch Firth mudflats. The friendly Sprinter rattled in well on time, nicely busy but with plenty of room for the bike. I sat back enjoying the experience of comfortable travel through frozen glens and across desolate moorlands on a black December night, especially appreciated since I didn't even have to pay for my ticket!

The Halkirk-Wick trail

Long distance paths are all very well, but they often take rather dull routes. Otherwise people might get lost, or stuck in bogs, or disturb important bird breeding sites. New footpaths cost a fortune to build... Which is why a superb route between Halkirk (Georgemas, to be precise) and Wick could never be an official route. Unofficially the route has always been there, is there now, anyone can take it. Indeed I never really see why we need official long distance paths; just get the maps out and choose a route from A to B to suit yourself. My roundabout route is perhaps 23 miles in length, goes a few miles south of the main road, crosses flow-country and moor and gives a completely different impression of the county from the 20 minute drive along the main road.

Early on the morning of 24th December it took me nearly 40 minutes just to reach Georgemas station on the bike in a south-westerly gale. Still in pitch dark, I left the bike and set off on foot, aiming to walk all the way to Wick and catch the afternoon train back. The first few hundred yards were along the A9 before turning left, up the road for a mile to Banniskirk Farm. At eight in the morning the red sky was gradually brightening, the farm still quiet – until the dogs started barking! A good (but wet) path links Banniskirk and Dunn, across the slopes of Spittal Hill; in the half-light I stumbled in and out of bogs before the track improved at Hillpark. The whole area is littered with abandoned and ruinous crofts.

After a short distance on tarmac I took the track past Markethill Farm to the Watten-Mybster road and the last bit of road walking for some 15 miles. A little further on I cut across fields to gain the hilltop just above the empty house at Backlass. It's a great shame this place is abandoned, it has one of the finest views in the county out over the moors. The wind had remained near gale-force and showers of stinging rain were moving in as I headed south along the track, a scrawny forestry plantation gave shelter for a second breakfast – then on, across half a mile of exposed wet fields to the ruined croft of Druimdubh. The roof was still precariously on, more or less, above a floor feet deep in dried manure and smelling strongly of sheep. Bits of worm-eaten wood remained from empty door and window frames, water dripped and ran from great gaps in the slates. I joined a sheep to shelter for another few minutes from the worst of the rain as clearer skies moved in from the west. The remains of the old hard farm track led down to Shielton farm, seemingly very isolated in the middle of the moor though only four miles from Watten. Skirting the farm buildings I crossed soaking fields to a footbridge over the swollen Acharole Burn and set off up over the moors. Another heavy shower was heading my way, so I wasn't hanging about, pushing hard through the heather and bog. On the crest of the hill, skirting the Dubh Lochs of Shielton, it was strange to think that this area would have looked almost the same 2000 years ago, even down to the shape of the pools. Ahead was the deserted farm of Kensary. Few crofts or farms would have been so close to the dubh-loch country as this one, with wild moorland just 100 yards from the buildings. The generations who carved out cultivated land from the peatbogs would be sad to see its state now. The farm track was a sea of mud leading to a deep ford – all the streams were very high – I crossed an extremely dodgy bridge a few yards upstream on the grounds that I'd get no wetter if the bridge gave way than if I'd waded through the young river. That bridge can't last much longer...

The weather had been steadily improving, now, the sun was shining brightly and the showers had gone, though it was still windy. It was an enjoyable walk down the track past another deserted farm, Rowans, to the Camster road, with another very dodgy bridge to cross over the upper Wick river. Here, any sensible long-distance route would turn south for a couple of miles then take the new forest road east. I preferred a more adventurous way across the pathless and soaking moors leading to the Flows of Leanas, then through new plantations to pick up the forest road further on. So straight across the road, over the crest of the hill, and into the moor again. It was wet, very wet. I skirted a forest corner, sloshed slowly through the bogs, climbed the forest fence and picked up a promising looking forest ride. The ride gave out into another bog and a push through lodgepole thickets, keeping an eye on the sun so as not to walk in circles. It was hot and sweaty going yet my feet were soaked and frozen – and there, at last, was the track, on the other side of a particularly impenetrable-looking bog. Paddling on Christmas Eve in freezing temperatures is not to be recommended. I stopped for lunch, wrung out my wet socks, and it was two hours before my feet were warm again.

Time was getting short, but the hardest part of the route was over. The track took me east for a mile before curving south, again I turned off onto a forest ride. Here, high in this out-of-the-way spot were old peat-workings, and, too, an old peat-track leading down to Blingery. Ahead was a most unusual view of Wick, still five miles away, framed in the trees. The Blingery track gave out at a gate on the other side of which was a deep muddy morass churned up by a herd of cattle. Through this I somehow clarted and plowtered to reach Blingery Farm and at last a good, if potholed, track past Refaithy to the Haster-Hempriggs Road (How many Wickers have walked out to Blingery? Do it – for yet another aspect of Caithness!) Just a four-mile walk remained, down to the town along the roads through Newton Hill on a fine afternoon with low sunshine and a following wind. There was now plenty of time, enough even to sit on a bench by the river, to change my wet socks, have a snack and then wander up to the station where the train was waiting. How nice to have just a 15 minute journey instead of the normal 12 hours! I heartily commend the journey from Wick to Georgemas, up the Wick river valley then along the very shore of Loch Watten, a good ending to the day after the long walk.

There will never be a long-distance path from Georgemas to Wick but my route is a good one to take, and there's nothing to stop anyone from walking it now!

Wild walking

This is the time of year for wild weather. Gentle, warm sunshine is just not appropriate at the end of December – gales, storms, sheets of driving rain, hail, blizzards – that's what we expect of a Highland winter. Yet rarely are things so bad that you can't go out and enjoy the elements. From indoors it often looks and sounds terrible but once you are outside, properly dressed, it's not half as bad and the conditions often turn out to be quite exhilarating.

With all the fancy outdoor equipment you can buy these days there is no excuse at all for venturing out only when the sun shines. Most of those fancy Goretex jackets costing hundreds of pounds are never worn in the conditions for which they were designed – presumably after spending that much, people don't want to get them wet and muddy! It always annoys me how people are conned into spending a fortune on gear which is rarely used. All you need to deal with 99% of our worst winter weather is sensible warm clothing and a lightweight waterproof cagoule with overtrousers which, between them, you can get for less than £50. Footwear is a matter of personal preference but unless you're climbing mountains in snow and ice, forget the expensive boots – they'll just get expensively ruined in the wet.

It so happened that a visit south, a week or two ago, coincided with one of those grand wild spells of weather when Atlantic lows were queuing up to sweep band after band of rain and gales across the western hills. All high ground needs to be treated with respect in such weather – but when you know an area of country really well you can enjoy a walk across the tops in stormy conditions without having to worry about route-finding. I was offered a lift across to the small town where the day's walk began, this meant however a late start and it was after ten before I set out. I'd be walking the last few miles in darkness. The wind would be mostly from behind, an important consideration in December with gales and rain forecast. It was very mild though, and in just a shirt I walked up the green path climbing steadily into the rounded, rolling hills. Cloud lay sullenly over all the higher ground with a base at about 1200 feet, the lights of the town on a dark December morning faded from sight as I entered the tearing grey mist. To me this was though all very friendly, well-known country, just follow the path, climbing easily till above 2000 feet. The first rain started, I donned cagoule and overtrousers and now, largely impervious to the weather, followed the up and down route across the plateau as a steadily rising wind hammered the rain in from the side. A triangulation column marks the highest point of this group of hills, a place I've visited in all seasons, all weathers, by day and by night, on foot and by bike – and a bit of mist and driving rain was nothing to worry about. The wind was still rising though, causing me to lean sideways with the rain roaring on my cagoule hood as the path contoured on round the hillside.

Long valleys led north, I could have tramped down the valley floor for four miles but chose instead to stay on a ridge in the wind and the cloud. A gully with views down to the valley gave shelter for lunch out of the wind. A trunk road ran through the valley ahead and as I came out of the cloud I could see the lights of the heavy traffic through the murk two miles away. The rain came on heavier than ever and the gale drove it in writhing columns across the hillsides as I splashed downwards through bogs and rising streams. Down in the wide valley the wind was roaring through the trees, howling past stone-built farms, the rain bouncing off the roads and hammering on windows. A great day for walking with the wind at your back! An underpass led beneath the main road – the rain blowing right through it – then my route led back up onto lower, grassy hills. A clearance seemed to be slowly coming in from the west and after another half an hour the rain stopped and the sky brightened, the wind however remaining strong. Now, taking it it easier, I made my way across two or three miles of grassy moorland passing another exposed triangulation column which I once reached on hands and knees on another, even wilder, day. Perhaps I wouldn't have lingered if I'd known what was yet to come.

It looked as if a shower was rolling in from the plain to the north-west, I'd seen the pink-white tops of cumulonimbus earlier on. On the last descent to the village it seemed to be getting dark very quickly even though it wasn't yet sunset. Just as I walked under the railway viaduct in the gloom a sudden flash of lightning made me jump, the thunder rolling about four seconds later – nearly a mile away. Suddenly the temperature dropped by about ten degrees and the village street literally disappeared in a haze of torrential driving rain and hail. I just walked on. Lightning flashed again ahead, and to the side – but after ten minutes all the fireworks were over. Water poured off the fields and ran across the road. Although the sun had set it was now getting steadily lighter, a great wall of cloud marking the cold front was moving away eastward leaving a clear sky behind it. As I tramped the last few miles along lanes and paths the wind dropped and the stars appeared – with Mars, Venus, Jupiter and Saturn strung out across the southern sky. In the distance could be seen lights of traffic pouring down the trunk road from the pass to the east, the hills there still enveloped in cloud with the odd flicker of distant lightning – driving conditions must have been horrendous. How much better to be out walking than manoeuvring a car through the juggernauts in clouds of spray – or sitting indoors saying: 'What a miserable day'!

Christmas ghosts?

I must have spent more nights alone in empty and reputedly haunted houses than most people. Many's the dark night I've walked alone through woods or over moors and mountains, or cycled empty, lonely roads. But never, even at Christmas have I met one real ghost. I've never believed in ghosts – perhaps that's why! Nevertheless I have had a few odd experiences.

Many people claim to sense an atmosphere to a place, or a building, perhaps friendly, or maybe sinister. I'm sure this is psychological, dependent on your state of health, how tired you are, the weather, the light, stories you may have heard and a host of other factors. I sometimes like to pretend I occasionally sense such things too, but don't really believe there's anything objective there. Take the little Binocular Lochs, five miles south of Reay. Unlike most Caithness lochs these are deep and dark in steep-sided rocky basins which suddenly interrupt the smooth sweep of the flow country. I've been there often, swum in both the lochs, skied across them when frozen, the location should be beautiful. Yet I tend to think of the place with a certain feeling of unease. Nothing objective, though once my digital watch reset itself to time zero just as I was approaching. Probably I'm doing my best to imagine something that's not there. I'll camp a night by the lochs sometime.

Ben Macdhui, the highest of the Cairngorms, has a reputation of being haunted by the infamous 'Grey Man', a huge shadow and footsteps which chase lone walkers in mist or at night. On my very first visit I found myself alone at the summit in mist – and fled, pretty quickly! But that was at the tender age of 18. Many years later I camped on the lower slopes of the mountain and had to answer the call of nature in the small hours on a snowy, moonlit night. I seemed to sense a brooding, sinister presence and was glad to get back to the tent – but then one is at one's lowest ebb at that time in the morning! Only once on the hills can I remember feeling the sense of oppression that people mention in places where dastardly deeds were done; this was on a glorious sunny day at a little-visited col in north-west Sutherland a couple of miles from the 'Robber's Pass'. On subsequent visits I noticed nothing at all. I don't know of any stories about the place, it must have been pure imagination.

Remote bothies at night can be anything but peaceful with wind howling through leaky windows, doors rattling, mice scratching, stags roaring on the hill, seals mooing on the seashore – but all are friendly sounds. (Mice can be worse than any ghost. Thirty years ago, alone at Camban bothy and sleeping in the upstairs loft, I heard mice scratching around the food I'd left down below. Half asleep and in a hurry to save my cheese and biscuits, I slipped and fell ten feet down the ladder onto a concrete floor, very fortunately sustaining nothing worse than bad bruising.) The closest I've come to a 'real' ghost was many years ago in the reputedly haunted Ben Alder Cottage, some ten miles west of Drumochter summit. Others were staying in the bothy and, tired and desirous of an early night, I retreated to the haunted back room. A series of scratching noises commenced, like a fingernail on glass, there was nothing visible to cause it, all my food and pans were out of reach of mice. Unable to sleep I was driven back into the main room. It was only years later that I found out that the bothy housed a colony of bats and that they typically made a scraping noise!

One winter evening in the near dark I was cycling towards the old Shebster school having just turned off the main Dounreay road. The sky to the west was still bright and, there in the field, silhouetted against the last of the light, was the tall black figure of a hooded monk. I pedalled on, and as the angle of view changed the apparition resolved itself into a large horse which had been standing with its back to me. Hundreds of times I've crossed Olrig Hill alone in pitch dark or full moonlight, via the fairy mound of Sysa, the Ghoul Law and the Gallows Hill and there is most definitely nothing remotely haunted or supernatural about any of them. The scream of a fox can sound blood-chilling if you don't know what it is, and there's a damp hollow below Sysa where a patch of cold mist can gather across the road on calm evenings which might, I suppose, have given rise to some stories.

A few years ago a new 'chicane' fence was erected along the road at Broubster to deter deer from passing through to the lowland fields – a cattle grid was deemed too pricey. It is said that early one dark December morning a Dounreay-bound cyclist heard a ghostly voice emanating from the darkness ahead. Being a hard-headed sort he carried on towards the voice and realised that it was annunciating the 'Today' programme on Radio Four! A jacket was hanging on the fence with a transistor radio in the pocket. There was nobody else about. It transpired that deer were still getting through so the ploy of leaving the radio on all night had been devised to scare them away.

One of my oddest experiences was on a frosty Christmas Eve by one of the remotest lochs in Caithness. A small dumpy bird (the books tell me it was a quail, but the bird experts say this isn't possible) flew straight towards me and landed right at my feet. It then scuttled a yard or so and settled down in a little peaty cleft right next to the loch; I could look down on it sitting there. Nothing supernatural, but no real explanation. My most recent 'ghost' sighting occurred in, of all places, the heart of Edinburgh. We had rushed up Arthur's seat to reach the top shortly after sunset and dusk was rapidly falling as we made our way back down towards the city lights and the rush hour. I noticed two large black birds, almost certainly ravens, hovering in the half-light in front of a rocky bluff where the figure of a man clad in black was standing, hands outstretched as if feeding them (perhaps he was). The dangers from real humans in cities are rather greater than from apparitions and I deliberately gave the chap a wide berth; he didn't look the sort of person you'd wish to pass a casual remark on how fine the evening was. Only later did it sink in that his clothes were rather strange – a wide-brimmed hat and what looked like a cloak. The official Keeper of the Ravens, perhaps? But no, not a ghost. They don't exist. Not even at Christmas!

A December ride

December is a month when it's especially worth making the effort to get out and about. Daylight is short and weather is usually stormy, wet, icy or snowy in any combination. Everyone is busy, tired, cross, working hard, preparing for the festive season, rushing from one thing to the next. The hills, moors and coasts by contrast have a refreshing quietness about them even in storm; time taken out to appreciate them is time well spent.

Even a couple of hours out of doors, cycling to work and back, is some help in maintaining the right perspective on life. The other morning it took me a couple of hours just to make it into Dounreay! Leaving home as usual around 6-30 it didn't seem too bad till Thurso but the westerly had by then risen to around force eight with occasional squalls of sleet and hail. I was well protected against the weather and knew that as long as the wind remained below force ten, cycling would be possible, if very slow. One advantage is that the roar of the wind drowns out the protests from the worn-out gears and chain of the old bike I use for winter cycling! The ride had it's moments though. Near the top of Scrabster Brae the side-wind from a passing van sent me onto the verge and the chain came off. In between the pitch dark and the dazzling glare of headlights from a stream of passing buses and cars I had to struggle to get the thing back on again, then wait for a gap in the traffic before wobbling back into the gale. A vicious squall hit near the bottom of Forss straight, the trees gave shelter but once over the bridge the wind, with sheeting hail and rain, was straight into my face and stopped me like a wall. I had to pull the bike off the road and, with the rain hosing off the road in the light of passing headlights, wait for a lull to get going again. There have been many, many rides like it, and harder, over the years. Such struggles however leave you not weaker but stronger to face the more insidious tribulations of life.

There are not many cycling days in December without problems of either ice or wind, but for once I was able to make the most of a rare interval between the snow and the gales. Leaving home at my usual time on a calm and frosty morning I had to take it canny for the first mile or two over hard-packed snow before reaching salted roads into and through town. The back road passed as normal, early traffic overtaking, dawn light gradually growing from behind. On many, many a fine day one turns into the Dounreay site wishing that one could just carry on west. (On the other sort of day the lights of the site gleam like a beacon promising shelter and a hot cup of tea, it is then with great relief that one at last reaches the haven of the main gate!) On this occasion I could carry on, and did, through Reay and up over Drumholiston as the dawn proper came up. Some early cloud was breaking, the day would be fine though a southerly wind was forecast for later.

There was a sprinkling of snow and a little slush on the road, but the snow-showers had kept near the coast and a few miles up Strath Halladale the snow had gone. I'd been too warm coming over the Drum but once down in the Strath started getting colder and colder, no matter how hard I pedalled. On frosty winter days, cold air pools in this valley and the temperature plummets; it was probably between -5 and -10C, I had to stop to put on another pullover and it took several miles to warm up my hands again. All the streams and the river were full, brown water rushing down, banks heavily fringed with ice. Frost, not snow, carpeted the landscape and even the Griams were only streaked with white. The school van passed, then overtook me going the other way half an hour later. On the 40 miles to Helmsdale probably no more than a dozen vehicles passed in both directions, mostly farmers. It was indeed a grand, quiet morning, sun now on the slopes but the valley floor still in shadow. The morning two-coach Sprinter to Thurso passed through Forsinard station just ahead of me, its journey from Inverness one of the most scenic in Britain on such a day. I carried on, slowly up to the bealach then onto the stretch I'd been looking forward to, downhill to Achentoul. The scene – long vistas across the flows to the Griams and the much whiter Ben Armine range – epitomised the remoter parts of the Far North.

Kinbrace is a favourite place of mine with that frontier-post combination of remoteness, self-sufficiency and eccentricity. Passing the school I could see into the cosy classroom with the children sitting round the table. Helmsdale was another 17 miles down the Strath of Kildonan, a valley which can evoke sad thoughts of clearances and evictions. Nothing can be done about the past, so it's perhaps better to be positive and accept Kildonan for what it is now, namely a very beautiful and peaceful valley, especially on a calm winter day. A rocky river, birch woods, mountains above, a few scattered farms, much of the valley floor in perpetual shadow and frost at this time of year. A perfect road for cycling.

Shortly after noon I joined the main A9 in Helmsdale and began the long climb up the Ord. It's perhaps easier in this direction than when coming south, except that there is a second big climb up the Berriedale Braes. Halfway up, getting really hot, I stopped, climbed over the roadside fence and sat down for lunch, high on the hillside with the sea stretching out in front of me. The air was clear to the distant Cairngorms with the sun gleaming on snowfields, skiing must have been good! I soon cooled off and was glad to get back on the bike for the rest of the climb. The road was in fact very quiet and gave good cycling, only a few lorries passing in two hours. Rather than take the Causewaymire I carried on to Lybster, reckoning that the single-track road via Camster would give a nice route in the late afternoon gloaming. So it proved, the yellow moors, flecked with white were beautifully lit by the setting sun with only the new forests spoiling the scene; these plantations within sight of the ancient Camster Cairns should never have been allowed. A light southerly wind provided a welcome helping hand along the miles of straight road across the empty moors, I've known purgatory here into a strong north-westerly! There was more snow inland, and for a mile or two the road was icy, demanding care, before it cleared on the descent towards the orange lights of Watten. The last ten miles were slow ones, but still to be enjoyed, especially on the Gillock road with Loch Watten reflecting a yellow sunset sky and the Caithness mountains in silhouette. Just 30 minutes earlier than on a normal workday I was home, having cycled 110 miles. Now that's what I call making the most of a December day !

Year-end

When I'm recovering from the flu or a bad cold there comes a time when some vigorous exercise will finally clear the worst of it. Not too soon, or it only makes things worse, but at the right time it gets me going again.

So, on Christmas Eve, a bit of gentle exercise on the mountain bike was in order. A settled, bright, mild day was forecast, and I set off down the hill in the dark without bothering to check how warm it actually was. The French call flu 'la grippe' – an apt description of the way the cold morning air seized my sensitive throat. I very nearly turned back – was this wise? But it wasn't that much below freezing and should warm up once the sun rose... I wrapped a scarf tightly round my neck and pedalled on, slowly. Dawn gradually came up on the familiar roads through Halkirk and past Loch Calder, wild geese flew overhead, their calls answering the occasional sneeze and wheeze from a definitely sluggish cyclist. I lifted the bike over the locked gate at Broubster and pedalled slowly up the forest road, past the lochs and up the hills across Clais Brice and Cnoc Luachair. Contractors had again been removing Christmas trees from what, until a few years ago, was deer-stalking and grouse country. The forest road from Broubster is a good route for anyone wanting a bit of very easy mountain-biking – once you've got your bike over that locked gate!

I wasn't going to return the same way, though, wheezing or not. It is only four miles of fairly easy bike-wheeling to Loch Caluim and the end of the Dorrery track, this would make at least something of the day. I changed into trainers and began a long paddle through the bogs. An open clearing between the plantations continues south for half a mile, very wet and much churned up by quads. It leads (cross the small loch at the middle, where it narrows) to the forest fence – another obstacle for the bike – then a wheel across rough peaty terrain to reach the top of Beinn Nam Bad Mor with Loch Scye below to the left. Many's the time I've crossed this top with a bike, usually returning down the track to Shurrery. One Christmas Eve, years ago, I watched the sun set over an arctic white landscape with temperatures to match and had to wheel the bike almost all the way down an ice-covered Shurrery track as the stars came out and everything froze solid. Today was mild by comparison, though the wind was cold and the sun had gone behind high cloud heralding the next rain.

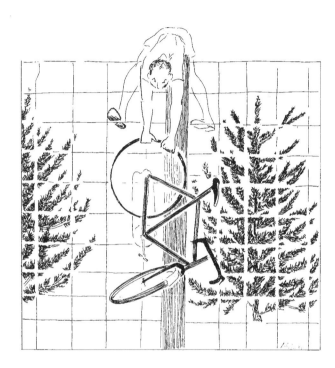

An easy descent through heather led to the track which I crossed, aiming for the green banks of a stream meandering down through the flows towards Loch Caluim. It looked like easy going, and so it was, until becoming very wet where sluggish, boggy streamlets joined the main watercourse; difficult with a bike. When hot, tired and covered in peat and with yet another morass to circumvent or plowter through – stop. Listen to the silence. Look at the clear moorland skylines, smell the fresh clean air, taste the peat in the icy water running gently over the stone, feel the wind in the face. Why else are you here? The shore of Loch Caluim also proved very wet but eventually I reached the end of the good track for an easy ride back through the mud and puddles to Dorrery. I was home by late afternoon, feeling more as if I'd done the Highland Cross than a gentle outing across a little bit of moorland. My cold was, though, definitely in retreat!

A week later, the last day of the year and another fine one. Not that it seemed that way early on with wind and rain hammering on the windows in the pitch dark; it always takes an effort to get out in such conditions but the weather is never as bad as it looks. By the time I'd driven to Berriedale it was getting light and the rain had stopped. I unloaded the bike from the car, tied on the rucsac and set off along the estate road up the Langwell Water to Wag, aiming to follow the river right to its source. The seven mile track up past the Langwell gardens and on along the river is an excellent easy cycling route, the track is so good that you don't even need a mountain bike. It's even better walked as the route mostly follows the river bank with very fine views and is full of interest with lots of deer, other wildlife and remains of clearance settlements. With a strong cold headwind I was slow, but there was no hurry.

The sky was clearing, to give a dry spell between the last of the rain and the first of the squally showers. A last steep climb took me over the shoulder of Sal-vaich then down the hill to Wag, an ugly ruin in a magnificent setting just below Morven. Leaving the bike I crossed the suspension bridge and followed the boggy south bank of the river for a couple of miles before striking up across the heather to the bare ridge of Creag Scalabsdale. This, the third highest peak in the county, gets a real battering from the weather with the mile-long ridge mostly scoured bare. I could see piled clouds over Sutherland rapidly advancing towards me and the bitter wind was rising. The summit cairn overlooks miles of remote moorland, with Loch Scalabsdale, the highest in Caithness and the source of the Langwell water, just below. The long vista from these hills across the vast Sutherland moorlands, lit by the odd gleam of low sun, to distant, enticing peaks partly obscured by snow-cloud always to me has something of a magical, almost haunting quality to it, hints of 'Over the Hills and far Away.'

A brief snatch of cheerful birdsong surprised me, a snow-bunting, with its unmistakable white wings, was emulating a lark as it fluttered high into the air above the summit. And, sure enough, the snow arrived two minutes later, heavy wet flakes blowing in the now near-gale. I hurried down, round the loch, and then across the atrocious bogs out of which the strange rocky peak of the Child's Seat rises like an island. As the shower petered out, the wind dropped and the sun projected the rainbow-fringed shadow of this little double peak onto a band of white mist which often settles across the ridge below Cnoc an Eireannaich to the north. There was good shelter below the top for a late lunch, then a simple tramp back through the bogs on a fine afternoon of low sun and lengthening shadows with the frost already settling. The prehistoric 'wheelhouses', a mile west of Wag, must be the best preserved in the county with low walls still standing. A following wind made for a fast, enjoyable cycle down the Langwell valley to Berriedale, always itself a lovely spot at dusk with the sound of rushing water below the old stone bridges and the scent of leaf-mould. Venus shone brilliantly, close to the new crescent moon, marking the end of the last day of the year.

Millennium night

Anyone out on the empty road from Dunbeath to Braemore – and there were only two vehicles in two hours – would have seen a heavily-laden walker heading into the hills as the dawn came up. Briefly the snow-streaked slopes of Scaraben gleamed red before the last sunrise of 1999 slipped behind the thickening cloud. Already the wind was near gale force, carrying with it the first spots of rain. The road was still icy on its higher stretches, there had been less of a thaw than expected. The effort of climbing to the top of the pass with a heavy pack had kept me warm but after descending to Braemore, into the bitter wind, I needed to stop at a sheltering patch of spruce to don more clothes under my waterproofs. The wind roared in the trees, Braemore in midwinter was pretty bleak.

Perhaps the gamekeeper watched, through his binoculars, a laden walker picking his way westward from the road-end along the ice-covered track and wondered where he was going on the last day of the old Millennium. Perhaps I had some misgivings – but the weather forecast had indicated nothing more severe than ordinary gales and rain and I was well equipped, if with old boots and no fancy Goretex. After a couple of miles I left the track and cut down to the Berriedale water, following deer-tracks up and down along the water's edge to reach the footbridge at Corriechoich. The rain had now set in but it had turned a little milder as I sweated up over the moor towards the foot of the Morven. There was a lot more slushy snow than expected and the steep slopes ahead looked very white... A 'cool-off' break was needed, to munch some sandwiches and a seasonal mince pie, take off a pullover (it would be needed, dry, later!) then, slowly, set off up those daunting slopes.

At this point anyone watching would have been puzzled. Why should a walker be wallowing upwards through wet snow and driving rain with a big pack at this time in the afternoon? It's a hard climb up the 30-degree slopes of Morven even when lightly laden and in good weather. On the lower slopes, amid the long heather, are large rocks and boulders with deep crevices and hidden holes. In rain with a 35 pound pack and thigh deep slushy snow in places, it was the hardest climb this walker has ever had up Morven. Yet upwards progress was slowly made, one step at a time, sometimes to put a leg deep into some hole, then to extricate it and find another way, to rest for a breath between each exhausting step as if on some Himalayan peak. To be pouring with sweat under my waterproofs wasn't good but there was little I could do about it. The higher slopes were, as expected, a bit easier, the snow had mostly been blown off and the heather was shorter. The wind was stronger though, forcing me to crawl the last stretch over the boulders to the eastern, subsidiary top. The summit slopes were still frozen, mostly bare of snow. A white ptarmigan sliced off sideways into the gale, I carefully picked my way, likewise leaning sideways, upwards through the tearing mist towards the main summit. Just below the top was a spot where it was almost calm, the wind being deflected upwards by the steep slopes below. This is a phenomenon of Morven I'd been relying on. I set the pack down, clambered up to the top then returned to what would be my home for the next 17 hours. Perhaps it was folly or madness – but the opportunity wouldn't come for another thousand years. I'd see in the new Millennium, alone, on the top of Morven.

Soon I had the tent pegs well into the frozen moss, on the edge of a cornice fringing a gully falling 1000 feet to the north. The tent was a 20 year-old model, a bit battered and stretched but I wasn't going to risk having my new one ripped to pieces. As the grey afternoon light faded I carried rocks to weigh down all the pegs and loose nylon, the wind could well change direction and give me an overnight blasting. There was no sunset, just wind and rain, but it was still most impressive to see the last light of the old year from the summit. Cloud came and went, revealing glimpses of a barren empty landscape, the white Knockfins fading out into dark flow country, streaked white and glimmering with frozen lochs. It was cold, my soaking feet were almost numb, my clothes wet with rain and sweat. Time to retreat to the tent for some dry clothes, a sleeping bag and a brew of hot sweet tea.

By 4-30 it was almost dark, now there was no alternative to staying put till 8-30 the next morning, alone in stormy midwinter weather on top of a high mountain in the Far North of Scotland on one of the longest nights of the year.

Tea was simple – I'd taken things I could eat cold if it was too windy for the stove – a tin of Macaroni cheese and half a steamed pudding (the other half for lunch the next day). The tent warmed up nicely with the Primus going but the outer tent was running with condensation. A gusty wind started picking up, the rain hammering on the nylon. By eight the wind had swung round to the west and was continuously shaking the tent. I ventured out after donning wet boots and jacket to see a brilliant starry night with the white glow of a faint aurora lighting up the northern sky. Round the horizons were patches of orange lights indicating the positions of Wick, Thurso, Lybster and the towns across the Moray firth, obscured from time to time by blowing cloud. A huge sea of darkness surrounded the peak, just a solitary light from Glutt Lodge, five miles away, and the orange flashing of a gritter somewhere on the CausewayMire.

A shower rattled on the tent. I tried to sleep but the cold and wind were to keep me awake most of the night. I wouldn't however be in worse shape than most other people when the first of January dawned! It turned colder. The inside of the tent was covered in frost, the wind blowing at least force eight. At about a quarter to midnight I prepared to venture out again, just as it started snowing... so at precisely midnight, between the two millennia, I stood on the very summit of Morven. It was foggy, freezing and blowing a gale, there was almost certainly no other human being within five miles. No fireworks, televisions, mobile phone or failing electronics!

'The Lord is risen, He is Risen Indeed!' I yelled into the gale – and retreated to the relative comfort of my flapping tent,

By two in the morning it was clear again, the aurora forming a narrow white band above the horizon, flickering and rolling upwards to evaporate into darkness, with the odd searchlight-like beam. Brilliant stars shone above the distant orange town lights; obviously the Millennium bug hadn't bitten! I dozed on and off, constantly wakened by the cold and by increasingly strong gusts of wind. There would be a lull, then the roar of an approaching gust which would whistle through the guy ropes and madly shake the tent. The wind appeared to be swinging back to the south-west, the lulls grew longer and the gusts more violent till around 5-30 when it suddenly turned wonderfully calm – but with a growing roar from just a hundred yards away. It would have been good to set off before the weather turned wet and stormy again but there was no point in trying to find my way down before it was light.

At 6-30 I brewed up tea, the hot drink and warmth from the stove restoring circulation to my feet and fingers. Breakfast was Weetabix and hot milk, then the slow process of sorting out and packing up. I was very lucky that the wind had turned back to the south or I'd never have got the stove going and packing up the tent would have been a desperate struggle, instead it was just cold. With feet in polythene bags to keep them from being immediately soaked by the wet boots, I set off downwards at 8-30. All around the wild and empty landscape of moor and mountain beneath a threatening sky, the wind already approaching force ten.

At precisely nine the first sun of the year 2000 rose over the sea before disappearing behind cloud.

Descent of those treacherous snow-covered boulder and heather slopes had to be very slow and careful; I didn't want to start the new Millennium with a broken leg and it was with great relief that I reached easier ground at the foot of the peak. Then just a long, easy, ten mile walk back to Dunbeath, over the moor, along the track to Braemore, across to the Dunbeath Strath and down the river to the village. The threatening weather turned out to be largely bluff though the wind remained strong, there was even some warm afternoon sunshine by the river. Cheerful, warmly dressed walkers were out first-footing the new Millennium. Never before had I spent a winter night on the top of a mountain – 15 stormy hours of darkness on the summit of Morven was certainly some experience. Once in a thousand years is perhaps often enough!

The winter way

It's a bit like climbing the munros. Sooner or later every Scottish hillwalker has to walk the West Highland Way from Glasgow to Fort William. I'd always thought of doing it in winter to provide a bit more of a challenge and avoid the crowds (I'm told that tens of thousands of people walk on the Way every year). Not that I'd have chosen January, except that I found myself with a few days to spare and a forecast of rain but not snow...

So with the late afternoon mid-January sun glowing on the slopes of the Campsies, I set off along the first yards of the path at Milngavie, through an underpass painted with scenes one might expect to encounter in the next hundred miles. I'd made no advance plans apart from booking a first night's accommodation near Drymen, glancing at maps and packing a rucsac with spare clothes, food and waterproofs. I aimed to finish the walk four days later; most walkers take seven or eight days but runners do the whole route in under 18 hours so I reckoned I'd set myself a reasonable target. I chickened out of camping in the probably wet and stormy conditions with long hours of darkness, choosing instead the luxury of B&B's, youth hostels and hotels where I could sleep and eat without having to carry tent, stove and sleeping bag.

The low sun soon went behind the hills as I tramped north; in the next four days I saw it again for at most a total of five minutes. Occasional showers blew over, just heavy enough to require waterproofs with the annoying business of putting them on and taking them off again – I was hurrying to make the most of the last daylight. Leg muscles, unused to steady tramping over level ground were already beginning to hurt. The path wound its way by pleasant woodland, a golf-course and fields, surprisingly rural but very much a local dog-walkers route. As dusk fell the route picked up the long-disused Aberfeldy-Glasgow railway line which keeps close to the main road with its steady roar of traffic; I didn't miss much by doing this stretch in the dark. I stopped for a picnic tea, under the stars, then carried on to where the route joined a back road and a two-mile walk to near Drymen where I'd arranged my first B&B. It had been a good day; I'd travelled by train all the way from Caithness and already covered the first 11 miles.

A comfortable night and a huge cooked breakfast stood me in good stead for the next day; I was going to need them. Rain was forecast but the morning should be dry so I was off at first light, soon into miles of boring forest tracks which emerged at last onto open moor and the first real climb, over the 1100-foot Conic Hill near the foot of Loch Lomond. Wind was rising, skies were a steely grey, all the higher peaks were hidden under cloud. Northwards, the long loch disappeared into grey murk. I should have had the sense to choose my own route but stuck to the official path which made a big detour south, joining the trippery loch shore before climbing steeply over a viewpoint by the pass of Balmaha. This was all new country to me, it would be packed with tourists in summer but in mid-January was deserted apart from a few locals. Car-parks were empty, paths unused.

It was after twelve. I'd fondly hoped to cross Ben Lomond but it had already taken me a lot longer than expected and the weather was deteriorating fast. For six miles up to Rowardennan the route followed the eastern shore of Loch Lomond, keeping close to the road but detouring through woods and along the loch shore. The rain started, I donned waterproofs and carried on. Many of the pine forests here have been cut down and are being replanted with native trees in a big native woodland restoration project. By three I'd reached a huge empty carpark at the foot of Ben Lomond. Rain was hammering down and it would be dark in under two hours; the lochside route to Inversnaid would be enough of a challenge. New boots were hurting my feet around the ankles and those road-walking muscles were sore, but otherwise I felt fit enough for the next eight miles up the roadless loch shore, through country as remote as any in the southern Highlands. This was all MacGregor country, yet an area where I'd never been before. A good, fast track climbed steadily, high above the loch, then, as dark fell, dipped back down to the loch shore. Now, totally reliant on torchlight (I'd taken both a head-torch and a hand torch, with spare batteries and bulbs to be on the safe side) I picked my way more slowly along the path. Although well made it twisted and turned, climbing up and down, round boulders and trees, crossing burns by bridges and fords. Some streams were already high with the rain, and difficult to cross. Torchlight shone on wet boulder and tree, on falling water and breaking wave. I was tired, footsore and wet and looked forward to a change of clothes and a good meal at the isolated Inversnaid hotel, whose lights I now glimpsed ahead through the trees. This is the only place where a road comes down to the eastern shore of Loch Lomond. A footbridge crossed a waterfall in roaring spate; I walked up to the hotel entrance. A little notice was there.

'Hotel closed. In emergency, contact reception.'

Reckoning that a pitch dark January night of driving rain, in the middle of nowhere, having already walked for over nine hours, was something of an emergency I went in. People were about. I asked someone,

'Is there any other accommodation around here?'

'No. Nearest is twelve miles down the road.'

'Oh dear... perhaps – could you find me a sofa to sleep on or something?'

'We're closed for renovations. Nobody can stay.'

Workmen were about, I tried again.

'You'll have to ask the hotel management.'

I approached a man who claimed to be the hotel manager.

'Look. I've walked over 20 miles up the West Highland Way. I'm tired and wet. There's even some sleeping bags here. Couldn't you find me a floor to sleep on?'

'Those are workmen's sleeping bags. I can't allow anyone to stay.'

'Perhaps the workmen might give me a lift down the road then?'

'You'd have to ask them. But they're not going anywhere, they're staying here.'

'Couldn't I stay with them then?'

I don't think they'd like you sleeping in their room.'

'What am I do to then?'

The man shrugged his shoulders, turned his back on me and walked away.

Evidently the hassle of helping me was greater than any worry he may have had that a benighted traveller could die of exposure on a wild January night.

To be fair to the hotel, I hadn't phoned to check it was open and couldn't really expect a stranger to be allowed to stay in an officially closed and unsupervised building. What was unforgivable was that the manager offered no help of any kind; he could at least have phoned a taxi to take me, at my expense, to the nearest accommodation and given me a cup of tea while I waited. Just because somebody gets into difficulty through being foolish or unprepared doesn't mean that you leave them to suffer the consequences. Particularly galling was that Inversnaid was, for years, a home of Rob Roy MacGregor – his house had, however, been burnt down twice by his enemies. MacGregors were clearly not welcome at Inversnaid (not that I'd revealed my name!) I sat down, ate a big hunk of Johnson's (of Thurso) black bun, and looked at the map. Five miles further on, along what was regarded as one of the more arduous stretches of the Way, was Doune bothy where I would at least get a roof for the night. I'd no sleeping bag but had plenty of spare clothes, food and a polythene survival bag. I was tired, but not exhausted and was reasonably fit and tough. Push on it was. If the ghost of Rob Roy haunts that unfriendly hotel for evermore they only deserve it.

I found the path leaving the carpark and was soon picking my way by torchlight along the route which weaved up and down, in and out, by boulder and tree and crag. Raindrops glistened in the light of the head torch, here a waterfall roared down, there the path climbed a slippery ladder and descended a cleft between boulders. At one point my torch shone on the black shape of a horned wild goat, sheltering from the wind and rain. Tantalisingly close, across the loch, was the main road with the lights of passing traffic. Above the road was the West Highland railway line; a four coach train was heading north. I thought of those passengers sitting cosily, looking out at the black wet night.

Hills of the North, Rejoice!

My father was a man of his time in retaining some old superstitions, one of which was that any MacGregor who crossed a certain stream on the east side of Loch Lomond would be haunted for the rest of his days. Ghosts were however the least of my concerns, a January night that would have suited Tam o' Shanter was positively friendly compared with that Inversnaid hotel. Indeed I was so annoyed that I hardly noticed the first few miles and surprisingly quickly was within striking distance of Doune bothy. At eight o'clock the dark outline of a building loomed ahead. It appeared to be shuttered and locked. Steel barriers were down over the windows and doors. With sinking heart I went round to the front of the building which was also shuttered. The shutters over the door were, however, half up. I pushed the door – and it opened. The place seemed very well equipped, furniture, armchairs, even beds and quilts upstairs. I'd get a far more warm and comfortable night than I'd been expecting. I ate cold bread and cheese and more of that marvellous Johnson's black bun, before going out to get some water, only then noticing another building... which was in fact the official bothy, cold and damp with the only furnishings a wooden sleeping platform. I must have gone into some private climbing hut.

In my first full day up the West Highland Way I'd walked much too far, almost 30 miles including most of the length of Loch Lomond. Sadly the most scenic stretch had been in the dark because of that unfriendly reception at Inversnaid. Never have I been more glad of shelter and a comfortable bed for the night, waking up only occasionally to the sound of heavy showers rattling on the skylights. All the ghosts in Scotland could have kept me company and I wouldn't have cared in the least. In the morning, snow was down to 2000 feet and occasional showers of hail and rain drove across the loch. A couple of walkers had arrived at the other bothy from the north and still huddled, cold, in sleeping bags in front of a little fire whose smoke mostly filled the room rather than going up the chimney. I didn't mention what a comfortable night I'd just had...

My second full day should have been the shortest with only ten miles to walk from Doune to Crianlarich. The previous day's rain had turned to occasional showers, I stopped to fill a water bottle then set off along the undulating path, enjoying the views across the loch to Ardlui and snow-dusted Ben Vorlich. After a couple of miles a heavier squall came on; I stopped to get my waterproof top out of the pack – and discovered it was missing. I'd left it where I'd stopped for water – and had to jog all the way back to the bothy to retrieve it. So five miles and an hour later I was no further on. Served me right. Still, it gave me a second look at the scenery I'd not seen in the dark!

From the end of Loch Lomond through Crianlarich to Tyndrum is perhaps the least interesting stretch of the West Highland Way. The best routes up the glen have already been taken by the main road and railway, so the path has to follow an artificial route, very undulating and usually not far from the road. It is however well constructed and maintained, indeed on one mile-long stretch complete resurfacing was in progress; half-ton bags of stone had been positioned every few yards, presumably by helicopter.

Showers became heavier and wetter as I tramped up above the roaring Falls of Falloch; an underpass below the main road gave brief shelter then the path climbed to make a muddy and cattle-churned circuit of the hillside above Crianlarich,with a descent through spruce woods to the village as hail roared down. Crianlarich Youth Hostel is a real haven for the hillwalker. The boot-drying cupboard and drying room actually dry, even when 30 or 40 mountaineers have been out on a soaking day. There's a well-equipped and spacious self-catering kitchen, a lovely bright clean dining room and a very comfortable and nicely decorated lounge. It's a real walkers' hostel, nearly everyone there is either climbing munros or doing the West Highland Way.

Come Sunday morning. When I stayed in youth hostels as a teenager, I liked to get out early but this would be impossible on a Sunday. Everyone, including the warden, would sleep in; nobody would be moving much before nine, especially on a dark wet winter morning. Times have changed. Those who've contrived a rare weekend away from work and family and have driven hundreds of miles to reach their chosen mountains mean business. About 30 people were staying in the hostel, mostly Englishmen, serious hillwalkers who were going to spend the weekend climbing their chosen munros come rain, snow, gale or even sunshine. It had rained all night; by Sunday morning the deluge had reached almost biblical proportions accompanied by a howling gale and pitch darkness. Not long after six, people were already getting up, by seven the kitchen was a hubbub of people making breakfast, packing lunches, filling flasks. Outside – still completely black and raining cats and dogs. A loud rumble of thunder around 7-30 did nothing to deter anyone, already the first walker had set off for an early start up his mountains in the wet and dark. The lights went out for five minutes, then came on again. I was in no hurry to leave; I'd be walking into darkness at the end of the day anyway so might as well wait for dawn and perhaps some improvement in the weather.

My ankles had been getting increasingly bruised by the padding on my boots. The only cure was surgery – on the boots that is; using my trusty Swiss army knife I cut out a big chunk from the ankle region of each. That felt better, even if it looked a bit odd – I'd just tell anyone who asked that they should have seen the size of the dog. By 8-30 many had already left for the hills, I could prevaricate no longer with over 25 miles to walk that day, so set out at dawn into something resembling a horizontal waterfall. There was little point in retracing my steps to pick up the official route winding through forests above the road, swollen streams would probably in any case be impassable. Instead I simply walked up the deserted main road, enjoying the wild scenes of driving rain with the river roaring brown below. I attempted to follow the path where it crossed the road but was turned back by a deep flood, so carried on along the road all the way to Tyndrum.

The rain briefly stopped; I just managed to take off my waterproof top before a heavy shower swept in. The route now closely followed the railway for the next six or seven miles to Bridge of Orchy, easy walking along a good track with fine views of the mountains rising into cloud and occasional driving rain. Bridge of Orchy was as quiet as it ever gets at a weekend, heavy hail hammered down as I climbed a hillside path out of the village. I stopped for a late lunch in thicket of sitka spruce, the last shelter for 12 miles. The tarred road ends at Victoria Bridge and the Way then follows the old military road for nine miles across bleak Rannoch Moor below the Blackmount, it was already turning towards dusk as I set off on this exposed stretch, meeting three bedraggled and exhausted-looking walkers heading back to their car after a battering on some munro.

The crossing of Rannoch Moor was just as I'd anticipated. Showers were funnelling up Glen Etive and building over the Blackmount, lashing me from the side with continuous sheeting rain. The moor faded into grey murk, the main road was only two or three miles away but the country felt much remoter. I tramped on, and on, thankful for the Ba Bridge across a swollen river which would have been completely unfordable, climbing steadily up to the highest part of the track at 1500 feet, thinking of all the thousands who must have tramped this way before the days of trains and cars, thinking of Kipling's poem, 'Boots, boots, boots, moving up and down again...' Now I could see the lights of the Kingshouse Hotel, three miles away – I'd phoned ahead from Crianlarich and knew it was open. There was still just enough light to manage without a torch, I came out on the empty road to the snowless Glencoe ski-centre and, as the rain sheeting up Glencoe blew straight into my face, stumbled down the last half mile of track to the hotel.

My reception was the exact opposite of that at Inversnaid. Although I was the only guest staying I was made most welcome, I enjoyed a huge bar meal, there was an open fire in the lounge, I soaked in a hot bath. Luxurious accommodation of which I don't normally partake, but this time I reckoned I'd earned it. The last day, 22 hilly miles to Fort William, would be a tough one too... The weather cleared late in the evening to give spectacular views, from the window of my room, of the moonlit Glencoe hills, especially the steep spur of Buachaille Etive More. In this sort of unsettled weather a fine night inevitably means a wet day to follow – and by morning, sure enough, steady rain was falling. At least the wind had abated, the last miles of the West Highland Way include some exposed stretches which could have been tricky in a January storm. The lounge of the Kingshouse Hotel, with its picture windows, was certainly a spectacular spot to eat breakfast, watching the light grow over the high peaks around. I thanked the staff for their friendly reception and set off in the only dry ten minutes I was to get for the next nine hours.

After a few miles towards Glencoe the path leaves the main road and climbs a few hundred feet to a col via a zigzag path known as 'The Devils Staircase'; I took it slowly so as not to overheat too much under my waterproofs. Here is one of the few places on the walk where the route passes through some wilder country away from the roads, the path though is very good and the walking easy. To the east, disappearing into the haze of driving rain was Blackwater reservoir; to the north, a long way down, was the town of Kinlochleven with steep mountains rising behind.

It rained. The path joined a track which hairpinned steeply down, through bare and dripping birch woods. I stopped for a snack where the track crossed a thundering waterfall. It still rained. As I splashed on downwards I thought of all the words that could be used to describe rain... It was becoming warm and muggy, more like June than January. No midges, anyway. The track emerged by the old aluminium works, I wasted half an hour in the town finding a shop to buy provisions for the rest of the day. Kinlochleven must have one of the most spectacular locations of any Scottish town with the Mamores and the Glencoe mountains rising steeply up to 3500 feet from the shores of the fiord-like loch. Having a strategic position on the West Highland Way has rejuvenated the place; hundreds stay there every night in the summer. Kingshouse to Fort William is really a bit far to do in one day...

In the muggy warmth and steady rain a steep, sweaty climb up through the winter birches was not much fun and I was glad at last to reach a track which climbed more gently over the 1100-foot Lairigmore, then beginning the descent towards Fort William. There were now four or five exposed miles to walk through a bare, empty glen between high mountains, before entering the shelter of the forests. The rain was turning heavier but it wasn't cold, I'd done a mile or so down from the pass when, with almost no warning, the wind suddenly picked up. Within two minutes a gale was sheeting cold rain up the glen, straight into my face. I just zipped up more tightly, pulled on gloves and rubber over-gloves (the Marigold variety, very effective!) and plodded on. It had taken less than five minutes to change from relatively benign conditions to the sort of weather where you'd rapidly get exposure if you weren't properly equipped. A local man had just over-taken me, out running in shorts, he stopped just ahead and wisely turned back.

After a couple of miles into the hosepipe rain, the track rounded the corner of the mountain to head north with the wind from the side again. A long mile of forestry led to a road at Blar a Chaoruinn with just five miles to go to the Glen Nevis Youth Hostel along a path through the forests. It was nearly four in the afternoon and starting to get dark, I reckoned I should reach the hostel by 5-30.

Hills of the North, Rejoice!

The West Highland Way had, however, a sting in its tail. On a fine June day, with the right company and a picnic lunch, it would be a lovely walk from Blar a Chaoruinn to Glen Nevis, a walk to spend a few hours over, enjoying the scenery and the well-made path which winds up and down through the woods. In the last hours of a long, wet day the endless ups and downs of the route were almost the last straw. There must have been about a thousand feet of climbing, up to a ridge, down into the forest, up a long forest ride, down another, steeply down steps into a deep gully with a bridge, steeply up the other side, down, up...

It was soon black under the trees so it was back to torchlight. Was this the descent to Glen Nevis at last? No, it wasn't, there was another 300 feet to climb before finally reaching the last 1000-foot col, with just a faint remaining glimmer of light in the sky. Across the glen the great bulk of Ben Nevis reared dimly into the cloud. The orange lights of Fort William shone brightly through the rain, four miles away.

The descent to the glen was by forest tracks, simple but frustratingly round-about. Careful map-reading in the dark was needed to find the spur leading down to the road and the hostel, it would have been all too easy to get tangled up in dense plantations at this late stage. The rain had at last stopped but I hardly noticed. Even on the road I found myself at a dead-end and discovered I'd inadvertently walked into the carpark of some closed hotel. At long last, an hour later than envisaged, I thankfully walked into the reception of the hostel. Those last five miles had been very long ones. Glen Nevis is a large hostel and normally one of the busiest but only about four others were staying and it was strange to have such a big place almost entirely to myself. A haven in which to change, cook a meal, shower, dry out clothes and boots...

By morning, you've guessed, it was raining again. There were just three miles to walk down to the town for the Inverness bus, and Lochaber was determined to show me what real rain was like. A horizontal downpour, goodness knows what it would have been like on the hills. It was still dark and the headlights of the odd passing car showed the sheeting, bouncing rain in sharp relief. In the half-light I just managed a quick photo of a sign marking the end of the West Highland Way, without getting the camera too wet, then made for the bus depot. After four and a half days of old-fashioned travel under everything the elements could throw at me (four days of rain!) it was a strange experience to step onto the comfortable, lit, heated coach and have all that wild weather reduced to just a little pattering on the side windows and the occasional swish as the wheels went through a deeper puddle.

I'd actually been lucky with the weather which can be truly apocalyptic in the January Highlands; indeed after my trip it worsened with high winds and continual rain or sleet which didn't relent till March. Recently I heard a radio warning for motorists to keep off the A82 over Rannoch Moor because of severe gales, snow, thunder and lightning! I met no weather with which I couldn't cope, and it was indeed a great experience just to walk for five days through the quiet winter Highlands. Until very recently, all journeys were made like this; now people grumble about the four hours it takes for the train to travel from Glasgow to Fort William. Winter is certainly the time to do the West Highland Way if you don't want to be in a crocodile of hundreds of other walkers; in summer I'd make my own route, away from such designated walks. Most people would probably want to take a bit longer than I did, seven or eight days is the usual. Or you could try to run the route in under 24 hours, as some have done...

Rain

(West Highland Way, January 2002)

Rainmaker!
Let it rain, let it rain, let it rain, let it rain, let it rain, let it rain...
Dripping and dropping, spitting and spotting,
Splishing and splashing, falling and plopping,
Smirring and sprinkling, drizzling, tinkling,
Pittering, pattering, pouring and blattering,
Cascading, sousing, pissing and dousing,
Swirling and sweeping, hammering, sheeting,
Bucketing, belting, flinging and pelting,
Stinging and lashing and driving and battering,
Sluicing, throwing, blinding and blowing,
Thundering, bouncing, flooding and hosing!

Rainmaker!
Let it rain, let it rain, let it rain, let it rain, let it rain, let it rain...
Let the heavens open, give us a deluge of truly Biblical proportions,
A waterfall, a welter of water,
A cats-and-dogs, thunderplump downpour,
A torrential, inundating, drowning cloudburst...

Rainmaker!
Let it rain, let it rain, let it rain, let it rain, let it rain, let it rain...
Scotch mist, precipitation, light and intermittent rain,

Small rain, gentle rain, moderate rain, steady rain,
Patchy rain, outbreaks, persistent and heavy rain,
Prolonged rain, sleety rain, blustery and squally rain,
Spells of rain, organised rain, horizontal, tipping it, chucking it down rain,
Wind-blown and curtains and stair-rods and drizzle,
Skin-off-your-nose, showers and mizzle!

Raining, raining, raining, raining, raining,
Damping,wetting, soaking, drenching, saturating,
Cold, dreich, dank, damp, moist,
Humid, muggy, sodden, sopping, waterlogged,
Wet, wet, wet, wet, wet...

That's odd, a patch of sky is turning a funny blue colour –
Or is it just my eyes? And what's that bright yellow thing starting to appear?
Don't worry, a friendly black cloud has hidden it again, whatever it was.
Weak showers? Sharp showers?
'Beefy showers packing in from the west,' they said...
And Eskimos have a few dozen words for snow?

Rain rain rain rain rain rain rain rain rain rain

Mike Tyson month

January is a Mike Tyson of a month. February by contrast seems more feminine, it can throw vicious tantrums but also give balmy spring-like sunshine even in Caithness – and each day is noticeably longer than the one before. January, though, has a hidden menace about it; even on rare quiet days there's a feeling of overwhelming power just waiting to be released. The days are very short, and as dusk falls one feels the latent threat of the winter stalking the hills and open country – and scuttles for shelter, light and warmth like a rabbit to its burrow. If someone from a couple of centuries back were to return, perhaps one of the things that would most surprise them is how the winter has been almost banished from the lives of most people. We live in exactly the same way in January as in July, the shops are well stocked with the same foods, we travel to the same work, the dark and cold and weather barely impinges. Modern society takes little notice of the seasons – until January suddenly throws one of its real knockdown blows. This year's end-of-the-month storm gave just a hint of the potential violence of the month.

Nobody these days thinks twice of travelling the length and breadth of Scotland in the depths of winter – a journey which would probably have been as dangerous 200 years ago as an ascent of Everest would be today. In a mere 10 hours of a January day the train took me from Caithness right through the Grampians and the borders to the north of England – it would have taken my ancestors weeks. It's a modern miracle I never take for granted.

I was trying out a new toy – a folding bicycle. It has become harder and harder to take bikes on trains. Somehow I never manage to book in advance and the bike space on modern trains seems to ever diminish. The bike looks a bit like one of those old shoppers with small wheels and tall handlebars and saddle – but is nevertheless a real bike you can ride for miles. It folds down and fits into a large bag – then behaving as a large, heavy and awkward suitcase, difficult but at least possible to take freely on public transport. James Bond had a folding helicopter – but even a folding bike has something of the same appeal – to leave the train at Penrith with a load of heavy and unwieldy luggage and know that soon I'd be pedalling freely through the lanes. 'Cool!' was the reaction of a young lady on the platform as I unfolded the bike. Ten minutes later, with pannier and rucsac strapped to the carrier, I was finding my way, more by good luck than judgement, out of the town via cul-de-sacs and footpaths away from the rush-hour traffic. The January night descended. After 20 miles cycling along the Cumbrian lanes it had turned very very dark. The black of the road was almost indistinguishable from the verges, hedges and walls in what was not the best of front lights (my fault). I pedalled through the occasional pool of light from a farm, cows milling in the yard after milking, then back into the blackness. The weather was calm, cold and quiet, but that veiled threat was still there.

On the Saturday I found myself with most of the afternoon to spare. The forecast was for gusts of 80 mph – surely just the weather for trying out the bike on a circuit of the highest and most exposed roads in the area! A little sticker on the bike warned: 'not intended for kerb jumping or other hard use'. A few steep hills climbing up and down to nearly 1800 feet in a January gale were just the conditions for riding a little folding bike and surely didn't constitute 'hard use'. The 'Tan Hill Inn' is famous as being the highest in England at 1750 feet above sea level, it's a favourite route of mine from Kirkby Stephen to take a 25-mile circuit passing the inn. First came a long, brutal climb up to 1700 feet above Nateby, the gale from behind pushing me up the easier gradients. The last stretch is 1-in-4 and I walked it to avoid overtaxing the poor bike (that's my excuse). A twisty, hilly road then winds down over the moors to Upper Swaledale, scenery more like northern Scotland. With a following gale it was a good test for the brakes. As if on a motorbike I coasted down for miles, just the odd easy pedal up a short hill. The young River Swale was full, roaring brown over waterfalls beside the road, around was the bleak winter landscape of moor, bare fields and stone walls, isolated trees swaying in the gale. The exposed stone-built farms are some of the highest habitations in Britain and must give some of the poorest living these days. Steep 1-in-4 zigzags had me walking again, then a long gradual climb up into the high moorland, the gale from the side, the bike handlebars flexing and the front wheel lifting off the road if I pushed too hard up the hills. I sailed past the Tan Hill Inn to the top of the road for a glimpse into grey County Durham, then turned back, fully expecting to have to walk for three miles where the road headed straight into the wind along the edge of an escarpment at 1600-1700 feet. Of course I'd have cycled it all on my normal bike (he says) – but did indeed manage to ride a fair bit where downhill or more sheltered. As dusk fell, January looked more and more menacing on those high moors – but the road then led steeply down, down into the bowl of the Stainmore country; almost suddenly I was back into the shelter of the village and the winter was, once more, at bay.

It was to be a few days of cloud and wind and rain, wind on which you could lean at times on the hilltops but still no stronger than I've met outside my own front door. Yet it was mild, the rain not that heavy, only the tiniest streak of snow visible on the highest hills. January this year was mostly bark with little bite. Came the ride back to Penrith – and another gale of driving rain. At least Cumbrian lanes are often well-sheltered by tall hedges, stone walls and trees but even so it took me nearly three hours to cover the 25 hilly miles. A change of clothes in the station toilet, pack the bike in its bag – and I was just another traveller with heavy luggage.

It was the first of February and back in Caithness the wind seemed fresh and invigorating rather than cold and menacing. The Olrig woods were carpeted in snowdrops, spring wasn't that far away.

A February night

I enjoy winter travel, especially if not by car! On a bleak, grey day in early February there was nothing better than to sit back on the Sprinter Express out of Inverness, as the east wind picked up and the country outside grew more wintry by the minute. The higher slopes of the Cairngorms could be seen fading out into a murk of drifting snow. Dalwhinnie – where I've sat awaiting the late afternoon train in blistering June sun – looked frozen, odd pellets of snow blowing on a near gale. To be able to ride over Drumochter on a warm, comfortable train, looking out at the frozen, snow-streaked slopes rising up into snowfields and drifting snow, is an experience I'll never be blasé about. It wasn't till south of Edinburgh that the real blizzard began. The train took no notice, hurtling over Beattock at 100 mph, straight into the gale and driving snow. Dimly could be seen the traffic on the A74, amid headlights and spray and slush. The journey would have made a good advertisement for the railways! There was someone I knew on the last train of the day, down into the Yorkshire Dales. He offered me a lift from the station; his car though wouldn't start after standing all day in the weather. We pushed it for 100 yards through the slush, feet sliding on the slippery ground, to a hill where we finally got it going. Trains are definitely the way to travel in winter.

On a bright, cold afternoon, four days later, I began the return journey north. Although the Highlands had been very white, the northern English fells only bore patchy snow, with the odd passing sleet or hail shower. The '125' from Penzance was 20 minutes late into Carlisle, however such a train can cross Beattock without even noticing and had up made up nearly all the lost time by Glasgow. A quick walk through the crowded streets led to Queen Street station and a packed rush-hour train to Inverness. Most of the commuters alighted at Stirling; once north of Perth it was again a Highland train. Deserted stations, a few lights from scattered houses, the odd pair of headlights on the roads. Just two hours from the crowded city I alighted at Blair Atholl, shouldered my pack and set off for a seven-mile walk into the hills. My aim was to spend the night at

a bothy I'd never before visited, walking down again early the following morning to continue my journey north.

The night was black, with no moon and broken cloud. I walked the first two miles along roads, passing the occasional cottage, lights gleaming from cosy interiors through closed curtains. I'd not been this way before, and careful map-reading was needed to find and follow the correct route. A good track led through dark woods, tall pine trees faintly silhouetted against the sky. Once out of the forest the track climbed steadily. It was, fortunately, a rare calm night. The ground was frozen now, the odd star gleaming between clouds. The occasional murmur of traffic on Drumochter drifted across the hills then, later, the unmistakable rattle of a train. Across the valley poachers were out, lamping after deer, or rabbits, their searchlight beam periodically stabbing upwards.

I tramped on. The ground was now white with snow, then a few hundred yards on, partly frozen drifts started appearing, covering the track. Soon I was crunching across deep snow, walking in the footprints of a group who must have descended this way the day before. It seemed a long way. At last, the crest of the pass. 10pm. Another mile downhill and there was the bothy, nestling into the hillside by the stream. The small, stone building was furnished simply with a table, a few chairs and a wooden sleeping platform. With a couple of candles lit, it was a haven indeed on a black snowy February night at nearly 2000 feet. Somebody had even left some coal and boxes of firelighters, I lit a very small fire and retired to my sleeping bag with the embers glowing, feeling very much at home.

By 5-30 the next morning I was up again. I'd not brought a stove and hadn't expected to be able to make a fire, so it was a bonus to be able to brew lots of tea over a couple of firelighters using an old pudding tin! With flask filled, and a good breakfast eaten, I set off again into the dark for the seven mile walk down to Blair Atholl. Sometime perhaps I'll see the bothy by daylight! Mornings start to lighten in early February, and as the dawn gradually came up it was nice to be able to see some of the country I'd walked through in the dark ten hours earlier. Low cloud on the hills was thinning, patchy blue sky appeared. It looked like the day might turn into a good one for the hills but, alas, there was a train to catch. In the words of Robert Frost, which often come to mind in such circumstances:- 'But I have promises to keep, and miles to go before I sleep, and miles to go before I sleep.'

The Broubster road

Just another ordinary ride home from work. After months of cycling to and fro in the dark it's good to be able to make the journey home by daylight. Yet it's been one of those brilliant sunny February days when it's torture to be stuck indoors. The sort of day when outdoor work is a pleasure and the lucky few are enjoying sun and snow on crisp winter hills. Four-fifteen arrives at last. The weather's changing now and a cloud-sheet has spread in – will the wind turn against me, round to the south-east before I get home? Dodging traffic I pedal down the site roads and out of the gate as fast as possible. Another, faster cyclist is ahead but I just manage to keep pace down the runway and up the hill to the Skaill junction; watch that the right-hand turn, the most dangerous part of the journey. Made it. Phew. I'm pouring with sweat after that 'race' but have at least got the unpleasant stretch over quickly. Now I can relax a bit, leaving the traffic to roar down the main road.

It's almost calm, and grey. Far west, the tops of Ben Hope and Ben Loyal glimmer white. A nice evening for the Broubster road, but it means pushing hard not to be late home, as at 20 miles it's the longest route. Watch out for hens and dogs and surprise cars on the Skaill bends then push on past the 5000 year-old cairns of Freiceadain (a very fine viewpoint) Standing on the pedals I sweat up the hill by the woods, then out into the open and over the top – there are Morven and Scaraben, still mostly white, and the top of Ben Griam Beg, snowstreaked across the moors. I sweep down the hill past the old stone barn (watch out for stray sheep on the blind bends) turn right at the main road then immediately left and speed down to the first dip on the Broubster road. There's the shepherd with his dog, it obeys orders but would LOVE to run at the bike – yes, he's got it well under control. I'm always very wary having been thrown off the bike by one dog and bitten by a couple of others.

A landrover passes then the road resumes its normal peace. Perhaps emptiness is a better word. Five thousand years of habitation has recently ended in this valley, and all around are the piles of stones, ridged fields and grassy mounds left by people who would mostly have regarded a bicycle as either magic or the invention of the Devil. The Forss is quite high, with melting snow – and why did someone have to adorn the fine old stonework of the bridge with ridiculous white and red reflectors? Thirty-five minutes gone, now a slight headwind. No slackening off! The moorland hills of Beinn Nam Bad pass to the right, still streaked with the snow which fell at Christmas. The old Broubster schoolhouse has gone, totally demolished. Ahead rises Dorrery, the road turns left to cross its southern flank to Brawlbin. The old manse is empty, the church now a barn. But the farm is inhabited again and strange breeds of sheep and goats wander around the road, a hazard for the unwary cyclist. I glance back for a last view of the Broubster hills (likely to be soon destroyed by over 50 giant wind turbines each over 400 feet tall), then follow the road through the plantation and up and down across the heather moors, Loch Calder ahead. To the left is Achins, a fine holiday cottage but used at most for a couple of weeks in the year. Are there any geese coming in to the loch? Not tonight. I hurtle down the steep hill to Brawlbin, watching out for stray sheep, then splatter through the mud around the farm. A field is white with gulls; the farmer's out ploughing.

The loch is mostly calm, with old ice still piled at the southern end. I pedal hard up the hill past the old farm and on by the new house, finely sited overlooking the loch. At night there is a brilliant outdoor light which illuminates the area for seemingly miles around. Most outside lights are used far too much – light pollutes too. Turning the corner I glance out across the quiet loch, the hills fading into the evening grey, then get down over the handlebars and head for Halkirk. A three-mile straight, more downhill than up in this direction. It's taken just under an hour to the village; not bad with a slight headwind. Dusk's coming on; I need the lights! On the road out of Halkirk are another two dogs I keep an eye out for. They're on a tight lead, and need it, as I pass. Why do so many dogs go for bikes? From the dip it always seems a long climb up across the level crossing to the Wick road, now beginning to feel tired and hungry, after a long day. By contrast, pedalling down the main road is almost effortless with the now following wind. Is my back light still on? Yes, and vital as the odd long-distance lorry comes roaring up from behind, eager to finish its journey.

Below, the green river valley winds its way down to the lights of Thurso. Turn off (beware more dogs!) and for the last two miles climb up through fertile farmland, mostly now empty of people. Some 20 ruined crofts dotted around the fields testify to former community. Commuters are starting to move back in though, with new bungalows replacing old stone.

Almost unbelievably, three local farmers are trying to put some 25 wind turbines, each 350 feet tall, into the rural landscape of farms, houses and fields around Durran. From this road, and indeed for miles around, they will dwarf everything else. As an experienced safety assessor it is beyond me how anyone can even consider having 150-foot long turbine blades rotating at up to 250 mph anywhere near habitations and roads!

Now I can see home, just over a mile away, but still a twisty road and quite a climb to get there. Sheep, mud and ice can all pose hazards but not tonight, a pair of mallard fly off from a field pond as I sweat up the last climbs. Nearly 90 minutes after leaving work and well on time. Another routine day over.

Stronsay sun, Rousay sleet

I've always fancied visiting Orkney during the winter. To cross from Scrabster to Stromness when it's *really* rough – to see the islands on the short dark days and in storm, when there aren't any tourists – to witness the midwinter sun shining down the passage of Maeshowe… needless to say I've never managed it; the Caithness weather can be off-putting enough. Coward as I was, it took a calm spell at the end of March before I finally made my 'winter' trip. A bike is the ideal way to see Orkney, the distances are short enough to manage even in a force nine gale and a bike is easy (and cheap) to take on the ferries. A journey to those outer Orkney Isles gives a taste of real travel right on our doorstep. Why do so many from Caithness go to far off holiday islands when such wonderful places are so near?

The sailing on the 'St Ola' from Scrabster at six in the morning did mean a very early rise but gave a flying start to an Orkney trip. By eight I was pedalling out of Stromness on a lovely calm morning of drifting low cloud with the odd gleam of sun. There would be plenty of time for a leisurely ride round the island before catching the 3pm ferry from Kirkwall to Stronsay. My favourite part of the Orkney mainland is the area of rolling hill country and big lochs stretching north from Stromness with its views of the high rounded Hoy hills just across the sound. I pedalled up the quiet main road, meeting just a little school traffic, to the right was the large saltwater Loch of Stenness and to the left the surprisingly high-looking hills of Yesnaby. In a remarkably short time (calm conditions for cycling on Orkney are a bonus indeed) I'd crossed over to the sandy Bay of Skaill, a typical Orkney crescent of beautiful white sand – perhaps Freswick is our nearest Caithness equivalent. Here too is the famous Skara Brae, an amazingly well preserved prehistoric village, 5000 years old. There is free entry before the tourist season so I could look around without having to queue or listen to commentaries in German! Indeed I had the place completely to myself; there was a tremendous atmosphere to the stone-age village in the quiet early morning.

Hills of the North, Rejoice!

The houses with their box-beds, stone dressers, hearths and passageways felt as if they had only just been left vacant, I had the feeling that I could meet one of the early inhabitants round any corner (others who have been there alone have also noticed this). A thousand years is like a day on Orkney.

An easy ride took me a few more miles to the far north-west corner of the Orkney mainland and the tidal island of the Brough of Birsay, reached at low tide via a slippery causeway. The tide was low. Once again entry was free; in the season, you have to pay £1 for the privilege of crossing. I jogged up to the clifftop lighthouse then back down to where a Viking settlement, church and small monastery have been excavated; dating from the eleventh or twelfth century they have connections with Hakon who built St Magnus Cathedral. A mere 1000 years old, the houses looked much the same as those at Skara Brae which were 4000 years older still. It's only really in the last couple of hundred years that the way of life on Orkney has changed. A thousand years is like a day, on Orkney.

On, eastward, inland from the north coast, then along the shore of the Loch of Swannay, more like a west coast loch with heathery slopes above. To the north was the holy island of Eynhallow in its tide-race channel with the hills of Rousay beyond. Southwards, huge windmills were being erected on Burgar Hill by a still taller crane. Much more elegant than the ugly two-megawatt brute which used to be here (it never worked properly and was recently demolished) they are prototypes designed for offshore wind farms. A long, long straight leads down through Rendall to Finstown, the scenery here's a bit scruffy and this road can be purgatory in a headwind. No problem though in the calm, soon I was through Finstown and heading east to Kirkwall. With the tide low it was possible to cross to the Holm of Grimbister, another small tidal island with a croft where a man was planting his early tatties. 'Mind the tide,' he warned me, 'you've got about an hour,' which was ample to walk round the little island and leave via the seaweed-covered gate on the causeway.

The magnificent St Magnus cathedral is a must for any visit to Kirkwall – if it's open. With lots of time to spare I read many of the inscriptions on the memorial stones set in the walls – typically to 'ane vertuos woman' who died aged 38 having 'procreated eight children sadly of whom but two are alyve'. 'Remember death,' they all warned. Yet, strangely, there was nothing depressing about it. Here too is a square hole in the wall leading to a cell where witches used to be imprisoned.

Down at the harbour I discovered a minor problem. The Sanday ferry had broken down so my Stronsay boat was going to have to visit Sanday in addition to Eday and Stronsay, and would leave 20 minutes late. There was lots of Sanday-bound traffic including a large lorry laden with bags of fertilizer. Also traffic for Eday and Stronsay. A few vehicles awaited pickup on both Eday and Sanday but a lot wanted to cross from Stronsay... these ferry operators would have no bother with those old puzzles about ferrying cannibals and missionaries. An hour after the boat was due to leave the car deck was packed full and three vehicles were still waiting to get on. The fertilizer lorry was persuaded to reverse off and await the next day's sailing, the cars drove on, and we were away. A glance at the map shows that the obvious route round the three islands is to Eday then Sanday then Stronsay. Logistics demanded otherwise. First Sanday – to unload the largest volume of vehicles. Position the few joining so that the Eday traffic could leave next. Finally call at Stronsay, let the traffic off and pick up the main contingent heading for Kirkwall. So by the time we'd made the third crossing of the stretch of water between the three islands I was getting to know the scenery quite well. 'It's all right when it's calm,' was the comment of one of the crew – and calm indeed it was.

It's always exciting to step onto an island you've never been to before. Shame on me for leaving it so long before visiting Stronsay! The main village, Whitehall, is right by the pier and looks across to Papa Stronsay, now owned and inhabited by an international order of monks. I'd planned to stay in the independent hostel but was surprised to discover that the hotel had taken it over during major renovations. There was a comfortable bed available, but no cooking facilities, a pity as I'd just bought all my food in Kirkwall! Ravenous after a long day it was however nice to get a fish supper instead. Before dark there was just time for a walk along the quiet grey seashore to the point of Grice Ness. The wind and sea were both flat calm with low cloud clinging to hills, the tang of seaweed and no sound but the odd curlew and the faint thud-thud of a generator on the monks' island. Like the first swallow in summer, I was the first tourist of the season on Stronsay.

The next morning was fine with a whole island to explore! Before eight I was cycling up the hill out of Whitehall village. The day was to be one of dappled cloud and sunny intervals, of rare calm. The views from the road which runs the crest of Stronsay – and from the school, and the manse, and the church, were some of the best I've seen on Orkney, a vista on both sides out over beaches and seas and islands for miles. The low, grassy island is well inhabited with many good farms and seems to retain the best of both the old ways of life and the new, a sensible pace of life and a real community but a modern primary school with computers. The few cars are mostly old with that characteristic small-isle rattle from the exhaust; there are no MOT's required here! Everybody passing gave me a big friendly wave. At the far end of the island I left the bike to jog round a few miles of the coast, low cliffs up to a hundred feet high with the best natural arch in Orkney at the 'Vat of Kirbister' (Caithness has better). The air was full of fulmars and black-backed gulls, a few black guillemots (tysties) were already installed on ledges but the bulk of the cliff-nesting birds had yet to arrive. Most of the open country was still brown and yellow after a hard, wet, windy winter – but this felt like the first day of spring and the moorland larks, curlews, peewits, oystercatchers and redshanks were singing out the joy of it. Wild geese, too, were present in considerable numbers.

Mid-morning and I headed back to Whitehall. I'd hoped to meet the monks who had recently bought the small island of Papa Stronsay, just across from the village. They currently live in the old farmhouse and are rebuilding other dwellings so that their whole order of Transalpine Redemptorists can move up from southern England. I was fortunate in seeing their little boat coming across and they very kindly agreed to take me over to the island for a couple of hours. They were however very busy – far from a contemplative life! They had a base at Whitehall where all mail and phone calls came and these had to be dealt with. There were supplies and building materials to be bought at Stronsay's two shops. There were clothes to be washed. Also, a barge lay in a bay on Papa Stronsay, laden with cement and such like, urgently needed unloading.

'It won't do it any good lying there with all that weight in it,' a local boatman advised, 'it'll get twisted.'

If that wasn't enough, one of the two milk cows of the island was in heat and somehow a bull had to be taken across. The four monks were learning to farm and were hoping to grow crops and vegetables in due course.

'We believe in doing things the old way,' they explained, as the battered boat pottered across the Papa Sound.

'Anything goes in monasteries these days. We follow the traditional Latin Mass, the traditional rule.'

Not that they could always keep to rigid timetables when they had to fit in with the weather and the needs of animals! Their role was to provide a contemplative, restorative base for visiting priests who would spend half the year on the island and the other half making exhausting world tours of mission and preaching. It was very important to them that Mass was now being held on the island for the first time since the old monastery was abandoned 700 years ago. Hardly a day on Orkney. I walked past the remains of the old monastery, the outline of the church clearly visible, and on round the shore of the low island. For almost the first time on the trip the sun emerged, giving a warm spot on a little beach to sit and eat lunch. The surroundings exuded peace – but I knew how wild the elements could be in different conditions (indeed just two days later).

The monks were taking a visiting priest back to Stronsay for the afternoon flight to Kirkwall and took me with them in the boat.

'It's a good life,' said one of them to me, 'but it wouldn't suit everyone.'

I wish them well.

The remains of old Christian hermitages on inaccessible sea-stacks and promontories are features of Stronsay, not to mention the usual chambered cairns and brochs. Late in the day I wandered along the Sand of Rothiesholm, a beautiful bay on a narrow spit of land linking the three 'legs' of the island. Here, where the dunes were eroding, was the unmistakable layer of dark sand containing limpet shells, bits of charcoal and bone indicating a Viking midden; the mounds of a buried settlement were in the dunes behind. Commonplace in these parts.

Just 36 hours later, another island, another season! I'd taken the morning boat from Stronsay back to Kirkwall, looked at ferry timetables and discovered that if I pedalled quickly up to Tingwall I could get a few hours on Egilsay and spend the night on Rousay. The weather had turned, and I'd spent my time on Egilsay jogging round much of the little island in the rain. Egilsay is a small, quiet island, poorer than many and with abandoned farms, it's a refuge for the corncrake and many other breeding birds. Here Hakon murdered St. Magnus in the twelfth century – Hakon subsequently repented and built the St. Magnus cathedral. A small church with a round tower was built on Egilsay in memory of

St. Magnus and has been a place of pilgrimage for 800 years. It's still in excellent condition, though roofless, with the round tower a landmark to mariners for miles.

I was the only person at the Rousay hostel, on an organic farm of ducks and geese and cows and glorious mud. Rousay is a delightful island of heather hills and moors, with a 12-mile road climbing steeply up and down, right round the island through the fertile fringe. I'd meant to cycle round the road in the evening but in the increasingly heavy rain and growing dark never even quite got round the hostel. There would be time before the morning ferry... By morning the wind was blowing strongly from the north-east and the heavy rain was mixed with blobs of sleet. Back to normal weather, so just ignore it and dress up in waterproofs to set off east into the near gale. It was invigorating. I climbed steeply to 500 feet at the north-east corner of the island, the rain at sea-level turning to heavy wind-blown sleet. The subsequent long downhill meant hard on the brakes to keep the speed below 40 mph with the wind from behind, then round the corner, the sleet stinging from the side, before coming straight into the face. Up and down, Eynhallow Sound below, vicious tideraces around the island of Eynhallow. A slow slog into the wind led back to the hostel.

The rough sea was nothing for the Orkney boatmen and the ferry crossed completely unconcerned back to the mainland. For once there was a strong following wind for the 20 miles back to Stromness so the precipitation was of little concern. Up from Tingwall harbour, out of the rain into the sleet across the Chair of Lyde then hurtle down to Harray to take a quick look at a cold wet deserted Maeshowe. Alas there was no free entry, it was locked. My favourite is the 800 year-old Viking graffiti in the 5000 year-old tomb. Sanitised translations used to be propagated such as: 'Ingebourd is the most beautiful woman there is.' The Vikings were however a coarse lot and a more accurate rendering is: 'Ingebourd is a horny bitch'! On, into Stromness where I could sit and eat my sandwiches in the warmth of the modern ferry terminal building. A set of Millennium posters on modern Christianity nicely rounded up the various Christian sites my four-day trip had taken in, including Brough of Birsay, St Magnus Cathedral, Papa Stronsay and Egilsay. No visit to Stromness is complete without a walk up to Brinkies Brae above the town, the sleet was dying out and the hills of Hoy were emerging white from the haze of falling snow which had earlier covered them. Winter had returned to Orkney; I must return again in winter!

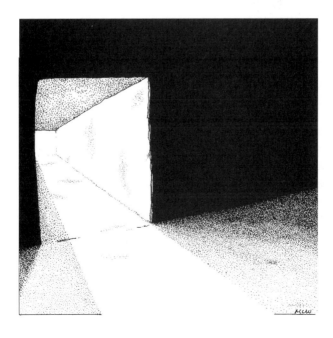

Ben Nevis hills

Warm rain had gradually turned to snow at higher levels, giving several inches lying above 2000 feet on the Lochaber Hills. After days of gales the morning dawned, for once, fine and frosty. Higher up it was still windy and from Fort William you could see the snow being whipped off the upper slopes of the Ben Nevis range. With a forecast for deterioration later, I set out before eight, wishing I'd been up earlier!

Ben Nevis in winter is not for the inexperienced or poorly equipped; instead I was making for the safer, neighbouring, top of Carn Mor Dearg. I probably would have been OK on the standard tourist route up the Ben, the danger lies in meeting severe weather or in going the wrong way on the summit and sliding over the edge of the cliffs. But I'd been that way before and instead wanted a good look (from a distance) at the North Face in winter. Under snow and ice these 2000-foot cliffs are famed as one of the most testing climbing areas in Britain, comparable with anything abroad and attracting climbers in droves from all over the country. At the foot of the cliffs, over 2000 feet above sea level, is the CIC climbing hut, about which countless stories and legends abound, and the base for many epic ascents – and rescues. Only the day before a climber had fallen in a gully near the summit and remained roped to the cliff for 18 hours in a blizzard before eventually being lowered 1000 feet down the face by the heroic rescue team. Climbing on the North Face is serious stuff.

Setting off before eight in early March would have given the hill to myself anywhere else. Not here, the climbers meant business. Already a number of cars and vans were parked, already fit and thoroughly equipped young men (mostly) were striding up the path past the distillery and along the Aluminium Company track leading towards the CIC hut. I pottered along as usual, letting myself be overtaken and hoping that nobody looked too closely at my boots. Some of these people were dressed almost like spacemen, most items of clothing probably costing over £100 and chosen from specialist mountaineering suppliers. (You could have bought everything I was wearing and carrying for less than than the cost of their crampons!) After a couple of miles and 1000 feet of climbing the track ended; a few vehicles were parked, the owners having presumably obtained permission from the Aluminium Company. Although it was only half past eight in the morning a lady with a clipboard was here, carrying out a survey of the climbers. How long had I been coming to the Ben? Er... actually it was a few years since I'd last visited – no I wasn't actually climbing the Ben today – fortunately she didn't start asking about the quality of my non-existent crampons or ice-axe or Goretex jacket.

Further on I was glad to turn off the path with its stream of climbers and start on the long gentle slopes of my hill. Even so, there were three people far ahead of me, above the snow-line and occasionally enveloped in clouds of drift. Views across the valley to the North Face were stupendous, steep white gullies separated by black rock ridges rising up into drifting snow and cloud which covered the summit. After the thaw and refreezing the crags would be coated in ice, giving severe climbing conditions. Black dots in twos and threes on the white slopes marked climbers heading up for the gullies and crags. My slopes were gentle, the only difficulty lay in picking my way across piled boulders partly covered by soft snow. The occasional stronger gust of wind would roar past in a cloud of white spindrift, but there was never anything as bad as I've seen outside my own front door at home. Just a question of plodding on, keeping well clear of the corniced edge, watching the Lochaber High School buildings on the edge of Fort William shrink ever smaller. Across the next valley to the east is Aonach Mor, with its new ski slopes. I know that the development gives local employment and provides enjoyment for many but I still don't like seeing a fine 4000-foot mountain destroyed with lifts and tows to its very summit. I could see some skiers hurtling down the summit runs amid clouds of blowing snow – Scottish skiing is a sport for the determined and dedicated and should never be marketed as anything else; Alpine conditions are rare!

On the 4000-foot summit of Carn More Dearg conditions resembled a severe January day in Caithness, a force eight gale and a temperature of perhaps -4C, yet bright and clear apart from some blowing drift. It was tempting to carry on to Ben Nevis... The infamous Carn More Dearg arête links the two mountains and is not particularly difficult itself; the danger is a steep snow slope leading onto the summit of Ben Nevis. Here it is essential to be well equipped and experienced with ice-axe and crampons or one risks joining the long list of people who have been killed by slipping and falling over 1000-foot crags. I was perfectly well equipped for what I'd done so far but not for going any further. So back it was, but not quite the same way, I turned back into the corrie to have a look at that CIC hut. Here again I started meeting those space-suited climbers. One man, a

professional guide with a younger couple in tow, asked if I was all right. I could see him looking at my worn-out £25 work boots 'Fine,' I said, striding on up as if making for the North Face (wearing my old, second-hand, framed rucsac, a pair of jogging trousers and no ice-axe to be seen). Once they were out of sight I turned back, taking the contouring path below the crags which crosses over to Glen Nevis.

In most pictures of Ben Nevis you see a shoulder on the lower slopes to the west, this is a little hill called Meall an t-Suidhe, only 2300 feet high (the same height as Morven). I'd been up before and now made the detour again to the quiet, attractive top of rocky outcrops and snow-covered grass, there are a couple of small cairns and no path. I'd be surprised if one in a thousand who climb Ben Nevis comes up here yet the views to Loch Linnhe and Ardgour, of the Mamores and up the Great Glen, are probably just as good and much more likely to be seen. Rather than join the tourist path I picked my way slowly down steep grassy gullies in the afternoon sunshine with Glen Nevis and a huge empty caravan site (sight) almost vertically below. The contrast between the gentle warmth of the valleys and the severity of the tops never fails to surprise. I enjoyed the walk down the riverside into the town, passing on the way the Fort William football ground where a few loyal supporters were watching the home team being beaten five-nil by Cove. Locals were out walking dogs along the seashore on a spectacular late afternoon with brown hills rising from the sea-loch to white summits and wisps of blowing snow. A yellow RAF rescue helicopter was making shuttle trips from the town into the corrie below the north face. Perhaps it was only a practice.

Swim Caithness!

It was, I realised, a situation to savour. Not every day did I find myself jogging across rough wet moorland in the rain, wearing nothing but bare skin and a pair of trainers! It was the logical (if not the sensible) thing to do when swimming in each of three closely situated lochs in a sudden shower of rain – if you're not wearing any clothes they can't get soaked!

But I often wonder what the RAF pilot made of a naked man running across the Caithness moors, miles from anywhere, early on an August morning... Very early I'd cycled and jogged out to the two remote flow country lochs of Loch Losgann, near Loch Caluim. Warm sunshine, and a breeze to subdue the insects, gave perfect conditions for a swim. At the western edge of the southern loch the reeds gave straight into four-foot deep water, just like a swimming pool. The base of the loch was firm and the swimming delicious. Wearing nothing but my old trainers I left the water and began to jog across the heather towards the northern loch – just as a low-flying jet screamed across from nowhere, turning on its side so that the pilot could have a good look.

There was another occasion when an observer would have seen some fine streaking through knee-deep heather. On an unusually hot and sticky August morning I'd cycled out to Quintfall and made my way out through heather and bog to the Black Loch. It didn't look particularly inviting; nevertheless I stripped off and wallowed out into the water. The bottom of the loch proved to be deep soft peat but near the middle I just about managed to swim, rather as in thick soup. Back on shore huge clouds of sweat-sucking flies descended to be followed by a ravenous horde of midges. I didn't hang about.

There was a Dounreay lunch-hour spent paddling around Loch Achbuiligan trying to find a spot deep enough for swimming – and another trying unsuccessfully to locate the Drumholiston Loch na Moin in thick fog. Lochs are not always easy to find, or reach – and are not always fit for swimming. It took two visits to locate the 'Black Loch' just east of the main A99 road near John O' Groats – to discover it was simply a damp, circular depression in the moor!

The Broubster Lochan Ealach gave one of the most nerve-wracking approaches. I detoured for a dip when cycling home from work and found the way barred by floating bogs – a mat of vegetation floating on deeper water with the whole surface dipping and quivering. In bare feet I pushed on, hoping I didn't suddenly drop forever out of sight – and found good swimming in a few feet of water when I finally reached the edge of the loch proper. Not I suppose, the sort of adventure most people encounter during routine commuting!

So what is this maniac trying to do??

A challenge for those who've climbed all the Munros and Corbetts and Donalds, visited every Scottish island, climbed the highest mountain on all six continents of the world and reached the summit of every state in the USA... is to swim in all the lochs in Caithness. Ideally to swim alone, and as nature intended – and certainly without a wetsuit!

At first sight it looks an impossible task. If you count the smallest dubh-lochans there would be thousands. However virtually all the nameless lochs and lochans in the middle of the flow country are completely unsuitable for swimming with no more than a foot or two of water above deep soft peat. As a general

199

rule, proper lochs have names – though not all named lochs are suitable for swimming! A reasonable list to attempt comprises all the lochs named on the 'Landranger' 1:50000 Ordnance Survey map, with a few other unnamed lochs if they are sizeable.

A few caveats in this litiginous age; I cannot recommend adventure without recounting the dangers! Obviously only a good swimmer should consider swimming in lochs, especially alone and in remote places. I would say that, in a swimming pool, you should be able to comfortably manage a kilometre, or 40 lengths. Breast stroke is a good idea so you can keep your head out of what can be very cold water. You should not, unless you are very accustomed to it, plunge straight into a loch. Go in slowly. Be very wary of lochs with soft bottoms. You can get stuck in deep gelatinous peat, not a nice prospect if alone, wearing nothing and miles from anywhere. Be wary too of hidden underwater boulders on which you can bang knees and legs, also of sharp stones, broken glass or fishing hooks on the loch bottom. I often wear old trainers to protect my feet. Beware of very steep shelves and sudden drop-offs into deep water – though these should pose no hazard if you are a good swimmer. If, like me, you have little body fat you will get cold very quickly. Do not stay in too long or venture too far from the shore. If I can manage five minutes in a loch I am doing well!

Attached as an appendix is Ralph's list of the Caithness lochs. It is (like the original Munro's Tables) a little arbitrary as to what is included or omitted. Some in the table, such as Loch nan Eun near Reay, are smaller than others which have been left out because they are unnamed. But then Loch nan Eun gives surprisingly good swimming. Sometimes (as at Loch Losgann) a name actually covers two or more lochs; you should swim or paddle in all of them unless they are very small and unsuitable. I have omitted the countless lochs and lochans on the Knockfin Heights, as well as other big areas of dubh-lochans, as dangerous to attempt and impossible in number. With the odd exception, of course... Others have been left out because they are simply marshes.

To become a 'compleater' you must swim, without a wetsuit or similar protection, in all the lochs in the table – unless they are too shallow, when they should be paddled. There are a few really dangerous lochs with very soft floors in which it is enough to just dip your toes. I have attached some notes especially to forewarn. Fishermen might wish to take up an alternative challenge of catching a trout – or at least casting a fly – in every one!

As with climbing the munros, swimming the lochs gives an excuse to explore country one might otherwise never visit. Late on a fine warm afternoon after a busy morning, I headed for the obscure lochans west of Loch More. Leaving the car at the road I pedalled for three miles down the Dalnawhillan track, then left the bike to jog across the moor to Lochan Chairn Leith. The going was rough and it took quite a while to find a way through a maze-like area of very fine dubh-lochans; the edge of the new forestry plantations lay just to the south but the spot was still relatively unspoilt. The loch, when reached, was ringed by rushes and bog with no sandy or stony beaches, the edge let down into three-foot deep water with a firm stony and peaty bottom. There's nothing better than swimming out into one of our moorland lochs on a fine day, the only pity is that I get cold quickly and can't stay in for long. The next objective was to investigate the little Lochan Dubh on the other side of the track, just above Loch More. There are a lot of Black Lochs and Loch (or Lochan) Dubhs and some can be little more than peat wallows. This one looked black and uninviting, completely ringed by heather and peat-hag. I ventured in one step, the bottom seemed firm – but when I carefully tried another, my foot disappeared into deep gelatinous peat. Venture any further and I'd probably never get out; the loch was a death-trap. Definitely no swimming or paddling there!

On a cool and breezy Saturday afternoon I found myself with some time to spare in Wick. I always like the Wick swimming pool, and although it was 3-15 I should have time for a good half-hour's swim as the pool didn't close till four. But no, 'Pool Closed', said the notice and there was no-one at reception even though quite a few adults and children were still enjoying their last 45 minutes. My fee would have contributed to the pool's running costs but I'd just have to get a free swim instead. So off to the Trinkie it was; the water was a bit cool with the sea breaking over the wall but in consolation I had this very fine 50-metre pool entirely to myself and enjoyed four lengths before getting too cold. A jog along to the Castle of Old Wick soon warmed me up again. Those who aren't local may not know of the Trinkie; it's a superb seawater outdoor swimming pool below the clifftop road reached by walking eastwards, south of the harbour, or by driving east from Pultneytown towards the Castle of Old Wick. Access is by steps a couple of hundred yards short of the carpark at the end of the road. The pool is very clean, with a sandy bottom shelving gently from paddling to swimming depth and is entirely free of charge for anyone to use, any time. It's an asset which perhaps Wick should publicise more!

On another day I made my target the highest loch in the county. I always forget just how fine are the woods of the Langwell estate, upstream from Berriedale. This is the only place in Caithness where you can see tall oaks and monkey puzzle trees! It was warm, but rapidly clouding over, the river was full after recent rain, with herons enjoying the fishing. From the end of the track at Wag I wandered up the river another mile or two then climbed to a rocky outcrop on the ridge of Creag Scalabsdale, easy stony slopes then led to the 1800-foot summit with a tremendous view over hundreds of square miles of empty and rolling moor and mountain. The weather had been closing in, cloud coming down on Ben Uarie and Ben Bhealaich across the deep Strath of Kildonan with grey murk moving in from the south-west. Now a cold rain started and the temperature dropped, as did my enthusiasm for a dip in Loch Scalabsdale which lay just below.

Perhaps it might yet clear. I wandered on across a peaty col and up the next top, Creag nan Gearr. It looked brighter now in all directions except to the south, where the weather was coming from. Showers seemed to be building off the sea over Ben Bhealaich then soaking me. I went down to the loch shore, it was flat calm with the rain hissing into the water. My enthusiasm for swimming doesn't extend to stripping off in cold rain at 1400 feet. It was though definitely brightening (I convinced myself). The loch is small, to walk round would take no more than 20 minutes; that would give time for improvement. I found a porcelain fishing float washed up in the peat; had anyone actually had a boat on this remotest and highest of Caithness lochs? Back at my starting point the rain had almost stopped with the sun bravely trying to make a showing. It was now or never... I managed about 20 strokes in the cold water. It would make a great place to swim on a rare hot day, high in its moorland basin with the rocky 'Child's Seat' just to the north. At least it wasn't snowing as it usually seems do when I'm in the Scalabsdale area.

More than once I've shared the water of a loch with a pair of red-throated divers and once even with a black-throated diver and its chick. Greylag geese, greenshanks, sandpipers, golden plovers – all will be commonly seen and heard around the moorland lochs. Remote Loch Rumsdale gives a fine swim with a sandy beach and a sloping sandy and peaty floor. It was lovely on a breezy morning in late July – however I looked carefully before sitting down; just ten minutes earlier I'd startled a large adder which had slithered off, hissing furiously.

202

Dunnet Head has a dozen swimmable lochs – but is the most northerly point on the British mainland, and surrounded by cold sea. When a warm sticky day comes these lochs are though surprisingly good. My favourite is Loch of Bushta, but some of the small ones such as Loch of Muirs give safe swimming better than any swimming pool. Indeed the most unlikely lochs can be good, for instance Loch a Mhuilinn on Dorrery Hill makes an excellent swimming pool, four feet deep with a soft but firm bottom. Then there is Little Loch Scye, where you might expect a peaty wallow but instead find a sandy shore and a fine swim in a lovely moorland setting.

Loch Beg, by Loch More proved a problem. This is really a large pool on the River Thurso and beloved by salmon fishermen. I did not fancy trying to explain myself to a water bailiff when caught wading in the loch! So in the end I went early on a cold Sunday morning and splashed a few strokes, fortunately not encountering any salmon. I'll not repeat the experience. Loch More is much better.

The Loch of Yarrows gave a nice swim at the southern end when I found a spot which was not overlooked. The day was though windy and rather cold and I was already shivering before tackling Loch Brickigeo to the east, just as the rain came on. This was insanity; jogging in bare nothings along the shore in rain and cold wind over carpets of scabious, twayblade and grass of Parnassus, managing eight strokes in icy water then coming straight out again into a wind which now seemed warm. After such an experience it can take me an hour to warm up properly. Even on a hot day, if I've been tempted to stay in the water too long, it can take half an hour's hard cycling or running to lose the white numbness in toes and fingers.

When the weather is warm in July and August you may have ferocious swarms of midges, clegs and sweat-sucking flies to contend with at the moorland lochs. But it is not always cold or midgey. In spells of sunny weather the shallow lochs warm up quickly and can give lovely swimming. To swim alone, out from the sandy beach of remote Loch Tuim Ghlas during a fine spell of weather, looking up at the sun and the sky and the empty moors stretching for miles all around, is swimmer's heaven. The whole chain of lochs south from here to Loch Slettil is delectable on a hot day; even if the flies and clegs pester. You enter the water and swim gently out, looking back to the quiet shore, and after a few dives underwater soon lose the insects. I remember a day in Northumberland, over 30 years ago. I was carrying a full camping pack over heather moors in a heatwave, pouring with sweat and pestered by the worst clouds of sweat-sucking flies I have ever met. Thousands of them, hundreds crawling over hands, legs, clothes, trying to settle on my face. Then I came to a loch – and I will never forget the sheer delight of swimming out into the cool water away from the heat and the flies.

In some lochs, such as Saorach, Broubster, you have to wade out for a long way to find deep enough water for swimming. In the Loch of Mey I made my way right to the middle of the loch (hoping I wasn't being watched!) and still found it only three feet deep. In Loch Rangag by contrast you are immediately in deep water from the broch. Loch Watenen is another surprise, instead of a shallow peaty pool in the high moorland it is straight into deep water; you can do widths just as in a swimming pool. You can never tell in advance. The western Loch Nan Clach Geala, in the heart of the flow country north of Beinn Ratha had a sandy beach instead of the expected deep peat and gave a delectable swim on a warm September morning – a loch on the plateau such as this one gives a real 'top of the world' swim with views all round! Quite different are the steep sided and very deep Binocular Lochs a mile to the south.

The combination of fine swimming weather with opportunity is rare in Caithness. Often it's grey and the loch looks cold and uninviting; it's then only the effort you've made to get to some remote spot like Loch a Cheracher and the thought that you'll soon be out again that makes you wade into the freezing water! Once you've enjoyed a few good swims in solitude in quiet, remote lochs you'll be hooked. Even if you're only in the water for a minute or two the experience can transform an ordinary day. But on balance I think the munros are easier!

Ralph's list of the Caithness lochs

(In roughly alphabetical order. Numbers in brackets are grid references.)

Loch Achbuiligan (988656) Only suitable for paddling.

Lochan Airigh Leathaid (990390) Three lochs. The fourth (second from north) is just a wet marsh. The two southern lochs are deep and fine for swimming with stony floors. The northernmost loch has a peaty/stony floor and is too shallow. Nice moorland location below the slopes of the Knockfins.

Loch Altain Dubh (991480) Too shallow for swimming. Stony bottom.

Chain of lochs north of Altnabreac:-

Loch Na Cloich (975475) Deep enough for swimming.

Lochan Ealach Mor (967480) Fine for swimming.

Lochan Ealach Beg (965495) Shallow and peaty.

Loch Torr Na Ceardaich (970510) Shallow and peaty.

Lochan Dubh Cul Na Beinn (984544) Peaty but deep enough for good swimming.

Loch of Auckengill (351652) Two lochs. Western loch is the only one fit for swimming; not very deep but a nice swim from the north shore. Reedy, soft bottom but not dangerous.

Loch Bad a Channain (934409) Shallow with reeds to east and stony bottom to west but deep enough for swimming. Nice setting rather spoilt by nearby forest fence. A lovely refreshing swim on a warm midgey late July morning.

Banniskirk Loch (177573) Too weedy for swimming. Managed a few strokes but only about three feet deep and weed growing everywhere – otherwise would be nice.

Loch Beg (by Loch More) (088463). Swum briefly from boat landing, cold water. Not worth it, although deep enough. Leave this one to the fishermen!

Black Loch (Quintfall) (312632) Shallow, very soft bottom, dangerous.

Black Loch (near Loch Scye) (998563) Good for safe swimming, three to four feet deep, soft (but not very soft) bottom. Warms quickly.

Black Loch (Scotscalder) (089548) Rather soft bottom with deep holes and lumps of peat near surface in middle. Definitely not for the novice but a nice swim.

Black Loch (Dorrery, north) (049578) A small peaty pool, only three feet deep in middle. Soft but firm bottom, a few stones. Possible to swim but not really deep enough. Nice moorland setting in spite of being near road.

Black Loch (John O' Groats). Just a dry – or boggy – circular depression in the heather. Not enough water for a frog when I visited!

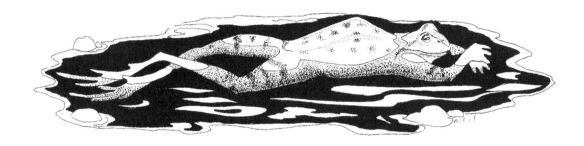

Binocular Lochs (Reay) (961566) Both tiny lochs shelve very steeply, but are good. Unique setting for Caithness.

Loch Bhraigh na h-Aibhne (998318) The source of the Dunbeath Water. Sandy beach. Very fine setting with Morven to south. A beautiful swim on a good day.

Borgue Loch (120270) Stony bottom, deep enough for good swimming.

Lochan Nam Breac (Altnabreac) (002478) Very marshy but loch has a stony bottom and is fine for swimming.

Loch Breac (Ben Alisky) (065375) Good loch for swimming, sandy beach sloping steadily, nice setting below steep slopes.

Lochan Buidhe (Forss) (038694) Agricultural loch surrounded by rushes, and marsh, very reedy but just about deep enough for swimming in middle.

Loch Caise (Altnabreac) (025468) Fairly soft bottom, shallow but deep enough and a good swim. Nice views to mountains.

Loch Calder (070610) No shortage of places to swim. A good place for a morning dip on the way to work. Probably ruined by gigantic windmills by the time this book is published.

Loch of Camster (263442) Peaty floor, rather shallow (three to four feet deep).

Loch Caluim (020520) Lovely swimming from beach at south end by fishing hut.

Caol Loch (Altnabreac) (025485) Good swimming. Good shelter in small fishing hut at south end. Fine views of hills and moors.

Catherine's Loch (043380) Very small, not really deep enough for swimming (three feet at most), bottom fairly soft and peaty but firm. Odd underwater boulder to scrape knees! Nice setting.

Lochan nam Bo Riabhach (038321) Good swimming, but high up and cold.

Loch a Chairn (south) (076494) Very boggy around loch but once in from east shore found a good stony bottom and deep enough for swimming.

(north) (074497) Has anyone else ever swum here? In spite of very boggy surrounds a good swimming loch from near north-east end where shelves a bit more steeply. Firm stony bottom.

Lochan Chairn Leith (058450) Maze of dubh-lochs between loch and track, large detours needed. Stony/peaty bottom, no beaches – in from rushes into three-foot deep water. Fine for swimming.

Loch a Cheracher (134395) Soft bottom but deep enough for swimming.

Loch a Cherigal (100488) Peaty, not really deep enough for swimming.

Loch a Chiteadh (040508) A nice moorland swim.

Lochan a Chleirich (north) (962453) Fine for swimming but was very cold indeed, managed most way across narrow end then retreated!

(south) (965550) has soft peaty bottom, gelatinous and very dangerous, almost certainly not deep enough for swimming.

lochan one mile to north-east) (975565) Really largest of dubh-lochs. About three feet deep then dangerous soft bottom, managed a couple of strokes!

Loch nan Clachan Geala (Broubster) (002585) Borrowed boat and swam from it. Quiet setting in new plantations.

Loch nan Clach Geala (Reay) (960578) Fine setting, grand views, lovely sandy beach.

Clar Loch (954443) Rough rocky bottom, shoes recommended but shelves from shore to plenty of depth for swimming. Nice loch.

Lochan Coire na Beinn (148398) Shelves steadily, stony then soft bottom, deep enough, for swimming, fine location. Danger of grazed knees on underwater boulders.

Lochan Croc nan Lair (040454) Deep enough for swimming, stony bottom.

Dhu Loch (Stirkoke) (339485) Attractive setting, rich in birdlife, should be visited but unsuitable for swimming or paddling as very marshy, shallow and reedy.

Lochan Dubh Cul an Loin (048523) Two lochs, both dangerous with very soft bottoms.

Lochan Dubh nan Geodh (060478) Deep enough for swimming but very rocky/stony bottom.

Loch Dubh (by Loch Ruard) (148435) Shelves steeply from east bank. Good swimming in deep water.

Loch Dubh (below Lochdhu Lodge, Altnabreac) (010440) Very overlooked by the lodge, choose a time of year when nobody is staying! Loch shallow with stony bottom, need to go in a long way before deep enough for swimming.

Lochan Dubh (near Loch More) (070448) Probably a death trap. Edge of loch seems firm then suddenly a very soft, sticky, and probably deep peaty bottom. Nowhere looks deep enough for swimming.

Lochan Dubh (north-east of Loch More) (094465) Shallow, peaty and reedy, not good for swimming and probably no more than three feet deep above soft bottom (could be dangerous). Not worth it, much better lochs near!

Loch Dubh (Ben Alisky) (053370) A good swimming loch but a bit bouldery to enter below the fishing hut – opposite shore looks better with sandy beach. A lovely setting.

Lochan Dubh na Cloiche (985485) A very out-of-the-way lochan beyond Altnabreac just inside the new forests. Good swimming from north-east bank, stony bottom, shelves steadily to deep water.

Lochan Dubh na Feithe Caoile (985443) A railway lochan, just below line west of Altnabreac. Not deep enough for swimming, perhaps two feet deep and bottom getting very soft once away from shore, could be dangerous.

Lochan Dubh a Chracairnie (065515) Nice, but nude swimmers watch out for the trains!

Loch an Duine (045507) Nice remote moorland loch.

Dunnet Head Lochs:- (some fifteen, most very good for swimming)

Loch of Bushta (195726) Good for swimming from south end where a nice sloping sandy bottom.

Loch of Easter Head (207763)

Long Loch (205760)

Loch Burifa (202762)

Sanders Loch (east) (210753)

Sanders Loch (west) (184748)

Nether Sanders Loch (190745) Only deep enough for paddling.

Many Lochs (200747) Three lochs, mostly not deep enough for swimming.

Black Loch (near Red Geo) (185736) Surprisingly good loch for swimming, like a large swimming pool, went in from north bank, peaty bottom but soon out of depth and fine for swimming. Nice location.

Grassy Loch (near road) (207743) Went in from south-east bank – a surprisingly good swim, stony/peaty bottom then deep, swam across to far shore which is a deep/floating bog suddenly ending in five-foot deep water. Could do widths!

Black Loch (near road, above Many Lochs) (203745) A good swimming pool, stony at south bank but shelves quite quickly into deep water, nice swim, some weed towards far shore.

Loch of Muirs (202734) A surprisingly good loch for safe swimming. From south-east bank, peaty/stony floor soon deep enough, could swim right across but still just touch bottom. Nice location.

(Courtfall Loch 214740 and Northern Gate Loch 209719 are reedy pools not suitable for swimming or paddling.)

Lochan Ealach (042603) Adventurous approach from Broubster road over floating bogs but fine for swimming if you manage to reach the water's edge!

Loch Eilanach (070475) Nice swim to island.

Loch Eun (Rumsdale) (983425) Good loch for swimming, soon deep enough from boat landing at end of path. Stony bottom.

Lochan Nan Eun (South of Reay) (982613) A small pool with bogbean and some weed but deep enough for swimming, quite good, nice setting partly surrounded by new plantations on hilltop. Soft but fairly firm bottom.

Loch nam Fear (025430) Good loch for swimming with sandy beach and gentle slope to softer bottom, nice views.

Loch Gaineimh (050470) A very good loch for swimming with a sandy beach and sandy bottom.

Loch Gaineimh (east, near Loch Eilenach) (077489) Very marshy and reedy around loch but good swimming when in from east bank, firm stony bottom.

Garbh Loch (Altnabreac) (037467) Stony rocky bottom and gentle shelving but good swimming once out.

Loch Garbh (Reay) (938606) Nice swimming pool, can do widths.

Glutt Loch (993374) Very much a private estate fishing loch with track, locked fishing hut, jetty and boat. A fine moorland location below the slopes of the Knockfins with Morven to the south – a very nice swimming loch if nobody is about! Stony floor.

Grassie Loch (by Caise) (030470) Too shallow to swim, very soft bottom. If full to top of old dam would be OK.

Groats Loch (Watenan) (315408) A marsh, completely unsuitable for swimming or paddling.

Loch Heilan (255685) Familiar farmland loch.

Loch Hempriggs (340470) Very gently sloping and stony bottom, from near main road. Otherwise access difficult through farmland or bog. Not my favourite.

St John's Loch (225724) Familiar fishing loch. Best go in from west shore.

Loch of Killimster (308560) A surprisingly good swim from the fishing jetty at the eastern end of the loch.

Knockfin Heights lochs. The Caithness swimmer is duty-bound to investigate but need not visit or swim all the lochs which are shallow with deep soft peat and potentially very dangerous. If determined it is just possible to swim in the larger ones. A better ploy is to ski across them when frozen.

Lint Lochs (378698) The southern one of the pair is deep enough for swimming, the other just a reedy pool. Nice but very small. Peaty bottom but not too soft.

Loch of Lomashion (386700) A nice loch for swimming, soft but firm peaty bottom, fine moorland setting.

Loch Losgann (027500) Two lochs. The southern loch is good, on the western edge the reeds give straight into four-foot water with a hard bottom, just like a swimming pool. The northern loch is not deep enough for swimming.

Margaret's Loch (976355) A small and remote lochan above Glutt Lodge, high on the edge of the Knockfin plateau with fine views. Unlike other very similar lochans nearby, for some reason this one is named. The loch is shallow with a stony shore and soft peaty bottom, just about OK for a paddle but unsuitable for swimming.

Loch Meadie (090480) Overlooked by the road so it is best to go in half way up the western shore where a forestry track gives access. Good swimming.

Loch Meadhoin (062517) Watch out for trains! Very boggy at southern end but deep enough for swimming.

Loch Mhadadh (south of Glutt) (998331) A very fine setting with Morven to south. Alas it is not deep enough for swimming, even in the middle. A fine sandy beach and soft sandy bottom.

Loch a Mhadaidh (Rumsdale) (980418) Not really deep enough, close to dubh-lochs and a bit like a large dubh-loch. A stony shore gives way to soft peat with big underwater hummocks of peat rising towards surface. I found nowhere over three feet deep.

Loch a Mhuilinn (Altnabreac) (018420) Good swimming but rather overlooked by road.

Loch a Mhuilinn (Dorrery) (060568) Small but a good safe swimming pool, firm but soft bottom, about four feet deep.

Loch na Moine (938658) Good swimming, unusual clifftop location.

Loch of Mey (273736) Only two or three feet deep even in the middle.

Loch More (080460) The classic swimming loch; you might even meet somebody else in the water off the sandy beaches along the eastern shore.

Loch na Nighinn (002417) A delectable high moorland loch with superb views to Morven, Ben Alisky and the Knockfin Heights. The stony east shore soon shelves to deep water, you can do widths as in a swimming pool.

Loch Olginey (090574) Shallow but shelves eventually to deep enough water for swimming. There is a small island but the water is too shallow for swimming there and just gives a muddy wallow.

Loch Rangag (178418) Shelves very steeply from the broch to deep water.

Loch Rumsdale. (967418) A good swimming loch with a sloping sandy/peaty bottom from a sandy beach. Nice setting.

Loch Ruard (143430) Went in from east bank south of fishing hut. Sandy beach steadily shelves, stony bottom. Good for swimming.

Loch na Saigh Glaise (013515) A bit disappointing. Loch shallow with soft silty/peaty bottom, never found it more than about three feet deep and peat getting soft in patches especially towards middle. Went in from west shore.

Loch Saorach (015605) A bit shallow at least at the southern end, with a stony bottom and a long wade out to reach deep enough water for swimming.

Loch Sand (098410) A nice loch with sandy beaches in a lovely setting. Unfortunately I've only managed to swim there, briefly, when it has been perishingly cold!

Loch Sarclet (343430) It is difficult to swim where not overlooked. At the southern end, you need to push through thick undergrowth to reach the bank. Once in, the stony bottom soon shelves to deep enough water for a good swim.

Loch Scalabsdale (963244) Stony bottom giving onto soft peat, deep enough for swimming. Grand setting but mostly very cold as the highest loch in the county.

Lochan Scrabach (025445) Not deep enough for swimming, mostly a rather soft peaty bottom which might be dangerous in places, otherwise stones/boulders.

Scrabster Loch (086704) Used to provide good swimming from east shore and was the most accessible loch for Thurso. The dam has recently been dismantled and the loch is probably now too shallow for swimming. Other lochans on Holburn Head such as Coghill Loch are just reedy marshes.

Loch Scye (005555) Swim at north end away from the boathouse and Shurrery lodge.

Little Loch Scye (012554) Remarkably good for swimming – sandy shore, deep enough, not very stony, good setting.

Loch Shurrery (045555) Best to swim from the southern end of the loch on the Dorrery side where there is a small sandy beach and you are not overlooked.

Skyline Loch west, Skyline Loch east (014478) Both give good swimming, both have rough stony bottoms. Eastern loch has some big rocks under the surface. Very boggy to the south of main loch.

Loch na Stairne (960303) Three or four lochs, little more than large dubh-lochs. The easternmost is just about deep enough for swimming with a soft peaty bottom. The others are shallow with deep soft peat and could be dangerous.

Loch Stemster (or Scarmclate) (190595) Shallow loch in farmland and woodland, rich in birds and wildlife. Muddy shores but good swimming once in.

Loch Stemster (Achavanich) (190425) Stony.

The Trinkie (376495) Excellent salt-water outdoor swimming pool.

Loch Thormaid (600015) Nice little sandy beach at southern end.

Loch Thulachan (105413) Good moorland loch below ruined lodge.

Loch Toftingall (190525) Now surrounded by plantations but still good for swimming from boat landing to west.

Loch Tuim Ghlais (978525) Perhaps the best loch of all.

Loch Watten (230560) The crannog at the eastern end makes a nice objective (but was overgrown with nettles on my last visit!)

Loch Watenan (319415) Rather reedy, not very good but deep enough for swimming, hard bottom.

Loch of Winless(293547) An attractive, very reedy loch with little open water. Bottom is soft but firm, water about three feet deep, swimming only just possible, lots of weed and mud. But nice for a quick dip early on a fine warm morning!

Loch of Warehouse (300424) Very steeply shelving but good.

Loch of Yarrows (310440) Nice at southern end where not overlooked. Also Loch Brickigeo (303437) just to east has fairly soft bottom, reedy, just deep enough for swimming.